The Bible Speaks Today

Series editors: Alec Motyer (OT)
John Stott (NT)
Derek Tidball (Bible Themes)

The Message of
the Resurrection

Titles in this series

The Message of the Resurrection

Christ is risen!

Paul Beasley-Murray

*Senior minister, The Baptist Church,
Victoria Road South, Chelmsford, England*

Inter-Varsity Press

InterVarsity Press
P.O. Box 1400, Downers Grove, IL 60515-1426
World Wide Web: www.ivpress.com
E-mail: mail@ivpress.com

Inter-Varsity Press
38 De Montfort Street, Leicester LE1 7GP, England

InterVarsity Press® *is the book-publishing division of InterVarsity Christian Fellowship/USA*®*, a student movement active on campus at hundreds of universities, colleges and schools of nursing in the United States of America, and a member movement of the International Fellowship of Evangelical Students. For information about local and regional activities, write Public Relations Dept., InterVarsity Christian Fellowship/USA, 6400 Schroeder Rd., P.O. Box 7895, Madison, WI 53707-7895.*

Inter-Varsity Press is the book-publishing division of the Universities and Colleges Christian Fellowship (formerly the Inter-Varsity Fellowship), a student movement linking Christian Unions in universities and colleges throughout the United Kingdom and the Republic of Ireland, and a member movement of the International Fellowship of Evangelical Students. For information about local and national activities write to UCCF, 38 De Montfort Street, Leicester LE1 7GP, England.

USA ISBN 0-8308-2401-4

UK ISBN 0-85111-508-X

Typeset in Great Britain by The Midlands Book Typesetting Company.

Printed in the United States of America ∞

British Library Cataloguing in Publication Data

A catalogue record for this book is available from the British Library.

Library of Congress Cataloging-in-Publication Data

Beasley-Murray, Paul.
  The message of the Resurrection : Christ is risen! / Paul Beasley-Murray.
    p. cm. —(The Bible speaks today)
  Includes bibliographical references.
  ISBN 0-8308-2401-4 (paper : alk. paper)
    1. Jesus Christ—Resurrection. I. Title. II. Series.
BT481 .B386 2001
232.9'7—dc21

00-047155

| 18 | 17 | 16 | 15 | 14 | 13 | 12 | 11 | 10 | 9 | 8 | 7 | 6 | 5 | 4 |
| 16 | 15 | 14 | 13 | 12 | 11 | 10 | 09 | 08 | | | | | | |

Dedicated to the memory of my father
George Raymond Beasley-Murray
10 October 1916 to 23 February 2000
'Thanks be to God! He gives us the
victory through our Lord Jesus Christ.'

Contents

General preface

THE BIBLE SPEAKS TODAY describes three series of expositions, based on the books of the Old and New Testaments, and on Bible themes that run through the whole of Scripture. Each series is characterized by a threefold ideal:

- to expound the biblical text with accuracy
- to relate it to contemporary life, and
- to be readable.

These books are, therefore, not 'commentaries', for the commentary seeks rather to elucidate the text than to apply it, and tends to be a work rather of reference than of literature. Nor, on the other hand, do they contain the kind of 'sermons' which attempt to be contemporary and readable without taking Scripture seriously enough.

The contributors to *The Bible Speaks Today* series are all united in their convictions that God still speaks through what he has spoken, and that nothing is more necessary for the life, health and growth of Christians than that they should hear what the Spirit is saying to them through his ancient – yet ever modern – Word.

ALEC MOTYER
JOHN STOTT
DEREK TIDBALL
Series Editors

Acknowledgments

There are a number of people to whom I wish to record my gratitude for the help they have given to me in writing this book: Tony and Audrey Pinkney of the Priscilla Trust for allowing me to stay for four weeks at their delightful property in the Dordogne; the Ministry Department of the Baptist Union of Great Britain for their kindness in giving me a sabbatical grant; the deacons and members of Victoria Road South Baptist Church, Chelmsford, Essex, for their generosity in granting me a sabbatical; Derek Tidball, the editor of this new series, for his guidance and encouragement; my friends Alan and Ursula Franklin, in whose home a good deal of the writing took place; my father, George Beasley-Murray, who in his books *Christ is Alive* and *The Resurrection of Jesus* demonstrated to me the importance of the resurrection; and above all Caroline, my wife, for her love and support.

Chief abbreviations

ET	English translation
GNB	The Good News Bible (NT, 1996, fourth edition 1976; OT, 1976)
LXX	The Septuagint (ancient Greek translation of the Old Testament)
NEB	The New English Bible (NT, 1961, second edition 1970; OT, 1970)
NIV	The New International Version of the Bible (1973, 1978, 1984)
NRSV	The New Revised Standard Version of the Bible (1989, 1995)
REB	The Revised English Bible (1989)
RSV	The Revised Standard Version of the Bible (NT, 1946, second edition 1971; OT, 1952)

Bibliography

N. Anderson, *A Lawyer among the Theologians* (Hodder & Stoughton, 1973).

G. Carey, *Jesus 2000* (HarperCollins, 1999).

P. Carnley, *The Structure of Resurrection Belief* (Clarendon, 1987).

S. T. Davis, *Risen Indeed: Making Sense of the Resurrection* (SPCK, 1993).

C. F. Evans, *Resurrection and the New Testament* (SCM, 1970).

D. Fuller, *Easter Faith and History* (Tyndale, 1968).

M. Green, *Evangelism through the Local Church* (Hodder & Stoughton, 1990).

R. Harries, *Christ is Risen* (Mowbray, 1987).

M. J. Harris, *Raised Immortal: Resurrection and Immortality in the New Testament* (Marshall, Morgan & Scott, 1983).

M. J. Harris, *From Grave to Glory: Resurrection in the New Testament* (Zondervan, 1990).

S. H. Hooke, *The Resurrection of Christ as History and Experience* (Darton, Longman & Todd, 1967).

G. E. Ladd, *I Believe in the Resurrection* (Hodder & Stoughton, 1975).

G. W. H. Lampe and D. MacKinnon, *The Resurrection: A Dialogue* (Mowbray, 1966).

P. Lapide, *The Resurrection of Jesus: A Jewish Perspective* (SPCK, 1983).

G. Ludemann, *The Resurrection of Jesus: History, Experience, Theology* (ET SCM, 1994).

W. Marxsen, 'The Resurrection of Jesus as a Historical and Theological Problem', in *The Significance of the Message of the Resurrection for Faith in Jesus Christ*, ed. C. F. D. Moule (ET SCM, 1968).

G. O'Collins, *Jesus Risen* (Darton, Longman & Todd, 1987).

A. M. Ramsey, *The Resurrection of Christ: A Study of the Event and its Meaning for the Christian Faith* (reissued Fontana, 1961).

A. J. M. Wedderburn, *Beyond Resurrection* (ET SCM, 1999).
N. T. Wright and M. Borg, *The Meaning of Jesus: Two Visions* (SPCK, 1999).

Introduction

'*The Lord is risen! He is risen indeed! Hallelujah!*' Every Easter I greet my congregation with this traditional Easter greeting. 'The Lord is risen!' I shout. 'He is risen indeed!' the people reply. But at this stage they seem only half-awake. So I shout out yet louder, 'The Lord is risen!' By now the church is beginning to get the message and with some fervour they shout back, 'He is risen indeed!' Excitement really is mounting. Yet once more I proclaim, 'The Lord is risen!' The congregation now has the message and roars back, 'He is risen indeed!' And together we lift the rafters, as it were, and praise God with an almighty 'Hallelujah!'

In this respect the story comes to mind of how on Easter Sunday 1960 the great Methodist preacher W. E. Sangster lay speechless and helpless. He was able, however, to write a message to his daughter, Margaret: 'It is terrible to wake up on Easter morning and have no voice with which to shout, "He is risen." But it would be still more terrible to have a voice and not want to shout.'

Easter Sunday is the most exciting Sunday of the year. It is the day when we sing almost non-stop hallelujahs to our risen Lord. I cannot understand any pastor wanting to be away from his or her church on that greatest of Christian festivals. Indeed, I find it difficult to understand church members who decide to take a holiday at that time. Easter is a day for celebration. If ever there is a day for popping the champagne, it is surely Easter Sunday. Or if champagne is not your thing, then on Easter Sunday find another way to party in your own manner – tie bunches of balloons (preferably helium-filled) to the pulpit, hand out Easter eggs galore to the children. In one way or another let joy be tangible, and let the world know that Jesus is alive.

And yet for all the excitement, preaching at Easter can be among the most boring of the year. For so much Easter preaching is predictable, simply more of the same, year by year. I know, because I've been a preacher for over thirty years. For my sins I've kept copies of all the sermons I've preached over the years. With a fair degree of embarrassment I've reread my Easter sermons and discovered that for the most part they have all been variations on a theme: 'Face the facts – Jesus rose from the dead. The evidence is incontrovertible. The tomb was empty. The appearances were for real. Jesus is alive. Hallelujah!' Even many of the illustrations get recycled. Perhaps after all there *is* a reason why church people go away at Easter time!

In one sense, of course, preachers need not be ashamed if their message is the same. There is but one message: 'The Lord is risen!' Yet somehow preachers need constantly to find new ways of repackaging the message, if the message is to remain fresh and vibrant in the hearts and minds of their congregations. I have no doubt that the best way to retain this freshness and vibrancy is to expound Scripture. For there is tremendous variety within Scripture. The four evangelists, thank God, do not repeat one another verbatim. Each has a different emphasis; each has a different point to make. What is true of the Gospels is true too of the rest of the New Testament. Paul, Peter, and all the other voices found in Scripture contribute to the kaleidoscope that is the message of the resurrection. Frankly, thematic preaching doesn't work – or at least, it doesn't work on an Easter-by-Easter basis.

But, of course, Easter preaching cannot – or rather should not – be limited to Easter Day. Nor indeed should it be limited to the fifty days in the liturgical calendar known as 'Eastertide', which stretch from Easter Day to Pentecost. Easter preaching is the call of the church throughout the year. When Paul visited Athens he preached 'Jesus and the resurrection' to such a degree that some Athenians became confused and thought he was preaching two gods – Jesus and Anastasis (Acts 17:18). The confusion was regrettable, but none the less instructive. Even for Paul, the great theologian of the cross, the message of resurrection was supreme. Sadly, my impression today is that preaching, in the Western world at least, has lost this Easter note. On those occasions when I have had opportunity to visit other churches and to listen to other preachers, the dominant note has not been that of Easter. In some circles the incarnation is the great miracle; in other circles the cross is the focus of attention. Not surprisingly there has been a notable absence of dynamism in many of these churches. The truth is, 'If the Church had contemplated the Empty Tomb as much as the Cross of its Lord, its life would have been more exhilarating and its contribution to the world more positive than has been the case.'[1] As it is, by and large, Easter hymns are restricted to

---

[1] G. R. Beasley-Murray, *Preaching the Gospel from the Gospels* (Lutterworth, 1956), p. 46.

Easter Day. Somehow we have forgotten that first and foremost we are Easter people. As Easter people we have an Easter gospel, a gospel which means good news every week, and indeed every day of the year.

In the first place, the Easter gospel is good news because it proclaims that Jesus is alive. The tomb was empty! The Lord appeared to Peter and the other disciples! Jesus Christ is the same – yesterday, today and for ever! In the second place, the Easter gospel is good news because it proclaims a risen Saviour. Our sins have been forgiven! God has set his seal of approval on the crucified! Jesus was raised to life for our justification! In the third place, the Easter gospel is good news because it proclaims a glorious hope. Death has been swallowed up in victory! We shall be with the Lord for ever! Jesus has brought life and immortality to light! In the fourth place, and of no less importance, the Easter gospel is good news because it proclaims a present power. The risen Lord Jesus is present with his people today! Already in the here and now we may begin to share in the risen life of Jesus! Even in our present moments of weakness we may experience the transforming power of his resurrection! Here is good news indeed. The resurrection is more than a past event and a future prospect; it is a present reality.

The conviction that underlies this book is simply this: the resurrection is the climax of the Christian gospel. Indeed, without the resurrection there would be no gospel. In the words of Michael Ramsey, a former Archbishop of Canterbury, 'The Gospel without the Resurrection is not merely a Gospel without its final chapter; it is not a gospel at all.'[2] Or in the words of George Carey, the present Archbishop of Canterbury, 'The fact is that without the resurrection of Jesus there would be no Christianity, no church, and certainly no millennium celebrations.'[3] Ramsey and Carey were in fact simply restating the thrust of Paul's argument in 1 Corinthians 15, which Eugene Peterson graphically paraphrases in the following way: 'If there's no resurrection for Christ, everything we've told you is smoke and mirrors, and everything you've staked your life on is smoke and mirrors . . . And if Christ wasn't raised, then all you're doing is wandering about in the dark, as lost as ever . . . If all we get out of Christ is a little inspiration for a few short years, we're a pretty sorry lot.'[4]

The resurrection is the first article of the Christian faith and the demonstration of all the rest. In the light of that conviction I have

[2] A. M. Ramsey, *The Resurrection of Christ: A Study of the Event and its Meaning for the Christian Faith* (reissued Fontana, 1961), p. 9.
[3] G. Carey, *Jesus 2000* (HarperCollins, 1999), p. 43.
[4] E. Peterson, *The Message* (Navpress, 1993).

sought to write a book for preachers, indeed for all who open up the word of God – a book that will, I hope, help preachers to preach the message of the resurrection. This book is different from most other books on the resurrection for several reasons.

First, unlike some books on the resurrection, this one sets out to expound a wide range of Scripture passages relating to the resurrection as distinct from a merely thematic and more general approach to the Scriptures. It is my conviction that expository preaching is the key to enabling pastors to remain fresh in their preaching Easter by Easter. Congregations can all too easily become bored if, for instance, their pastors preach what are in effect variations on the theme of the empty tomb or of the appearances of the risen Christ. By contrast, the interest of congregations is much more likely to be roused when they discover, for example, that the four evangelists all have slightly different approaches to the resurrection of Jesus. This book seeks to take seriously the diversity as well as the unity of Scripture.

Secondly, precisely because this book seeks to expound a variety of Scripture passages, it differs from many other books on the resurrection in so far as it does not focus just on the more narrow interests of apologetics, but rather seeks to paint the message of the resurrection on a larger canvas. If the truth be told, much Easter preaching treats the Scriptures as a peg on which to hang the arguments for the historicity of the resurrection yet again. The choice of Scripture texts may vary from year to year, but the content of the preaching is for the most part unvaried. The upshot is again a sense of boredom on the part of the congregation. My conviction is that although expository preaching should never neglect the need for an apologetic approach to the resurrection (and in this book, in the course of expounding Scripture, we shall discover good reasons for believing in the resurrection of Jesus), apologetics should not be allowed to become an unhelpful straitjacket for the message of the resurrection.

Thirdly, this book differs from some other books on the resurrection in so far as the overall concern is not with the minutiae of scholarship, important though such matters may be in other contexts, but with the Easter message itself. Sadly, so many commentaries and works of scholarship appear to have anybody but the preacher in mind. Much, if not most, of their material is totally irrelevant to the needs of those who come to worship in our churches. This, however, is where this book is different. For although I was trained in the academic rigours of New Testament research, above all I am a pastor; and it is as a pastor with the needs of my people in mind that I have sought to write this book. My conviction is that although there is a place for scholarly interaction, this place is not the pulpit. The task of preaching is not to expound the latest views of scholarship, but rather to expound Scripture itself. This, however, does not mean that I have adopted a negative approach toward scholarship. Indeed, rightly understood, the task of theological scholarship is to be a vehicle of the Spirit, guiding us into 'all truth' (John 16:13). As a careful reading of the text will I hope show, although the bulk of this book is relatively light on footnotes, I have consulted and absorbed the works of scholars. Furthermore, in the final chapter I have sought to give an overview of the wider theological debate on the resurrection of Jesus.

One of the difficulties I have faced in writing this book has been the selection of passages on which to comment. Clearly the resurrection narratives were 'musts'. So too the two key Pauline texts in 1 Corinthians 15 and 2 Corinthians 5. But what else? At a very early stage I set out to make a list of those Scripture passages where the message of the resurrection was to the fore. The list proved far greater than could finally be encompassed in this book:

John 2:18–22; 10:14–18; 11:1–44

Acts 2:22–26; 3:13–15; 4:1–4, 8–12; 5:27–32; 10:37–43; 17:2, 18; 23:6–8; 24:15–21; 25:13–22; 26:6–8

Rom. 1:3–4; 4:25; 6:1–14; 8:11, 33–34; 10:6

2 Cor. 4:7–18; 5:14–15; 5:17

Gal. 1:1–3

Eph. 1:13–14, 15–23; 2:14–18, 19–22; 3:14–19; 4:7–11

Phil. 2:8–11; 3:8–11

Col. 1:18–20; 3:1–17

1 Thess. 1:9, 10; 4:13–18

1 Tim. 3:16

2 Tim. 1:8–10, 12–14; 2:8–13; 4:7–8

Titus 2:11–14

Heb. 6:1–3; 9:24–28; 12:1–3, 22–24; 13:20–21

1 Pet. 1:1–11, 13; 3:18–22

Rev. 1:1, 2; 1:12–18; 5:6–14; 7.9–17; 11:15–18; 15:3–4; 19:5–8; 20:4–6; 21:1–7, 22–23; 22:3–5, 12–13, 16–17

This was just the initial list. No doubt, had I given further attention to developing the list, more passages could have been found. In the end, for reasons of space, I decided to limit myself. As will be seen, I have grouped my selection of passages into seven main sections.

The first four sections involve a detailed investigation of the resurrection narratives as found in Mark, Matthew, Luke and John. Needless to say, the witness of the Gospels to the resurrection is not limited to these climactic narratives. The very existence of the Gospels is a witness to the resurrection of Jesus. The Gospels are 'good news' only in so far as the Jesus of whom they speak is the risen Lord. Had the story of Jesus ended with the cross, there would have been no gospel – nor would there have been four Gospels.

The fifth section examines the witness of Paul to the resurrection. Paul is often portrayed as the theologian of the cross, and yet all his teaching on the atonement would have been as nothing without the resurrection. The Christ crucified whom Paul proclaimed (see, e.g., 1 Cor. 1:18 – 2:5) was at one and the same time the risen Christ. Indeed, it was his encounter with the risen Christ that led to his conversion and proved to be the basis for his calling as an apostle: 'God . . . was pleased to reveal his Son in me, so that I might preach him among the Gentiles' (Gal. 1:15–16). The resurrection of Jesus was of the essence of the Pauline gospel.

In the sixth section, entitled 'The witness of Peter and his friends to the resurrection', we study a variety of passages found in the remaining letters, Acts and Revelation. We shall see, for instance, how the book of Acts may be termed 'the Gospel of Resurrection'. Similarly, we shall see how the book of Revelation is dominated by the image of the risen, reigning, and returning Lord Jesus. The fact is that with the exception of the eight shortest and arguably least important books of the Bible (2 Thessalonians, Titus, Philemon, James, 2 Peter, 2 and 3 John, and Jude), the resurrection of Jesus receives explicit and emphatic mention in all the other sixteen books of the New Testament

Then, under the heading of 'The witness of other voices to the resurrection', we look at the way in which some of the hymns and confessions of the early church speak of Jesus as the risen Lord, and discover that from the very beginning the resurrection was at the heart of Christian worship.

Finally, we consider the more mixed voices of recent theologians, concluding that the only proper theological response to the resurrection of Jesus from the dead is doxology.

As a result of this wide-ranging, albeit selective, study, one thing, I hope, will become clear: the message of the resurrection permeates every stratum of the New Testament. The resurrection of Jesus is its key message.

1. The witness of Mark to the resurrection

1. The empty tomb (16:1–8)

When the Sabbath was over, Mary Magdalene, Mary the mother of James, and Salome bought spices so that they might go to anoint Jesus' body. ²Very early on the first day of the week, just after sunrise, they were on their way to the tomb ³and they asked each other, 'Who will roll the stone away from the entrance of the tomb?'

⁴But when they looked up, they saw that the stone, which was very large, had been rolled away. ⁵As they entered the tomb, they saw a young man dressed in a white robe sitting on the right side, and they were alarmed.

⁶'Don't be alarmed,' he said. 'You are looking for Jesus the Nazarene, who was crucified. He has risen! He is not here. See the place where they laid him. ⁷But go, tell his disciples and Peter, "He is going ahead of you into Galilee. There you will see him, just as he told you."'

⁸Trembling and bewildered, the women went out and fled from the tomb. They said nothing to anyone, because they were afraid.
[The shorter ending of Mark]

The resurrection of Jesus is at the heart of our faith. Christianity is above all a religion of resurrection. The church is called primarily to be the community of the resurrection. All this makes Mark's account of the resurrection so strange. For Mark appears to end his Gospel with the words, *Trembling and bewildered, the women went out and fled from the tomb. They said nothing to anyone, because they were afraid* (Mark 16:8). What an anticlimactic way to end a Gospel!

Perhaps not surprisingly, at a very early stage in the copying of Mark's Gospel, two attempts were made to round it off in what seemed a more fitting manner. One attempt is known as the 'longer ending' of Mark and appears in most Bibles as Mark 16:9–20. These verses tell of Jesus' appearance to Mary Magdalene, then of his appearance to two disciples, followed by an account of his appearance to the Eleven, and finally of his ascension. However, as is indicated in most modern versions of the Bible, the earliest and therefore the most reliable of Gospel manuscripts do not have Mark 16:9–20. It is almost universally agreed among New Testament scholars that these verses are a later addition to the Gospel. The style and vocabulary of these verses are in fact very different from the rest of Mark. They were probably added some time before the middle of the second century.

But to return to Mark 16:1–8. Did Mark intend to finish his Gospel where it currently appears to end? At this point there is a division of opinion. Many, if not most, scholars believe that Mark's Gospel ends prematurely. It is possible, for instance, that the original ending was lost. Perhaps the original papyrus version of the Gospel got damaged and mutilated. Alternatively it has been suggested that for some unknown reason Mark failed to finish his work. Certainly it does seem difficult to believe that Mark would have ended his Gospel in its present form. Indeed, the reference to Jesus' going ahead to Galilee (v. 7) tends to imply that Mark ended his Gospel – as the other evangelists did – with at least one actual appearance of Jesus to his disciples.

Not all are convinced, however, that Mark's Gospel ends prematurely. There are scholars who believe that Mark deliberately intended to end in this abrupt manner. They argue that Mark's failure to give an account of a resurrection appearance of Jesus to his followers does not mean to say that Mark did not believe in such appearances – they are in fact implied here in these first eight verses. Mark dispensed with any such account, they suggest, because he wanted to put the emphasis elsewhere. In particular, Mark wished to emphasize the cost of Christian discipleship.

It has to be remembered that Mark was writing to the church at Rome at a time when the church was about to enter a violent period of persecution, when many Christians, the apostle Peter included, were to lose their lives. Mark, it is argued, arranged his material in such a way as to underline the fact that the church's lot was to be no different from that of its Master. To follow Jesus is to go the way of the cross (Mark 8:34). The church is called to live under the cross – true, a cross bathed in resurrection glory, but a cross nevertheless. This emphasis, it is suggested, accounts for Mark ending his Gospel in the way he did. An overtly triumphal conclusion to the story of Jesus would have been inappropriate.

Whether or not Mark did intend to end his Gospel at 16:8, there is something to be said for this emphasis today. For although, in the Western world at least, Christians may no longer face persecution, there is a tendency in the churches of the West to centre on glory, and to pass over the themes of suffering and self-denial. But in the words of the old Negro spiritual, 'we cannot wear the crown if we do not bear the cross'. Cross-bearing is never an optional extra.

a. Mark's account of the empty tomb

Each Gospel account of the first Easter differs from the others. The differences between the Gospel narratives, however, are relatively slight (e.g. the number and names of the women, the number of angels, their varied reaction to the angelic message) and can be fairly easily reconciled. We should not be unduly disturbed by these differences. In the first place, we need to remember that from beginning to end of their Gospels each evangelist has a different emphasis to make, because each has a different audience to address. In the second place, the very differences are indications of historical reliability – where witnesses agree in every respect, suspicion arises that there may have been an attempt to make up a story. In this respect Professor Sir Norman Anderson, the former Director of the Institute of Advanced Legal Studies at the University of London, had some wise words to say:

> It is common experience for a lawyer to note how a number of witnesses will almost invariably give accounts which differ widely from each other, initially at least, about any incident at which they have all been present. Each individual will see it from a different angle (both literally and metaphorically); will note some, but by no means all, of the relevant facts; and will usually be highly selective in what he actually remembers. To a considerable degree, therefore, minor differences in some of the resurrection stories may be regarded as actually strengthening the evidence rather than weakening it; for if a number of witnesses tell exactly the same story, with no divergences, it is nearly always a sign that they have been 'coached' as to what they would say, or at least have conferred together on the subject.[1]

All four Gospels agree that women were the first to discover the empty tomb and to receive the news of the resurrection. Here in Mark we are told that there were three: *Mary Magdalene, Mary the mother of James, and Salome* (v. 1). In Matthew only two are named: 'Mary

[1] N. Anderson, *A Lawyer among the Theologians* (Hodder & Stoughton, 1973), p. 109.

Magdalene and the other Mary' (Matt. 28:1). In Luke there are more: 'Mary Magdalene, Joanna, Mary the mother of James, and the others with them' (Luke 24:10). In John only Mary Magdalene is mentioned (John 20:1), although others are implied (John 20:2). The only woman who is therefore common to all four accounts is Mary Magdalene. However, ultimately it is not the names that count, but rather the sex. No first-century Gospel writer would ever have dreamt of mentioning women as witnesses of the empty tomb unless it happened to be true. For women did not count. The rabbis used to say, 'Sooner let the words of the Law be burnt than delivered to women.' In the Jewish Morning Prayer there was a line in which the men said, 'Blessed art thou, O Lord our God, King of the universe, who hast not made me a woman . . .' But God was not – and is not – bound by human prejudices. God was pleased to allow the women to have precedence over the male apostles that day.

These women *bought spices so that they might go to anoint Jesus' body* (v. 1). Some have questioned whether the women actually went with the purpose of anointing the body of Jesus, on the ground that in a hot country the body would well and truly have begun to rot. This objection carries no weight, however, since it can be quite cool in mountainous Jerusalem in early spring. A more significant objection might have been the fact that, according to John 19:38–42, Joseph of Arimathea and Nicodemus had already anointed the body with about 75lbs (34kg) of spices. However, even this objection is not decisive. Sometimes love for others causes people to go 'over the top' in expressing their love. But here the important thing to note is that for the women this last act of devotion was the closing of a final chapter. There was no thought in their minds of resurrection. As far as they, and indeed others, were concerned, Jesus was dead and buried, and would remain so.

It was not until the Saturday evening, *when the Sabbath was over* (v. 1), that the women had an opportunity to go out and buy spices with which to anoint Jesus. They had to wait, however, until the night itself was over before they could venture out to the tomb. At this point there is no mention of men. The disciples had heard Jesus talk of service (Mark 10:42–45), but it was the women who truly put the teaching of Jesus into action. In spite of the teaching of church history, where male figures dominate, the true heroes of the Christian church were and still are women.

The women made their way *very early on the first day of the week, just after sunrise* (v. 2). According to John, the women went 'while it was still dark' (John 20:1). This need not be viewed as a major contradiction, however. We can well imagine the women setting out in the dark, but arriving in the light.

Their destination was *the tomb* (v. 2) where the body of Jesus was laid. It was the custom of the citizens of Jerusalem to bury their dead outside the city walls (see Mark 12:8; Luke 7:12; Acts 14:19) – to this day ancient rock-cut tombs surround the walls of Jerusalem on all three sides (but not on the west, from where the prevailing winds blew!). These tombs were normally intended to hold a number of bodies and often had a series of burial chambers leading off the main antechamber. Sometimes the bodies were buried in tunnels ('kôkîm') cut in a 'pigeon-hole' arrangement, 2 metres or more deep into the rock, and about 60 cm wide and high. At other times the bodies were laid in semicircular niches (*arcosolia*) formed by cutting away the side walls of the tomb to a depth of up to a metre and about 75 cm up from the ground level. The niche was cut to leave either a flat shelf or a trough on which a body could be placed. There were also 'bench' tombs where the body was laid on a bench that ran around three sides of the tomb. These tombs were cut into the soft limestone rock (15:46). The entrance of such a tomb was blocked by a rounded stone, like an upright millstone, which was rolled in a groove before the entrance. A heavy stone (see 16:3) would not only keep out wild animals, but also discourage theft.

As they went, *they asked each other* – more accurately, 'they were asking each other', for the Greek verb is in the imperfect (*elegon*) – *'Who will roll the stone away from the entrance to the tomb?'* (v. 3). In their concern to anoint the body, the women had apparently not given any thought to the question of how they might shift the *very large* (v. 4) stone blocking the door of the tomb. But once on their way to the tomb, this question repeatedly came to mind. The clear implication is that the stone was too large for women to move. This was men's work.

When they arrived, however, they discovered that *the stone . . . had been rolled away* (v. 4). In fact this was not men's work at all. This was God's work. The passive tense here would have been understood by readers of Mark's Gospel as a 'divine passive'.

They entered the tomb (v. 5). As they did so, they must have had to crouch, for the entrance to such a tomb tended to be small and low. Inside there would probably have been room to stand. A simple burial chamber would perhaps have been 2 metres or so square and the same height.

There in the tomb *they saw a young man dressed in a white robe* (v. 5). In the present context the 'young man' is clearly an angel. In the Gospel narratives of the resurrection the task of the angels is to be the link between the events of the resurrection and the women. For the resurrection of Jesus itself was not witnessed by human eyes. The angels alone were witnesses. In this capacity of witnesses they

25

act as 'messengers' (the literal meaning of the word for 'angel') conveying the news of the resurrection of Jesus from the dead.

The sight of an angelic figure is no everyday occurrence. Perhaps not surprisingly the women were *alarmed* (v. 5). Indeed, 'frightened out of their wits' might be a better expression. Mark is the only evangelist to use such a strong word (*ekthambeō*) to convey fear and amazement.

The angel immediately sought to reassure the women: *'Don't be alarmed . . . Jesus the Nazarene, who was crucified . . . has risen!'* (v. 6). With hindsight the juxtaposition of crucifixion and resurrection would bring reassurance. At the time, however, the turnaround in Jesus' fortunes disturbed the women even more. Even today a dead Christ is easier to come to terms with than a living Lord. The former offers stability of a kind, the latter never ceases to surprise. Stability rather than surprise is still the preferred option in many a church.

'He has risen!' (v. 6), declared the angel. Or perhaps more accurately, 'he has been raised' (*ēgerthē*). Mark uses here a passive tense. Although it is possible for the passive tense not to be given its full force (see 2:12), almost certainly Mark is using a 'divine passive'. In the New Testament the resurrection is above all an act of God (e.g. Acts 3:15; 4:10; Rom. 4:24; 8:11; 10:9; 1 Cor. 6:14; 15:15; 2 Cor. 4:14; 1 Pet. 1:21). Jesus does not rise from the dead of his own accord; rather, it is God who raises Jesus from the dead. This is true even in the Fourth Gospel, where the resurrection is depicted as the completion of the works given by the Father to the Son to do (see John 10:17–18). Like the rest of those works, the resurrection is ultimately the work of the Father through the Son (see John 5:19–30). Although the perspective may be slightly different, the resurrection of the Son is certainly not independent of the Father.

'He is not here' (v. 6). Ironically, for the women the first experience of the resurrection of Jesus was not his presence, but his absence. The tomb was empty. The appearances of Jesus to his disciples came later.

'See the place where they laid him' (v. 6). The empty tomb is in itself strong evidence of resurrection. Nevertheless, there have been many who have sought to throw doubt on the evidence. It has, for instance, been suggested that the women went by mistake to the wrong tomb, and that a young man directed them to the right tomb with the words, 'He is not here: behold, there is the place where they laid him.' This explanation, however, takes no account of the fact that Mark tells us that Mary Magdalene and Mary the mother of Joses had seen where the body of Jesus was laid (15:47). Furthermore, it involves reworking the words of the angel, including

removing all reference to resurrection. To tamper with the evidence in such a way is not a mark of critical historical enquiry but rather a sign of prejudice and partiality.

The angel declared, *'He is going ahead of you into Galilee. There you will see him, just as he told you'* (v. 7). According to Mark 14:28 Jesus on the way to the Mount of Olives had already told his disciples, 'But after I have risen, I will go ahead of you into Galilee.' Now just three days later the women are reminded of this promise of Jesus. Some commentators have questioned the veracity of Mark's account and have sought to limit the appearances of Jesus to Jerusalem. There is no logical reason, however, why the appearances should be limited to one geographical place. Although the Gospels record Jesus initially appearing to his disciples as also to the women in Jerusalem (e.g. Matt. 28:9; Luke 24:34, 36–49; John 20:14–17, 19–23, 24–29) and on the road to Emmaus (Luke 24:13–31), they also tell of his appearing to his disciples in Galilee (e.g. Matt. 28:16–20; John 21:1–23). The traditions of appearances in Jerusalem and in Galilee are equally legitimate.

Instead of joy, fear and bewilderment were the paramount reactions of the women to the angelic message (v. 8). The last thing the women expected to see was an empty tomb, and even more amazing was the thought of resurrection. Those who loved Jesus, who were prepared to give their all for him, did not expect a miracle, did not expect God to be at work. Instead, like the disciples in the Garden of Gethsemane (14:50), *they fled from the tomb. They said nothing to anyone, because they were afraid* (v. 8). As the other Gospels make clear, their silence was not to last long. They were soon to tell the disciples. But initially words failed them. They were stunned by God's mighty act of resurrection.

b. The women were the true heroes

With hindsight it is easy to scoff at the women. Fancy their setting out for the tomb without having first considered how they might roll away the large circular stone that guarded the entrance! If they had had any sense, they would have brought one of the male disciples along with them. Fancy too their being afraid of the angel and the empty tomb! Surely they should have been overjoyed at what they saw. Rather than keeping quiet, they should have rushed to tell the disciples that Jesus had risen from the dead. These women were pretty slow!

But to scoff at the women is to misunderstand the story. For in contrast to the disciples, the women were the real heroes. Indeed, have not women always been the real heroes? Whether men like it or not, when it comes to devotion to Christ, women win hands down. During the ministry of Jesus, it was women who provided economic support for Jesus and his disciples (Mark 15:41; Luke 8:2–3). At the crucifixion, when all save the Beloved Disciple had deserted Jesus, women were there (Matt. 27:55–56; Mark 15:40–41; Luke 24:49; John 20:25–27). Even when Jesus was dead, the women were the first to go to the scene. As Mark reminds us, it was the women who *bought spices so that they might go to anoint Jesus' body* (16:1). Strictly speaking, this task was unnecessary – Nicodemus together with Joseph of Arimathea had already seen to it (John 20:38–42). What was more, in a climate such as Palestine's, to anoint a body that had already been dead two nights and a day could well have been viewed as a useless task. But these women were devoted to Jesus. It was love for Jesus that prompted them to go what may have seemed a worthless extra mile.

No, we dare not scoff at these women. Rather, we should admire them. We should allow their devotion to challenge our devotion. Our question should be, 'Do we love Jesus in the way they loved him?' Perhaps it was because of their devotion to Jesus that they were given the privilege of being the first to receive the news of his resurrection. It was not Peter, James or John who first found the empty tomb, but the two Marys and Salome.

c. The stone was rolled away

Mark tells us that as the women made their way to the tomb, they were asking, '*Who will roll the stone away from the entrance to the tomb?*' (v. 3). And well might they ask! For the stone was *very large* (v. 4) – indeed, according to one New Testament manuscript (Codex Bezae) twenty men could hardly have moved it.

We build our tombs differently today. No cool cave for us. Rather, for some of us a damp hole 2000 × 60 cm in the ground; and for an increasing majority of us an even smaller hole where our cremated remains will be laid to rest. And yet for all of us that cartwheel of stone is a meaningful symbol. It speaks of the death that must come to each one of us. It doesn't matter who we are or what we have done, death will come to us. However much power we may exercise in this life, there will be a day when our power comes to an end. No human power has been found to defeat the power of death. This is the message of the stone.

But thank God, the stone didn't have the last word. For when the women came to the tomb they discovered that the stone had been rolled away. What was beyond their means was not beyond the means of God. '*He has risen!*' declared the angel (v. 6). God had raised his Son from the dead. Death may mark the end of our power – but not of God's power. Death was not the end for Jesus – neither need death be the end for us.

d. The crucified Nazarene is the risen Christ

The message of the angel closely combines the themes of crucifixion and resurrection. Punctuation apart, in the Greek text the two verbs *was crucified* and *has risen* follow each other without a break (v. 6). Here surely is a lesson for any preacher.

Preachers are called to sound the note of vindication. The Nazarene, crucified so ignominiously, had been raised from the dead. The verdict of the centurion, 'Surely this man was the Son of God!' (Mark 15:39), was confirmed on Easter Day for all to see. Furthermore, as Peter made clear on the day of Pentecost, God did not abandon Jesus to the grave (see Acts 2:31). Appearances can be misleading: God may have seemed to have forsaken his Son (Mark 15:34), but in fact the very reverse was true – for God raised Jesus from the dead. The powers of evil did their worst, but they did not – and never will – have the last word.

For Mark's readers, undergoing the fires of persecution, this will have been a powerful message of encouragement. God will have the last word! Those who commit their cause to him will be vindicated! It is a message of encouragement that many also need to hear today. For life can be tough. Indeed, life can become tough precisely because we seek to follow the Lord Jesus. This is not surprising – Jesus called his followers to a life of cross-bearing (Mark 8:34). But, as Jesus went on to say, it is in losing our life that we find it (Mark 8:35). The cross is not the end of the story. Those who know the darkness of Good Friday may draw comfort – Sunday is coming!

The crucified is also the risen Lord. Here too is a reminder to preachers never to overemphasize the cross to the detriment of the resurrection. 'For even the Son of Man . . . [came] to give his life as a ransom for many,' said Jesus (Mark 10:45), but this act of self-giving was not the end of the story: 'the Son of Man must suffer . . . and rise again' (Mark 8:31; cf. 9:10, 12). 'We preach Christ crucified,' declared the apostle Paul (1 Cor. 1:24), but the crucified Saviour is also the risen Lord. The cross is always bathed in resurrection glory. When at the table of the Lord we remember the death of the 'crucified Nazarene', it is always too the death of the one who was raised to life. For it is the resurrection that transforms and completes the work of Christ on the cross. It is the resurrection that is the climax of the gospel story.

e. The first day of the week

All four Gospels mention that it was *on the first day of the week* (Mark 16:2; Matt. 28:1; Luke 24:1; John 20:1) that the women discovered that the tomb was empty. At one level the day may well appear to be an insignificant accident of chronology. The basic message of the resurrection would have remained the same, whether the empty tomb had been discovered on a Monday, Tuesday or indeed any other day of the week. And yet the chronology is rich with symbolism. For, as the book of Genesis makes clear, it was on the first day of the week that God began his work of creation (Gen. 1:3–5). Now in the Gospels we discover that it was on the first day of the week that Jesus rose from the dead. From this we may rightly infer that in the resurrection of Jesus God was setting about his work of new creation. Jesus is the 'beginning' of a new order of life (Col. 1:18). In the words of the apostle Paul, 'if anyone is in Christ, he is a new creation; the old has gone, the new has come!' (2 Cor. 5:17).

Very quickly the 'first day of the week' became the day when Christians met for worship. Luke, for instance, tells us that it was 'on the first day of the week' that the church at Troas came together to break bread (Acts 20:7). When Paul came to give instructions for taking up the collection for the poor of Jerusalem, he urged the Corinthians to set aside money in proportion to their income on 'the first day of every week' (1 Cor. 16:2). By the time the book of Revelation was written the 'first day' was known as 'the Lord's Day' (Rev. 1:10). This was the day when the lordship of Jesus over sin and death was celebrated. Unlike the Jewish Sabbath, Sunday is not primarily a day of rest. In one sense the slogan 'Keep Sunday special' is misleading, for the special quality of Sunday has nothing to do with shops being closed or with the family being together. Sunday for Christians is a day of celebration. It is the day when the church is called to celebrate God's mighty act in raising Jesus from the dead. In this sense every Sunday is an Easter Day. Every Sunday is a day for the church to sing its Easter 'hallelujahs'. To restrict Easter hymns to Easter Day is to fail to perceive the overriding importance of the resurrection. The church by definition is the community of the resurrection.

Sadly, for most people Sunday is no longer the first day of the week. Diaries today print Monday as the first day of the week. Sunday is the last day of the week, now just part of the weekend. Shop assistants and essential workers apart, Sunday has entered the private domain and has become a day of leisure, a day when people can do their own thing, whatever that might be. Not surprisingly the worship of God on a Sunday has become an optional extra even for some Christians: if, for instance, friends or relatives visit, churchgoing tends to go by the wayside. As Christians, however, we need to recover the controlling significance of Sunday. Sunday worship is a priority, for it is on this day that we celebrate the power of God to raise Jesus from the dead and so we are able to put all our concerns into perspective. Furthermore, Jesus is the risen Lord, and as such has a claim not only on what we do together in church, but also on how we live and work from Monday to Saturday.

f. 'Go, tell ... Peter'

The women were told by the angel to take the message of the resurrection to the *disciples and Peter* (Mark 16:7). The word order is surely significant. Had the angel said, 'Go, tell Peter and the disciples,' the emphasis would have been on Peter as if he were the most important disciple. As it is, there is a different emphasis. Peter is not to be forgotten: 'Go and tell his disciples – and don't forget Peter.' Peter is singled out, because he was the disciple who had most failed Jesus.

What a wonderful message this must have been for Peter! How it must have cheered his heart when he received it! He must have been tortured with the memory of his disloyalty. How could he have denied his Lord, not just once, but three times? And suddenly there comes this message, a special message for him. He, of all the disciples, is picked out. Here is a message of forgiveness. Peter may have turned his back on his Lord, but his Lord has not turned his back on him. The message of the angel assures Peter of love and of forgiveness.

What a wonderful message for Peter – and in turn what a wonderful message for us! We may not have literally denied Jesus three times, but in one way or another all of us have failed him. Furthermore, we have failed him as his disciples. Like Peter we have professed our love and devotion for him, and yet we, his followers, have let our Lord down. The message of the angel speaks to us about new beginnings – it is about forgiveness, hope, renewal.

To put it another way, the message of the angel is about *grace*. The women may have deserved to be the first to receive the news of the resurrection; but Peter didn't deserve his special message of cheer. Neither for that matter do we. For we too are men and women who know what it is to boast and to betray, to declare and to deny, to strut and to weep bitterly. Yet God in his love acts beyond our deserving. The message of Easter is a message of grace. There is one who understands, forgives and restores. Easter is a time of new beginnings.

g. *The risen Christ goes ahead of us*

The angel declared, *'He is going ahead of you into Galilee'* (v. 7). Not 'he will go' or 'he has gone', but 'he *is going* ahead of' his disciples. In other words, the present tense is used. At one level this was a purely factual description: Jesus, says the angel, is already on the move, making his way to Galilee.[2] It may well be, however, that in his Gospel Mark intended to convey something more.

In the first place, Mark may have seen this instruction as having significance for all who would follow Jesus. For he uses the same verb (*proagō*) in Mark 10:32. There, just before the passion, Mark records that the disciples 'were on their way up to Jerusalem, with Jesus leading (*proagōn*) the way'. It may well be that Mark intends us to see here a picture of Christian discipleship. For disciples are by definition followers of Jesus (see Mark 8:48; John 10:46). This comes to expression, for instance, in Mark 10:52, where the healed Bartimaeus follows Jesus on the 'road' (or 'way', *hodos*). Christians do not just recite a creed; they follow a person. There is a dynamic element to Christian believing: for as Christians we belong to 'the Way' (Acts 9:2: see also 19:23; 22:4; 24:14, NRSV); as Christians we belong to a movement, and not to an institution. If Christian discipleship means following a Lord who goes ahead of us, then this means that we cannot – at least should not – live in the past. We are constantly on a journey. We can never stand still, for we have never arrived. Our experience of the Lord Jesus should never remain in the past, but rather should always be in the present.

In the second place, Mark may have seen significance in the very word 'Galilee'. Galilee for Mark may not just have been a physical location. Certainly, as far as the disciples and the women were concerned, Galilee was the place of every day. It was the place from which they came; it was their home turf; it was the place of work, the place of daily routine. With this in mind, Easter becomes more than a celebration that Jesus appeared to his disciples at particular times and in particular places; it becomes a reminder that Jesus goes ahead of us and meets us in the places where we live and work. Just as Jesus invited his disciples to meet him in Galilee, so he invites us to meet him in our Galilees. Jesus invites us to find him within our daily routines. Jesus is not just present with his people when they

---

[2] According to John Calvin, 'When the angel sent the disciples into Galilee, he did so, I think, in order that Christ might make himself known to a greater number of persons; for we know that he lived a long time in Galilee. He intended also to give his followers greater liberty, that by the very circumstances of their retirement they might gradually acquire courage. Besides, by their being accustomed to the places, they were aided in recognizing their Master with greater certainty.'

gather together in worship; he is present with his people as they disperse into their various walks of life. The Christ of Easter Day is the Christ of every day!

But there may be yet another aspect present. In Matthew's Gospel, and maybe in Mark's too, Galilee is the place of mission. Matthew, for instance, in his Gospel, links a quotation from Isaiah 9:1–2 with the beginning of Jesus' ministry:

> When Jesus heard that John had been put in prison, he went away to Galilee . . . This was done to make what the prophet Isaiah has said come true . . .
>
> 'Galilee, land of the Gentiles
> The people who live in darkness will see a great light.
> On those who live in the dark land of death
> the light will shine.'
>
> From that time Jesus began to preach . . .
> (Matt. 4:12–17).

It is perhaps not without significance that it was in Galilee that, according to Matthew, Jesus issues his Great Commission, adding 'and I am with you always' (Matt. 28:18–20, GNB). From this we may infer that Jesus goes before us into the Galilees of this world – those 'dark' places where 'death' reigns. Furthermore, Jesus assures us of his presence as we go to share the good news of his death and resurrection.

h. Emotions on Easter Day

Easter Day is traditionally a day of great joy. According to Mark's Gospel, however, fear and bewilderment characterized the women on Easter Day. The discovery of the empty tomb and the sight of the angel caused the women to be *alarmed* (v. 5). When they heard that the crucified Jesus had risen from the dead the women fled *trembling and bewildered* (v. 8). To cap it all, Mark records that, initially at least, *They said nothing to anyone, because they were afraid* (v. 8).

These twin emotions of 'fear' and 'bewilderment' (the latter at times translated 'amazement') frequently come to the fore in Mark. Jesus constantly surprised and disturbed his contemporaries. The stilling of the storm (4:41), the healing of the Gerasene demoniac (5:5), and the experience of the transfiguration (9:6; cf. 9:15) all caused people to fear. The driving out of an evil spirit (1:27), the healing of a paralytic (2:12), the raising of Jairus's daughter (5:42), the walking on water (6:51), the healing of a deaf and mute man (7:37), all caused people to be bewildered and amazed. These emotions, although perhaps understandable, are not to be commended. According to Mark's Gospel such emotions were symptoms of a failure to understand (Mark 6:51–52; see also 8:21) and to believe (Mark 6:2, 6). In the light of such an assessment, it is possible that by their reaction the women also were showing signs of a failure to understand and to believe.

And yet we surely must not be too hard on these women. They were in the process of grieving a loved one. They were experiencing all the pain, confusion and emotion of bereavement. They were reacting in an honest and natural way to the news of Easter Day. Our difficulty today is that we have heard the story so often that we fail to react. We are like people reading a novel who have already read the last page and so know how it ends. The fact is that the bewilderment of the women is totally natural. Dead people don't rise. The message of the angel was totally unreasonable. From a human perspective it was absurd to declare that Jesus had risen from the dead. True, they believed in a resurrection, but it was a belief in a general resurrection on the last day (see John 11:24), not a resurrection in the here and now. The news of Jesus' resurrection therefore understandably amazed the women. Would that on Easter Day we could wonder a little more! In this respect we need to heed the advice of Stephen Davis: 'I believe that Christians need to recover a sense of the shocking absurdity of the very idea of the resurrection.'[3]

On Easter Day there is likewise a place for 'fear', or at least 'fear' in the sense of holy awe. The resurrection of Jesus is truly 'awesome'. God was at work. As with Moses at the burning bush, there is, as it were, a place for taking off our shoes, for it is holy ground (Exod. 3:5). Similarly, the 'fear' of the women is in some ways commendable, in the sense that it testified to the mystery and awesomeness of the event. There is a place for awe when God is at work. Alas, the happy-clappy nature of much modern worship today tends to miss this note of awe. Easter is perhaps a time when we need to pay attention to the injunction of the author of Hebrews: '... let us ... worship God acceptably with reverence and awe' (Heb. 12:28).

---

[3] S. T. Davis, *Risen Indeed: Making Sense of the Resurrection* (SPCK, 1993), p. 168.

2. Jesus appears to his disciples (16:9–20)

When Jesus rose early on the first day of the week, he appeared first to Mary Magdalene, out of whom he had driven seven demons. ¹⁰*She went and told those who had been with him and who were mourning and weeping.* ¹¹*When they heard that Jesus was alive and that she had seen him, they did not believe it.*

¹²*Afterwards Jesus appeared in a different form to two of them while they were walking in the country.* ¹³*These returned and reported it to the rest; but they did not believe them either.*

¹⁴*Later Jesus appeared to the Eleven as they were eating; he rebuked them for their lack of faith and their stubborn refusal to believe those who had seen him after he had risen.*

¹⁵*He said to them, 'Go into all the world and preach the good news to all creation.* ¹⁶*Whoever believes and is baptised will be saved, but whoever does not believe will be condemned.* ¹⁷*And these signs will accompany those who believe: In my name they will drive out demons; they will speak in new tongues;* ¹⁸*they will pick up snakes with their hands; and when they drink deadly poison, it will not hurt them at all; they will place their hands on sick people, and they will get well.'*

¹⁹*After the Lord Jesus had spoken to them, he was taken up into heaven and he sat at the right hand of God.* ²⁰*Then the disciples went out and preached everywhere, and the Lord worked with them and confirmed his word by the signs that accompanied it.*
[The longer ending]

These twelve verses, found in the Textus Receptus and thus in the Authorized Version of the Bible, almost certainly do not belong to the original text of Mark. The very first of these verses (v. 9) has, for instance, an unannounced and awkward change of subject, and unnaturally reintroduces the news of Jesus' resurrection and the character of Mary Magdalene. The longer ending is possibly a second-century addition made by some unknown scribe who clearly was unhappy that Mark's Gospel ended at verse 8. Strictly speaking, therefore, these verses, like the story of the woman caught in adultery (John 8:1–11), do not form part of the New Testament canon, for both passages are not to be found in the earliest manuscripts. Almost certainly, however, both contain genuine Gospel material. In the case of Mark 16:9–20, these verses 'show us how the Church continued to think of Easter as central and decisive, as the hinge of its history and belief and above all of its missionary proclamation and service'.[4] In

---

[4] H. Anderson, *The Gospel of Mark* (Oliphants, 1976), p. 31.

essence what we have in verses 9–20 is a summary of material contained in the other Gospels, perhaps drawn up with the needs of instructing new Christians in the faith. The appearance to Mary Magdalene (vv. 9–11) is reminiscent of John 20:11–18; the appearance to the two travellers (vv. 12–13) is reminiscent of Luke 24:13–32; the appearance to the Eleven (v. 14) is reminiscent of Luke 24:36–43; and the account of the ascension (v. 19) is reminiscent of Luke 24:50–21.

Of particular interest is the form of the Great Commission (vv. 15–18). Although parallels are often drawn with Matthew 28:18–20, verse 15 in particular is distinctively 'Markan' in style. Indeed, it can well be argued that verse 15 is an authentic summary of the message of Jesus as found in Mark. For that reason, these verses repay study and exposition.

a. The good news is Jesus

The risen Lord commands his disciples to *preach the good news to all creation* (v. 15). Good news (*euangelion*) is one of Mark's favourite words. Whereas in all his twenty-eight chapters Matthew uses the term only four times, Mark in just sixteen chapters uses it seven times, (1:1,14,15; 8:35; 10:29; 13:10; 14:9). If we add 16:15, then the total rises to eight times; that is, it is found twice as often in Mark as in Matthew. As for Luke and John, the noun does not appear once (although Luke does employ the cognate verb *euangelizomai*). From all this we deduce that, for Mark in particular, the story of Jesus was 'good news'. It was good news for the church at Rome, to which tradition has it that Mark was writing; it was good news too for the world, of which Rome was the centre and focus.

Mark indeed begins his Gospel with the words, 'The beginning of the gospel about Jesus Christ, the Son of God' (1:1). Although there was no such literary form as a 'Gospel' in our sense of word when Mark began to write his Gospel in the mid-60s, he was none the less clear that his work was 'good news', for it centred around Jesus.

This word 'gospel' was rich in associations. In the Old Testament, for instance, the cognate verb is frequently found in the latter chapters of Isaiah, where it is used of God's bringing his people from Babylonian captivity back to the Promised Land. For example,

> How beautiful on the mountains
>   are the feet of those
> who bring good news,
>   who proclaim peace,
>   who bring good tidings,

who proclaim salvation,
who say to Zion,
'Your God reigns!'

(Is. 52:7)

Or,

The Spirit of the Sovereign LORD is on me,
because the LORD has anointed me
to preach good news to the poor.
He has sent me to bind up the broken-hearted,
to proclaim freedom for the captives
and release from darkness for the prisoners.

(Is. 61:1)

These Old Testament associations of *euangelion* immediately help us to unpack something of the thrust of Mark's message. The 'good news' is that God has acted again; in Jesus, his Son, he has come to bring release to the captives. This time, however, it is not Babylon holding men and women prisoner, but the dark forces of sin and death.

But Mark did not simply write his Gospel against the background of the Old Testament. He was also writing against the background of his day. Almost certainly his readers would have noticed another contrast. For inhabitants of the Roman Empire, *euangelion* had special associations with the emperor cult, where it was used of the birth of an heir to the throne, of his coming of age, and of his accession to the throne. For example, here is a well-known decree of the Greeks of the province of Asia c. 9 BC, marking the birthday of Augustus (23 September) as the beginning of the civil year:

It is a day which we may justly count as equivalent to the beginning of everything – if not in itself and in its own nature, at any rate in the benefits it brings – inasmuch as it has restored the shape of everything that was failing and turning into misfortune, and has given a new look to the universe as a time when it would gladly have welcomed destruction if Caesar had not been born to be the common blessing of all men . . . Whereas the providence which has ordered the whole of our life, showing concern and zeal, has ordained the most perfect consummation for human life by giving to it Augustus, by filling him with virtue for doing the work of a benefactor among men, and by sending in him, as it were, a saviour for us and those who come after us, to make war to cease, to create order everywhere . . . and whereas the birthday

37

of the god [Augustus] was the beginning for the world of the glad tidings [*euangelion*] that have come to men through him . . . Paulus Fabius Maximus, the proconsul of the province . . . has devised a way of honouring Augustus hitherto unknown to the Greeks, which is, that the reckoning of time for the course of human life should begin with his birth.

Here the birth of Augustus, described as 'god' and 'saviour', is said to mark 'the beginning for the world of the glad tidings', for Augustus is seen as having ushered in an age of gold; so much so that 'the reckoning of time for the course of human life should begin with his birth'.

'No,' says Mark, as it were, 'the beginning of the gospel is found not in Augustus, but in Jesus. And furthermore, the good news centres not so much on his birth as on his death and resurrection. Jesus – through his life, death and resurrection – has ushered in a new age, the age of the Spirit; in Jesus God has begun to bring about his kingdom.' That is, when we proclaim good news, we proclaim that in Jesus the course of history has been changed. That is why all history is reckoned as BC and AD. Jesus is more than a personal saviour – he is Lord of the world. Jesus, through his death and resurrection, has begun to take up his reign. Here is good news!

b. The good news of Jesus needs to be preached

The risen Lord commands, '*Go . . . and preach the good news*' (v. 15). The verb 'to preach' is another favourite word of Mark's. It is found twelve times in Mark's Gospel (fourteen times if we include Mark 16:15, 20), as compared to nine times in Matthew and Luke.

Mark's use of this term is instructive. In the first place, he highlights the fact that Jesus came preaching; for example: 'After John was put in prison, Jesus went into Galilee, proclaiming [preaching] the good news of God' (1:14). This is a fascinating summary statement. Mark was aware that Jesus was more than a preacher – he includes many miracles of healing – but first and foremost he describes Jesus as a preacher. The primacy of Jesus' preaching ministry is illustrated in Mark 1:25–39. The previous evening Jesus had exercised a wonderful healing ministry (see vv. 32–34a): news spread like wildfire, and next day the sick descended on Capernaum in their droves in hope of healing. But Jesus went off to 'a solitary place' (v. 35). When Peter and the disciples caught up with Jesus, they could not contain their frustration: 'Everyone is looking for you!' (v. 37). Jesus replied, 'Let us go somewhere else . . . so that I can preach there also. That is why I have come' (v. 38). Yet again Mark depicts Jesus as primarily a preacher. Yes, Jesus was concerned for people in their physical need, but above all he was concerned for their spiritual need.

In the light of this emphasis it is not surprising that Mark highlights the fact that Jesus sent his disciples out preaching. For example, 'He appointed twelve . . . that they might be with him and that he might send them out to preach . . .' (3:14); 'They went out and preached that all should repent' (6:12). True, the disciples were also involved in casting out demons and healing the sick (3:14; 6:13), but these activities followed on the preaching.

Furthermore, in Mark preaching was not limited to Jesus and his disciples. Those whom Jesus helped were so full of what he had done for them that they had to share 'good news' with others. This was true, for example, of the leper (1:40–45) and the deaf-mute (7:31–37).

This emphasis of Mark's on preaching is surely still needed. Yet today considerable controversy surrounds preaching. Preaching, it is said, because it is non-cooperative communication, is no longer suitable for our time. It is like using a paraffin lamp in the age of electric light. The sermon is 'a monstrous monologue by a moron to mutes'.[5] But if preaching has had its day, then what would we put in its place? How else would the gospel be communicated? The discussion group might supplement the sermon, but it can never replace the sermon. Preaching takes different forms. Sermons, as the Acts of the Apostles reveals, do not have to be stylized and divided into three headings. But in one way or another the gospel needs to be presented. For the gospel is about 'news' – about what God has done in Christ – and not about 'views'. Inevitably, therefore, there has to be a place for 'one-way communication'. What is questionable, however, is whether today's formal preaching actually fulfils the mandate to 'preach the good news to the whole creation'. All too often the good news is restricted to the church. Somehow we need to find ways of communicating the gospel to those without the church, and to do so in ways that are authoritative yet meaningful.[6]

---

[5] H. D. Bastian, cited by K. Runia, *The Sermon under Attack* (Paternoster, 1983), p. 9.

[6] J. C. Hoekendijk once cited a one-time prisoner of war from Russia who gave him the following impression of the church as he found it on returning to freedom: 'There is a preacher talking from behind the pulpit. We don't understand him. A glass cover has been put over the pulpit. This smothers all the sound. Around the pulpit our contemporaries are standing. They too talk and they call. But on the inside this is not understood. The glass cover smothers all sound. Thus we still see each other talk, but we don't understand each other any more.' Hoekendijk went on to comment that it is not ordinary glass that separates people on the inside from those on the outside, but distorting glass. The people outside receive the strangest images of what is going on inside.

c. The good news of Jesus is for all

The risen Lord emphasizes the universality of the gospel: *'Go into all the world and preach the good news to all creation'* (v. 15). Not once, but twice, the word 'all' occurs. Again, this is very much an emphasis of Mark's. Although the early ministry of Jesus was limited to Israel, in no way could the good news be restricted to a particular race or group of people. In Mark's Gospel we find Jesus very aware of the universal implications of his mission. For example, in his eschatological discourse he tells his disciples that 'the gospel must first be preached to all nations' (13:10). Later he looks forward to the day when the gospel would be 'preached throughout the world' (14:9). In other words, whether or not Mark 16:15 is an authentic word of Jesus, it is certainly true to the spirit of Jesus.

Amazingly, it took centuries before global mission really came on to the church's agenda. The modern missionary movement did not come into being until 1792, when William Carey and his friends founded what was first known as 'The Particular Baptist Society for Propagating the Gospel Among the Heathen'. That year Carey published his *Enquiry into the Obligation of Christians to Use Means for the Conversion of the Heathen.*

Today the word 'missionary' can no longer be restricted to Christian work beyond our shores or borders. We are realizing afresh that churches are by definition 'missionary congregations'. No church can exist for itself. Rather, as individuals and as churches we must have the world in view. Nor can the good news be restricted to a particular group of people today. Jesus died and rose for people of all cultures, all races, all ages, and all sociological groups.

d. The good news has to be received

The gospel is experienced as good news only as it is received and believed. In Mark's Gospel we read: 'Jesus went . . . proclaiming the good news of God. "The time has come," he said. "The kingdom of God is near. Repent and believe the good news!"' (1:14–15). A little later Mark records that the disciples likewise 'preached that people should repent' (6:12). Mark's version of the Great Commission retains this emphasis: *'Whoever believes and is baptised will be saved, but whoever does not believe will be condemned'* (v. 16). The 'good news' is described very much in life-and-death terms: people are either saved or they are condemned. In this respect Mark differs from the other evangelists, whose variations on the theme of the Great Commission fail to mention the possibility of condemnation and hell.

The tense employed here is significant: '*Whoever believes and is baptised . . . whoever does not believe . . .*' In our English versions the tense appears to be in the present. The Greek actually uses a special past tense (aorist) which brings out the thought of the decision that has to be made in response to the preaching. Faith is of course more than a matter of a moment: those who follow Christ are called to live a life of faith. But that faith must have a beginning – there must be a time when the will is surrendered and the heart opened to Christ. Much today is made of the fact that conversion is often a process: however, within that process a decision to follow Christ has to be made.

Such a decision is here linked to baptism. '*Whoever believes and is baptised will be saved.*' Faith, on the one hand, clearly precedes baptism. On the other hand, baptism is part of the salvation process. Baptism is in fact the moment when faith comes to outward expression. Yet, although baptism is here viewed as part of the natural process of becoming a Christian, it does not of itself make a person a Christian; there is nothing magical about it. Thus it is not the unbaptized person who is 'condemned', but the person who 'does not believe'. It is unbelief that is the reason for condemnation, not the failure to be baptized.

e. The good news will be confirmed

The risen Christ continues: '*And these signs will accompany those who believe: In my name they will drive out demons; they will speak in new tongues; they will pick up snakes with their hands; and when they drink deadly poison, it will not hurt them at all; they will place their hands on sick people, and they will get well*' (vv. 17–18). At this point many Christians begin to feel uncomfortable. The fact is that on the whole these signs are not our experience. What then are we to make of them? Are we simply to write them off as not belonging to the original Gospel of Mark, and therefore of no significance?

The way forward is to realize that what we have here is descriptive rather than prescriptive: these words describe what happens when the good news is preached. Mark's version of the Great Commission does not actually tell us to drive out demons, to speak in new tongues, to pick up snakes, to drink deadly poison, and so on, but rather it says that where the good news is proclaimed, there signs will follow. In this respect the final verse of the longer ending is apposite: 'Then the disciples went out and preached everywhere, and the Lord worked with them and confirmed his word by the signs that accompanied it' (v. 20).

What we have here in verses 17–18 is a summary of life in the early church. The early Christians did drive out demons in Jesus' name (see Mark 3:15; 6:7, 13; Acts 8:7, 16, 18; 19:12); they did speak in new tongues (see Acts 2:4; 10:46; 19:6; 1 Cor. 12:10, 28; 14:2–40); they did on at least one occasion pick up a deadly snake (see Acts 28:3–6); they did place their hands on people to heal the sick (see Acts 28:8). As for drinking deadly poison without taking harm, there is no New Testament instance. It is possible, however, that this is an allusion to the story told by Eusebius, the early church historian, on the authority of Papias, according to which Justus, surnamed Barsabbas, drank a deadly poison, and yet, by the grace of God, suffered no harm.[7]

If we take these signs to be prescriptive, then we end up in snake-handling and other aberrations which have been the mark of certain enthusiastic sects. But to see these words as not being prescriptive is not to cease to take them seriously. The principle behind this promise is that if we truly give ourselves to faithfully preaching the good news of Jesus, crucified and risen, then we shall find the preaching confirmed in all kinds of tangible ways. Lives, for instance, will be changed, relationships transformed, and the community of the church will in itself become a sign pointing to the risen Lord. The Swiss theologian Emil Brunner once wrote: 'People draw near to the Christian community because they are irresistibly attracted by its supernatural power. They would like to share in this new dimension of life and power, they enter the zone in which the Spirit operates before they will have heard a word about what lies behind it.'[8]

Sadly, this is not always true. In many places the Christian church has become so institutionalized that it has ceased to be a living, vibrant organism. In principle, however, the church is called to be a sign of the living, risen Christ.

---

[7] Eusebius, *Historia Ecclesiastica* III.xxxix.9.

[8] Quoted by W. Abraham, *The Logic of Evangelism* (Hodder & Stoughton, 1989), p. 156, n. 17.

2. The witness of Matthew to the resurrection

1. The empty tomb (28:1–10)

¹*After the Sabbath, at dawn on the first day of the week, Mary Magdalene and the other Mary went to look at the tomb.*
²*There was a violent earthquake, for an angel of the Lord came down from heaven and, going to the tomb, rolled back the stone and sat on it. *³*His appearance was like lightning, and his clothes were white as snow. *⁴*The guards were so afraid of him that they shook and became like dead men.*
⁵*The angel said to the women, 'Do not be afraid, for I know that you are looking for Jesus, who was crucified. *⁶*He is not here; he has risen, just as he said. Come and see the place where he lay. *⁷*Then go quickly and tell his disciples: "He has risen from the dead and is going ahead of you into Galilee. There you will see him." Now I have told you.'*
⁸*So the women hurried away from the tomb, afraid yet filled with joy, and ran to tell his disciples. *⁹*Suddenly Jesus met them. 'Greetings,' he said. They came to him, clasped his feet and worshipped him. *¹⁰*Then Jesus said to them, 'Do not be afraid. Go and tell my brothers to go to Galilee; there they will see me.'*

On the first day of the week, *Mary Magdalene and the other Mary went to look at the tomb* (v. 1). In common with all three other Gospels Matthew mentions that Mary Magdalene went to the tomb. Whereas Mark mentions 'Mary the mother of James, and Salome', here Matthew mentions only *the other Mary*. The latter was presumably 'Mary the mother of James and Joses' (Matt. 27:56), who had been present at the crucifixion.

Unlike Mark and Luke, Matthew does not mention that the women went to anoint the body of Jesus. Instead, Matthew just states that they *went to look at the tomb* (v. 1). In view of Matthew's almost certain knowledge of Mark's Gospel, this omission might seem strange. It may be that in the light of the Jewish allegation that the disciples had stolen the body (v. 13), Matthew thought it might be unhelpful to mention that certain followers of Jesus, by their own admission, planned to interfere with the body. The viewing of the tomb within a matter of two or three days after burial would not have seemed strange, since it was customary for Jews to visit graves 'until the third day' in order to ensure that the person laid in the tomb was really dead (*Semahoth* 8.1). Indeed, according to one rabbinic source (the *Midrash Rabbah* c. 7 on Gen. 1:10), mourning was at its height on the third day. The women therefore came with great sadness to the tomb of Jesus, expecting to see the cause of their grief only too well confirmed.

Matthew alone of all the Gospels mentions *a violent* (literally, 'great', *megas*) *earthquake* and the angel's subsequent rolling back of the stone from the tomb (v. 2), just as Matthew alone of all the Gospels records an earthquake at the time of Jesus' death (27:51). The nearest parallel to the event described in verses 2–4 is in the *Gospel of Peter*, of which a lengthy fragment was discovered in the tomb of a Christian monk in Upper Egypt:

Now in the night in which the Lord's day dawned, when the soldiers, two by two in every watch, were keeping guard, there rang out a loud voice in heaven, and they saw the heavens opened and two men come down from there in great brightness and draw nigh to the sepulchre. The stone which had been laid against the entrance to the sepulchre started of itself to roll and gave way to the side, and the sepulchre was opened, and both the young men entered in. When now those soldiers saw this, they awakened the centurion and the elders – for they also were there to assist at the watch. And whilst they were relating what they had seen, they saw again three men come out from the sepulchre, and two of them sustaining the other, and a cross following them, and the heads of the two reaching to heaven, but that of him who was led of them by the hand overpassing the heavens. And they heard a voice out of the heavens crying, 'Have you preached to those that sleep?'; and from the cross there was heard the answer, 'Yes.' Those men therefore took counsel with one another to go and report this to Pilate. And whilst they were still deliberating, the heavens were again seen to open, and a man descended and entered into the sepulchre (9:35 – 11:44).[1]

---

[1] See E. Hennecke, *New Testament Apocrypha* 1 (SCM, 1963), pp. 185–186.

In so far as the account of the resurrection in the *Gospel of Peter* is clearly legendary in character, many believe that Matthew's account of an earthquake is legendary too. Earthquakes were not unknown in Jerusalem, however. Furthermore, if an earthquake did indeed take place on Good Friday, then it is possible that the earthquake on Easter Day was some kind of aftershock. Or was Matthew, so steeped in the Old Testament, simply seeking to underline in a symbolic manner that God was at work in a special way (see Is. 24:19; 29:6; Jer. 10:10; Amos 8:8; etc.)? Certainly, in the Old Testament, changes to nature that accompany the coming of the Lord are there to underline that when God comes, he comes to act. Similarly the earthquake in Matthew's account may well be a pointer to the world-changing implications of the resurrection of Jesus.

The chronological relationship of verses 2–4 is disputed. At first sight it might appear that the women were witnesses of the earthquake and of the angel's rolling away the stone from the tomb. If this were so, it would directly contravene the testimony of the other Gospels. Another explanation is possible, however. In the New Testament the aorist past tense can often be translated by an English pluperfect. If this is so, then we can regard verses 2–4 as an insert: 'There had been a violent earthquake . . .'

The earthquake is accompanied by the descent of *an angel of the Lord* (v. 2). The last time an angel of the Lord had appeared in Matthew's Gospel was in the birth narratives (1:20, 24; 2:13, 19). An angel by definition is God's 'messenger'. Not only through his words does he convey the triumph of Jesus over death; his very action of sitting on the stone appears to symbolize that death has been routed.

Only Matthew records that it was the angel who *rolled back the stone* (v. 2). There is no need to assume that the angel did so in order to allow Jesus to come out. As John makes clear, locked doors were no barrier to the risen Lord (John 20:19, 26). The stone was surely rolled away for the sake of the women, so they could see that the tomb was empty.

The description of the angel (v. 3) is reminiscent of heavenly beings in Daniel 7:9 (*his clothes were white as snow*) and Daniel 10:6 (*His appearance was like lightning*), and is no doubt intended to convey a sense of awesome otherness. The combination that night of the earthquake and the sudden arrival of an angel in brilliant light must have been unnerving, to say the least. No wonder the guards *were so afraid of him that they shook and became like dead men* (v. 4). There is here a touch of irony. It is not Jesus, but those sent to guard the body of Jesus who now appear dead!

The message of the angel (vv. 5–7) in Matthew is considerably longer than that found in Mark. Although the basic thrust of the message is the same, there are differences of detail. For instance, the phrase *just as he said* (v. 6) now refers not just to the promised appearance in Galilee (26:32), but to more general predictions of the resurrection (16:21; 17:23; 20:19 and, by implication, 12:40). The women are told to *tell his disciples* (v. 7) that Jesus has been raised from the dead, but by contrast with Mark's Gospel Peter is not singled out specifically. This may seem a little strange, since Matthew tends to take a particular interest in Peter (10:2; 14:28–31; 16:16–19). Another difference of detail is that whereas in Mark the angel simply declares, 'He has risen!' (or, 'He has been raised!'), in Matthew the message of the angel is slightly extended: he has risen *from the dead* (v. 7). The addition of this phrase *from the dead* may indicate a desire on Matthew's part to point to Jesus as the first to rise from the dead, and so becoming the 'firstfruits' of a more general resurrection (see 1 Cor. 15:20). Indeed, the fact that Matthew records that 'many holy people . . . came out of the tombs . . . after Jesus' resurrection' (27:52–53) is perhaps an indication that Matthew saw the resurrection of Jesus as bringing in a new era.

In response to the angel's command to *go quickly* (*tachy*) (v. 7), the women *hurried* (*tachy*) *away from the tomb*. Indeed, Matthew tells us that they *ran* to tell the disciples the news (v. 8). As in Mark, the women are understandably 'afraid', but by contrast with Mark's account they are also *filled with joy* (literally, 'with great joy') (v. 8). Their joy is reminiscent of the joy of the wise men when they saw the star (Matt. 2:10). The star and the empty tomb, both signs of God at work, brought 'great joy' to those privileged to see God at work in incarnation and resurrection.

On their way back to the disciples, the women suddenly encountered the risen Lord himself. '*Greetings*,' said Jesus (v. 9). In itself there was nothing unusual about this form of address. Jesus had greeted Judas, for instance, with the same term in the Garden of Gethsemane (Matt. 26:49; see also 27:29). But in this particular context, this may have been more than a formal greeting. For the term literally meant 'Rejoice' (*Chairete*), and as such is reminiscent of the joy (*chara*) experienced only a little earlier by the women (v. 8). The women had indeed cause to rejoice that Easter Sunday morning.

They *clasped his feet* (v. 9). The precise significance of this action is uncertain. It has been suggested that we have here an act of supplication (see 2 Kgs. 4:27), but if so, then what were the women wanting? Others have drawn attention to the fact that in much folklore ghosts have no feet: if Matthew were aware of this tradition, then perhaps he intended the grasping of the feet to indicate that Jesus was not a spirit (see Luke 24:37–43). In the light of John 20:11–18, however, which is probably an expanded version of this story, the women, like Mary Magdalene, were perhaps simply expressing their wish not to let Jesus go (see John 20:17). At the same time they *worshipped him* (v. 9). The Greek verb designates the custom of prostrating oneself before a person and kissing his or her feet or the hem of his or her garment. The disciples in Galilee were later to do the same thing (v. 17).

Like the angel, Jesus tells them, *'Do not be afraid'* (v. 10; see v. 5). Again, along similar lines to the angel's command, Jesus orders them to tell his disciples to go to Galilee, for *'there they will see me'* (v. 10; see v. 7). Somewhat unusually, however, he terms his disciples *'my brothers'* (v. 10). The same expression is found in the parallel passage in John 20:17. This intimate description of the disciples had been used by Jesus at an earlier stage during his ministry (12:49–50; 25:40). In using this term of his disciples now, Jesus is perhaps indicating that he has forgiven them for having forsaken him at the time of his arrest (26:56). Maybe too we have an allusion to the fact that the new community Jesus is forming is a community of brothers and sisters. He, however, is the firstborn (Rom. 8:29; Heb. 2:11).

a. Just looking?

The two Marys early that Easter Sunday morning symbolize blind devotion. They undoubtedly loved Jesus, but they had no expectations of him. Matthew tells us that they went to *look at (theōrēsai) the tomb* (v. 1). As far as they were concerned, there was nothing to see. Or if there was anything to see, then it was the body of *Jesus, who was crucified* (v. 5). In Matthew's Gospel there is no mention of the anointing. They simply went to look, and perhaps had nothing more in mind than paying their respects to Jesus.

The same Greek verb is found in Matthew's account of the crucifixion: 'Many women were there, watching (*theōrousai*) from a distance . . . Among them were Mary Magdalene, Mary the mother of James and Joses . . .' (Matt. 27:55–56). The two Marys were in the business of looking on that occasion. But what did they learn? What did they understand? Almost certainly they looked at Jesus without comprehension. They were just spectators, involved and yet not involved. The same was true on Easter Day. They came to look, without any comprehension of what had happened to Jesus.

In some ways the two Marys represent a good number of people who Sunday by Sunday go to church. It would not be true to say that they go to church purely out of habit. It is devotion that takes them to church. They would say that they love Jesus, and they probably do. But they have no expectations of him. They would not put it this way, but nevertheless, to all intents and purposes, as far as they are concerned, Jesus is still in his tomb – or, if not in his tomb, then he is shut up in his church. In worshipping Jesus on Sunday mornings they are in effect politely paying him their respects.

Somehow a shift needs to take place in their understanding. It is an interesting fact that the Greek verb used here for watching (*theōreō*) can be used in the sense not just of 'looking at', but of 'perceiving', 'noticing', 'finding'. For instance, as her conversation with Jesus develops, the Samaritan woman at the well exclaims, 'Sir ... I can see that you are a prophet' (John 4:19). Comprehension had begun to take place.

Looking is not enough. Understanding, comprehension, is needed. The apostle Paul wrote to the Ephesians, 'I pray also that the eyes of your heart may be enlightened in order that you may know ... his incomparably great power for us who believe. That power is like the working of his mighty strength, which he exerted in Christ when he raised him from the dead' (Eph. 1:18–20). If the resurrection is to mean anything at all for us today, then we must understand that Christ's resurrection power is not buried in some time capsule, but rather is available to us today. This kind of comprehension leads to expectation, and where there is expectation, experience of the risen Christ's power quickly follows too.

b. Easter magnitude

When Jesus rose from the dead, there was *a violent (megas) earthquake* (v. 2). No doubt, as when an earthquake accompanied the death of Christ, the 'earth shook and the rocks split' (27:51). Nature itself testified to the earth-shattering nature of the resurrection.

Today many feel embarrassed by this peculiarly Matthaean addition to the Easter story. But in fact it is a great symbol of the effect that the resurrection of Jesus has had on the world stage. For although the tremors of this particular earthquake may have been localized and perhaps would have rated only a minor reading on the Richter scale, the tremors of the aftershock of the resurrection are of the greatest magnitude and continue to reverberate down through the course of history. In a sense the very foundations of the world were rocked, and the world has never been the same. For the resurrection of Jesus was no one-off feat; rather, its repercussions are there for all to experience. Furthermore, unlike any other earthquake, which normally leaves havoc and devastation in its train, the 'seismic' repercussions of the resurrection are life-creating and hope-inducing. For in rising from the dead, Jesus broke death's defences once and for all. The only destruction brought about by the resurrection is the destruction of 'him who holds the power of death – that is, the devil' (Heb. 2:14). The earthquake recorded here in Matthew anticipates the theologizing of Paul: 'For as in Adam all die, so in Christ all will be made alive' (1 Cor. 15:22). On Easter Day the claim of Jesus to be the resurrection and the life (John 11:25) is vindicated. The resurrection of Jesus has cosmic significance. All this is symbolized by the earthquake.

Is it therefore just coincidental that along with the great earthquake, which made them afraid, there was also great joy (v. 8) that Easter Day? In one sense, yes. The women who experienced great joy that day had little inkling of the difference the resurrection had made to life and to death. Neither were the disciples initially any wiser: they were simply 'overjoyed' to see the Lord (John 20:20; see also 16:22). Only later did the full implications sink in. Peter, for instance, began his first letter with a hymn of praise to God for 'the resurrection of Jesus Christ from the dead' and for the 'living hope' of eternal life inherent in the resurrection for those who believe (1 Pet. 1:3). Not surprisingly he went on to write, 'you believe in him and are filled with an inexpressible and glorious joy' (1 Pet. 1:8). Yes, the resurrection brings great joy. William Tyndale was right when he described the Christian gospel as 'good, merry, glad and joyful tidings, that makes a man's heart glad and makes him sing, dance and leap for joy'.

2. The report of the guard (28:11–15)

While the women were on their way, some of the guards went into the city and reported to the chief priests everything that had happened. ¹²When the chief priests had met with the elders and devised a plan, they gave the soldiers a large sum of money, ¹³telling them, 'You are to say, "His disciples came during the night and stole him away while we were asleep." ¹⁴If this report gets to the governor, we will satisfy him and keep you out of trouble.' ¹⁵So the soldiers took the money and did as they were instructed. And this story has been widely circulated among the Jews to this very day.

This story of a guard being posted at the tomb (see Matt. 27:62–66 and 28:2–4), and then of the guard being subsequently bribed, is found only in Matthew. The authenticity of this story has often been questioned, the suggestion being made that it is a creative piece of Christian apologetic. The story's apparent naïvety, however, serves to reinforce its trustworthiness. The early Christians would have had nothing to gain by inventing the story of a closely guarded tomb, only to undermine it by introducing the idea that the guards had been 'sleeping'.

An indirect confirmation of the story of the guard may perhaps be found in the so-called Nazareth Inscription. In this imperial edict belonging to the reign of either Tiberius (AD 14–37) or Claudius (AD 41–54), Caesar decrees death for disturbing the tombs of the dead:

> It is my pleasure that sepulchres and tombs, which have been erected as solemn memorials of ancestors or children or relatives, shall remain undisturbed in perpetuity. If it be shown that anyone has either destroyed them or otherwise thrown out the bodies which have been buried there or removed them with malicious intent to another place, thus committing a crime against those buried there, or removed the headstones or other stones, I command that against such person the same sentence be passed in respect of solemn memorials of men as is laid down in respect of gods. Much rather must one pay respect to those who are buried. Let no one disturb them on any account. Otherwise it is my will that capital sentence be passed upon such person for the crime of tomb-spoliation.

It has been suggested that news of the empty tomb had got back to Rome in a garbled form – hence the decree.[2]

When the guards came to, they immediately *reported to the chief priests* (v. 11), and not in the first place to Pilate. For although they were ultimately accountable to Pilate, the mission to which they had been assigned had been initiated by the chief priests (27:62–66).

The response of the Jewish authorities was yet again to stoop to bribery: *they gave the soldiers a large sum of money, telling them, 'You are to say, "His disciples came during the night and stole him away while we were asleep"'* (vv. 12–13). The line the guard was to take was pretty unconvincing. Not only did it require people to believe that all the soldiers had fallen asleep while allegedly on guard; it also required people to believe that not one of the soldiers had woken while the tomb was being robbed. A highly improbable story!

The Jewish authorities further assured the soldiers that if Pilate were to hear of what had happened, they would not be punished for sleeping on duty and for allowing the tomb to be robbed. *So the soldiers took the money and did as they were instructed* (v. 15). Clearly the Jewish version of the theft of the body was very current at the time Matthew was writing, and was no doubt the reason for its inclusion.

---

[2] See F. F. Bruce, *New Testament History* (Pickering & Inglis, 1982), pp. 284–286.

a. The case of the disappearing body

In all four Gospels, the empty tomb is the great discovery of Easter Day. Perhaps Matthew, more than the other three evangelists, however, encourages his readers to examine the evidence. The words of the angel, *'Come and see the place where he lay'* (v. 6), may be construed as an invitation to check the facts. Likewise his inclusion of the story of the bribing of the guard (vv. 11–15) can be seen as an invitation to the reader to reflect on the evidence. This invitation needs to be taken up by all, recognizing with Sherlock Holmes that 'when you have eliminated the impossible, whatever remains, *however improbable*, must be the truth'.[3] Such evidence does not do away with the need for faith, but it does show that there is a reasonable quality to faith.

Over the years all kinds of explanations for the empty tomb have been given. For the sake of integrity we shall examine five of them.

The women went to the wrong tomb

Kirsopp Lake, a professor at Harvard, maintained:

> Comparative strangers to Jerusalem, and coming in the uncertain light of early morning, they missed their way; but a young man who was lurking around realised their purpose and said, 'You seek Jesus . . . He is not here . . . See (pointing to another tomb) the place where they laid him.' The women were terrified and ran away. Subsequently they came to believe that the young man must have been an angel, and his words an announcement that their Lord had risen from the dead.[4]

Others, although not adopting Lake's theory in its entirety, have also gone along with the idea that the women went to the wrong tomb. Indeed, Dominic Crossan, an American professor of biblical studies who is part of the radical Jesus Seminar, has argued that 'Nobody knew what had happened to Jesus' body . . . By Easter Sunday morning, those who cared did not know where it was and those who knew did not care.'[5]

But this argument that the women went to the wrong tomb is fatally flawed. First, *it takes the women to be fools*. According to Matthew 27:61, Mary Magdalene and the other Mary were present when Joseph of Arimathea and Nicodemus placed the body of Jesus

[3] A. Conan Doyle, *The Sign of the Four*.
[4] K. Lake, *The Historical Evidence for the Resurrection of Jesus Christ* (Williams & Norgate, 1907), pp. 248–253.
[5] J. D. Crossan, *The Historical Jesus* (T. & T. Clark, 1991), p. 394.

in the tomb. Similarly Mark 15:57 and Luke 23:35 state that the women saw the tomb where Jesus' body was laid.

Secondly, *it takes Peter and John to be fools.* Luke (24:12) and John (20:3–9) record that they came to verify the story. Would these two men, as well as the women, have made this mistake?

Finally, *it takes no account of others' checking the story.* Surely Joseph of Arimathea would have verified the story – it was his tomb! So too Nicodemus, and most certainly the Jewish authorities, would have investigated it. Any of them could have checked and discovered the mistake, if mistake there had been. The fact is that the message of the apostles could not have been maintained in Jerusalem for a single hour, let alone a single day, if the emptiness of the tomb had not been established as a fact for all concerned. It was not as if any great distance was involved. Anyone could have visited the tomb and come back again between lunch and whatever may have been the equivalent of afternoon tea.

Jesus never really died
Almost from the beginning there have been those who have maintained that Jesus did not die on the cross – he simply fainted from exhaustion. According to Celsus, a second-century opponent of the Christian faith, Jesus did not die, but was nursed back to health by Mary Magdalene. Forty days later, however, his wounds got the better of him, and he died and was buried secretly, but not before he had assembled his friends and walked off into a cloud on a mountain top.[6]

According to H. E. G. Paulus, a nineteenth-century German scholar, Jesus' 'death' was only a trance. The loud cry uttered shortly before 'death' shows that his strength was far from exhausted. The thrust of a spear in the side of Jesus was no more than a surface wound. The cool grave and aromatic spices contributed to the process of resuscitation, and finally the storm and earthquake roused Jesus to full consciousness. The earthquake also had the effect of rolling the stone away. Jesus stripped off his grave-clothes and put on a gardener's outfit – that is why Mary mistook him for a gardener![7]

In the early 1990s the Australian Barbara Thiering developed even more bizarre theories about Jesus. She suggested, for instance, that Jesus ended up marrying Lydia, Paul's first convert in Philippi, whom Thiering believes became a bishop. She too has claimed that

---

[6] Cited by Origen, *Contra Celsum* 2. 55.
[7] H. E. G. Paulus, *Das Leben Jesus als Grundlage einer reinen Geschichte des Urchristentums* (C. F. Winter, 1828). See further W. L. Craig, *The Historical Argument for the Resurrection of Jesus During the Deist Controversy* (Edwin Mellen, 1985), pp. 393–400.

the crucifixion did not result in Jesus' death. The supposed rising was effected by a medical antidote to the drug which had caused Jesus apparently to 'die'.[8]

There are strong grounds, however, for ruling out these theories. First, *the Roman soldiers thought he was dead.* They should have known, for death was their business. But, to make doubly sure, one of them thrust a spear into Jesus' side (John 19:33–34). Secondly, *Joseph of Arimathea and Nicodemus thought he was dead.* They should have known, for they took the body of Jesus down from the cross, wrapped it in grave-clothes and laid it in the tomb (John 19:38–42).

David Friedrich Strauss, a nineteenth-century German sceptic, had many doubts about the gospel story, but even so he scorned any 'swoon theory':

> It is impossible that a being who had stolen half dead out of the sepulchre, who crept about weak and ill, wanting medical treatment, who required bandaging, strengthening and indulgence . . . could have given the disciples the impression that he was a Conqueror over death and the grave, the Prince of Life, an impression which lay at the bottom of their future ministry. Such a resuscitation . . . could by no possibility have changed their sorrow into enthusiasm, have elevated their reverence into worship.[9]

It is perhaps significant that neither the Jewish historian Josephus nor the Roman historian Tacitus had any difficulty in accepting the death of Jesus. For both Josephus (*Antiquities* 18.63–64) and Tacitus (*Annals* 15.44) record that Jesus was crucified on the orders of Pontius Pilate.

The body was stolen by the disciples

This 'official' Jewish explanation (Matt. 28:13) was revived by Hermann Reimarus. According to Reimarus, after the death of Jesus the disciples were unwilling to abandon the kind of life they had led with him, so they stole the body and hid it, and proclaimed to all the world that he would soon return as the Messiah. But they waited for fifty days before making this announcement in order that the body, if it should be found, should be unrecognizable.[10]

More recently A. N. Wilson has come up with a similar story, in which he maintains that the disciples took Jesus' body back to

[8] B. Thiering, *Jesus the Man* (Corgi, 1993).
[9] D. Strauss, *A New Life of Jesus* (London, 1879), p. 412.
[10] H. Reimarus, *The Goal of Jesus and his Disciples* (1778).

Galilee for burial. James then reassured his followers that all had happened 'according to the Scriptures'. Due to family likeness and general confusion, James was mistaken for Jesus, and the story got around that Jesus himself had been raised from death.[11]

Apart from the fact that this theory flies in the face of all the evidence of the Gospels, there are other difficulties. First, *the practical difficulty of rolling away the stone and getting the body of Jesus out without attracting the attention of the Roman guard.* Even if the soldiers had all dozed off, it is highly unlikely that not one of them would have woken up if the disciples had suddenly tried to snatch the body.

Secondly, *the difficulty of motivation.* All the Gospels record that the disciples abandoned Jesus in confusion and fear. If that were so, it is impossible to imagine that within a matter of hours of his death they would have planned such a daring coup of raiding the tomb.

Thirdly, *the difficulty of preaching a lie under the pain of death.* While people are ready to suffer for something they believe in passionately, few – if any – are prepared to suffer for something they know to be untrue. People tell lies to get out of trouble. Nobody in their right mind tells lies to get into trouble. Pascal, the French philosopher, was surely right when he said, 'I readily believe those witnesses who get their throats cut.'

Joseph Klausner, himself a Jew, refused to accept this explanation: 'Deliberate imposture is not the substance out of which the religion of millions of mankind is created . . . The nineteen hundred years' faith of millions is not founded on deception.'[12]

The body of Jesus was stolen, but not by the disciples

Tertullian mentions that according to one story that was going the rounds in his day, the local gardener, fearing that many visitors would come and damage his vegetables, removed Jesus' corpse from the tomb. On finding the tomb empty, the disciples wrongly concluded that the resurrection had taken place. Apparently the gardener was supposed to have said nothing to disturb their 'good faith'.[13] Others have suggested that the Jews removed the body, but if so, why? Yet others have suggested that Joseph of Arimathea removed the body, but again, if so, why? And if they did so, then why did they not produce the body of Jesus and nip the preaching of the resurrection in the bud? It just does not make sense!

---

[11] A. N. Wilson, *Jesus* (Flamingo, 1993).
[12] J. Klausner, *Jesus of Nazareth* (Macmillan, 1953), pp. 357, 359
[13] Tertullian, *De Spectaculis* 30.

The body of Jesus remained in the tomb

According to certain radical theologians today, there never was an empty tomb. The story of the empty tomb was an invention of the early church. The evidence of the Gospel writers is to be discounted.

Apart from the high-handed way of treating the integrity of the first Christians, this suggestion runs into other major difficulties. First, if the story of the empty tomb were invented by later Christians, why is the story made to hang so crucially on the testimony of women, whose evidence was not legally admissible in Jewish courts of law? Secondly, if Matthew were making up the story of the resurrection, why did he in effect give a handle to the opposition by suggesting that the disciples stole the body while the guards were asleep?

Indirect confirmation of the story of the empty tomb is to be found in the fact that the tomb of Jesus did not initially become a place of pilgrimage. Tomb veneration was common at the time of Jesus, and people would often meet for worship at the grave of a dead prophet. But there is no evidence whatsoever that the earliest Jewish Christians did such a thing. The tomb was empty because God raised Jesus from the dead.

The sceptics push their arguments much too far: they need to learn to become sceptical of their scepticism! Somewhat surprisingly, this was the opinion too of an orthodox Jewish scholar, Pinchas Lapide, who examined the evidence for the resurrection of Jesus and who, although refusing to accept the messiahship of Jesus, came to the following conclusion: 'I accept the resurrection of Easter Sunday not as an invention of the community of disciples, but as a historical event . . . I cannot rid myself of the impression that some modern Christian theologians are ashamed of the material facticity of the resurrection.'[14]

We need to hear again the words of the angel, *'Come and see the place where he lay . . . He has risen from the dead'* (Matt. 28:6–7).

3. Jesus appears to his disciples (28:16–20)

Then the eleven disciples went to Galilee, to the mountain where Jesus had told them to go. [17]*When they saw him, they worshipped him; but some doubted.* [18]*Then Jesus came to them and said, 'All authority in heaven and on earth has been given to me.* [19]*Therefore go and make disciples of all nations, baptising them in the name of the Father and of the Son and of the Holy Spirit,*

[14] P. Lapide, *The Resurrection of Jesus: A Jewish Perspective* (SPCK, 1983), pp. 13, 131.

²⁰and teaching them to obey everything I have commanded you. And surely I am with you always, to the very end of the age.'

Neither Matthew nor indeed any other Gospel specifies the *mountain* (v. 16). The message the women had brought to the disciples was to go to *Galilee* (vv. 7, 10; also 26:32). Mountains for Matthew are places of revelation: it was on a mountain that Jesus revealed his new 'law' (5:1); it was on a mountain of transfiguration that Jesus revealed himself to Peter, James and John (17:1); now as risen Lord he was to reveal yet more of himself and of his intentions for disciples.

It is understandable that the disciples should have *worshipped* Jesus (v. 17; see also v. 9), for he was now the risen Lord. But why should some have *doubted* (v. 17)? The Greek verb (*distazō*) occurs in the New Testament only here and on the occasion when Peter sought to walk on the water, but then began to sink: 'You of little faith . . . why did you doubt?' (14:31). The verb indicates hesitation and indecision rather than actual unbelief. Thomas doubted, but that was before he saw the Lord (John 20:24–29). Luke records that when Jesus appeared, 'they still did not believe it because of joy and amazement' (Luke 24:41). One possibility is that some failed to recognize Jesus because there was still some distance between them and him (v. 18 indicates that Jesus then moved towards them). Another possibility is that some, while recognizing Jesus, were nevertheless confused about what had happened to him and therefore not a little hesitant about how to react. Whatever the case may be, for some at least there was an initial degree of uncertainty.

That uncertainty was surely dispelled as the Lord revealed himself in all his glory to his disciples: *'All authority in heaven and on earth has been given to me'* (v. 18). What a claim! Already something of his 'authority' had been displayed in his earthly ministry (see, e.g., 9:6; 11:27), but Jesus now enters into another league. For in virtue of his death and resurrection 'all authority has been given' (the Greek aorist tense, *edothē*, indicates a particular occasion) to the risen and soon-to-be-exalted Lord (see Phil. 2:9–11). The language used here is reminiscent of Daniel's exalted Son of Man: 'He was given authority, glory and sovereign power; all peoples, nations and men of every language worshipped him. His dominion is an everlasting dominion . . .' (Dan. 7:14). Others have seen an allusion to Psalm 2:7–8:

> He said to me, 'You are my Son;
>   today I have become your Father.
> Ask of me,
>   and I will make the nations your inheritance . . .'

Or to Psalm 110:1:

> The Lord says to my Lord:
> 'Sit at my right hand
> until I make your enemies
> a footstool for your feet'.

Maybe all three passages underlie this assertion of authority!

Because he was invested with such universal authority (hence the Therefore) Jesus could now say, *'Therefore go and make disciples of all nations . . .'* (v. 19). Here we have what has been traditionally regarded as 'the Great Commission', or as the Duke of Wellington called these words, 'the marching orders of the church'.

Up to this point a limitation had been imposed on the extent of the preaching of the gospel (see 10:5; 15:24), but now, after the death and resurrection of Jesus, that limitation is removed. From now on, 'The field is the world' (13:38). The good news of the kingdom is to be shared with all. There is a signal difference here between the 'universalism' of Jesus and the 'universalism' of the Old Testament. The prophetic vision of the last days was of a pilgrimage of the nations to Jerusalem, when Mount Zion would be exalted as chief among the mountains and 'all nations' would 'stream to it' (e.g. Is. 2:2). But Jesus here commands his disciples to *go* to the nations. The nations will not come, unless his disciples go.

Jesus further commissions his followers to *make disciples*. This is a characteristically Matthaean word (e.g. 13:52; 27:57). However, the term 'disciple' appears as a regular term for Christians, and is found some 146 times in the New Testament. The disciple-making process begins with *baptising them in the name of the Father and of the Son and of the Holy Spirit* (v. 19). Baptism had its roots in Judaism. Indeed, in the earlier part of his Gospel Matthew has described how John the Baptist had been baptizing in the Jordan River (3:6). The early church took over this rite of baptism and it became part of the normal process of becoming a Christian (see Acts 2:38, 41; etc.). Unlike John's baptism, however, Christian baptism was more than an expression of 'repentance' (see 3:11); it was an expression of faith, in which people were baptized with a view to belonging ('in the name of') to Jesus – or as here *in the name of the Father and of the Son and of the Holy Spirit*. This trinitarian formula is unique in the New Testament.[15]

---

[15] Some have raised questions about the authenticity of the text. However, although this precise trinitarian formulation is found nowhere else, the doctrine of the Trinity is implied in such passages as Rom. 8:9–11; 1 Cor. 12:13–4; Eph. 2:18.

The disciple-making process also included *teaching them to obey everything I have commanded you*. This commitment to teaching is reflected in Acts 2:42, where those baptized at Pentecost 'devoted themselves to the apostles' teaching'. For Matthew such teaching would surely have included the way of life expounded by Jesus in the Sermon on the Mount (chs. 5 – 7). Presumably it would also have included obedience to the command to 'make disciples'!

Jesus concludes his commission with a promise: *'And surely I am with you always, to the very end of the age'* (28:20). It is not only when his followers meet in his name that he is there (18:20); it is also when they go out in his name. In the original Greek the 'I' is emphatic (*egō*): 'I myself, the risen Lord, to whom all authority has been given, will be with you always.' The one whose name is 'Emmanuel, God with us' (1:23), promises to be with his people right to the end of time. What a confidence this must have given to the tiny nucleus of his disciples as they faced the pagan masses! What a confidence it gives us too as we go out to make disciples!

a. A necessary precondition for making disciples

In the Great Commission the main verb is 'make disciples'. The other verbs are in participle form. A key participle is the very first, *go*, literally 'going'. It is only as we 'go' that we can hope to make disciples. If we are to win the world for Jesus, we must first go into the world and encounter people where they are. It has been said that when the risen Christ commanded his followers to make disciples, his first word of commission was not 'Preach' but 'Go'. We are to follow the example of Jesus himself, who was known as 'a friend of tax collectors and "sinners"' (Matt. 11:19), and build bridges of friendship with people who would normally never darken the door of a church.

In recent years there has been much talk of '3-P' evangelism: namely presence, proclamation, persuasion. All three elements are needed if evangelism is to be effective. For people are not going to respond to the gospel unless they hear the good news of the kingdom proclaimed. Often proclamation is not enough: people need to be persuaded of the truth as it is in Jesus. But before there can be proclamation and persuasion, there must be 'presence', for people are not going to listen to the gospel until they see its reality in our lives. This was the experience of evangelical Christians in the closing years of the apartheid era in South Africa: 'Our proclamation has been so swallowed up by the cries of the poor and the oppressed that it is now even impossible to hold conventional evangelistic campaigns in this war situation. These voices have become so loud that it has now become impossible to hear the church preach.'[16] In this respect some words from the Sermon on the Mount are apposite: 'let your light shine before men, that they may see your good deeds and praise your Father in heaven' (5:16).

b. Disciples, not decisions

Jesus calls not for decisions, but for disciples. Gospel preaching involves far more than simply calling men and women to decide for Christ – it involves calling men and women to a lifetime of following Jesus and learning from him. On more than one occasion Jesus said, 'If anyone would come after me, he must deny himself and take up his cross and follow me' (16:24; see also 10:38). On another occasion Jesus invited his listeners to 'Take my yoke . . . and learn from me' (11:29).

Disciple-making cannot be limited to preaching. It involves mentoring – the establishing of a personal relationship with a view to helping to shape the life of a younger disciple. In the words of the South American theologian Orlando Costas, 'Discipling is not the transmission of a body of knowledge; rather it involves the introduction of material in such a way that the receiver can retain and incorporate it into his life.'[17]

Disciples are by definition learners. What is more, this process of learning never ends. For instance, disciples of an eminent rabbi would come to the end of their training and set up their own schools – but we have never learnt all that Christ has to teach us! We never graduate from the school of Christ. This truth was well expressed by Samuel Rutherford, who wrote to a Christian woman of his day, 'Madam, you must go in at heaven's door at the last with the Book in your hand, still learning.'

---

[16] *Evangelical Witness in South Africa: A Critique of Evangelical Theology and Practice by South African Evangelicals* (Evangelical Alliance, 1986).

[17] O. Costas, *The Church and its Mission: A Shattering Critique from the Third World* (Tyndale House, 1974), p. 75.

3. The witness of Luke to the resurrection

1. The empty tomb (24:1–12)

> *On the first day of the week, very early in the morning, the women took the spices they had prepared and went to the tomb. [2]They found the stone rolled away from the tomb, [3]but when they entered, they did not find the body of the Lord Jesus. [4]While they were wondering about this, suddenly two men in clothes that gleamed like lightning stood beside them. [5]In their fright the women bowed down with their faces to the ground, but the men said to them, 'Why do you look for the living among the dead? [6]He is not here; he has risen! Remember how he told you, while he was still with you in Galilee: [7]"The Son of Man must be delivered into the hands of sinful men, be crucified and on the third day be raised again."' [8]Then they remembered his words.*
>
> *[9]When they came back from the tomb, they told all these things to the Eleven and to all the others. [10]It was Mary Magdalene, Joanna, Mary the mother of James, and the others with them who told this to the apostles. [11]But they did not believe the women, because their words seemed to them like nonsense. [12]Peter, however, got up and ran to the tomb. Bending over, he saw the strips of linen lying by themselves, and he went away, wondering to himself what had happened.*

Whereas Mark 16:1 states that it was after the Sabbath that the women bought spices, Luke gives the impression that spices had already been bought before the Sabbath (23:56). Whatever may have been the case, both Gospels agree that it was not until the *first day of the week* that the women went to the tomb (v. 1).

Luke also diverges from Mark in so far as he omits the questioning of the women as to who would roll away the stone. However, this is but a minor detail. In line with all three other Gospels Luke does record that on their arrival they *found the stone rolled away from the tomb* (v. 2). Already there is a hint of the resurrection.

The evidence for the resurrection begins to pile up. For when the women entered the tomb, *they did not find the body of the Lord Jesus* (v. 3). We are so used to reading the Gospel story that perhaps we do not feel the full force of this punchline. The body had gone – it had disappeared! Luke is the only Synoptic evangelist to say explicitly at this stage that the tomb was empty, and that the body was not there. In Mark, for instance, it is left to the angel to point out that the body was gone (Mark 16:6). Significantly Luke does not simply write that they did not find 'the body of Jesus', but rather *the body of the Lord Jesus.* Luke is choosing his words carefully. The very phrase *Lord Jesus* denotes the new status that now belongs to Jesus. He is now 'Lord', for he has risen from the dead. As Peter was later to declare on the day of Pentecost, 'God has made this Jesus . . . both Lord and Christ' (Acts 2:36).

Not surprisingly the women were *wondering* (v. 4) at their failure to find the body. The Greek verb (*aporeisthai*) indicates that they were 'at a loss' to know what had happened. They were perplexed and uncertain. They could not think of any rational explanation as to why the tomb should be empty. By contrast with the versions in Mark and Matthew, the angels are not already on hand to give an account of what had happened.

But *suddenly two men in clothes that gleamed like lightning stood beside them* (v. 4). As Luke later makes clear, these two men were indeed 'angels' (v. 23). Again, there is another divergence between Luke and the other evangelists. In Mark and Matthew only one angel is mentioned, but Luke mentions two such heavenly figures. Why should Luke seek to 'correct' Mark's account in this way? Some have suggested that Luke introduced a second angel in order to ensure the presence of the minimum number of witnesses required by Jewish law (Deut. 17:15). This argument is not compelling, however, in so far as for Luke the prime witnesses to the resurrection are human, not divine (see, e.g., Acts 1:22 where being a witness of the resurrection is the key qualification for an apostle). Others have suggested that Luke's account of the resurrection has been influenced by the transfiguration (Luke 9:30) and the ascension (Acts 1:10), where on each occasion two heavenly figures were present. However, the parallelism is not as strong as is sometimes alleged. For example, at the transfiguration the two who appeared 'in glorious splendour' were not angels, but Moses and Elijah. Perhaps the ascension offers a stronger parallel, for then 'two men dressed in white' were present. The most likely explanation for the presence of two angels at the tomb – rather than one – is that Luke was simply being true to one of his sources (see 1:1–4), a source John in his Gospel also appears to have followed (John 20:12). This apparent discrepancy between Luke and John on the one hand, and Mark and Matthew on the other, is not of major significance. Some, indeed, have sought to overcome the discrepancy by pointing out that Mark does not explicitly say that only one angel was there! The most honest course, however, may be to remain agnostic about the discrepancy: we do not really know the truth of the matter.

In none of the Gospels do the women take the angel(s) in their stride. Instead, fear is their reaction. According to Luke, *'In their fright the women bowed down with their faces to the ground'* (v. 5). It was almost certainly this fear, rather than the brightness of the angels' clothes, that induced the women to look away. The presence of the angels proved unnerving.

Whereas in Mark the angel declares, 'You are looking for Jesus the Nazarene, who was crucified' (Mark 16:6), Luke turns Mark's statement into a question, and in so doing exposes the nonsensical nature of the women's quest: *'Why do you look for the living among the dead?'* (v. 5). Why indeed should one look for the living in a graveyard?!

The empty tomb witnesses to the resurrection: *'He is not here; he has risen!'* (v. 6) – or rather, 'he has been raised'. Once again, we probably have a 'divine passive'. For Luke, God is the one who raises Jesus from the dead (see Acts 3:15; 4:10; 10:40; 13:30, 37).

In Matthew and Mark the angel at this point mentions Galilee as the place to which the risen Jesus has gone on ahead. In Luke, however, there is a radical shift of emphasis. For the angels continue, *'Remember how he told you, while he was still with you in Galilee* ...' (v. 6). Galilee, in Luke's account, is no longer the place of future meeting, but rather the place of past teaching. Luke does not record any appearances in Galilee. Jerusalem is the place where the risen Jesus meets his disciples. This is not necessarily because Luke was not aware of the Galilean appearances. Rather, Luke's selection of material has to do with his theological emphasis, and in particular with his emphasis on Jesus as the Saviour of the world (see 24:47; also 2:32; 3:6; 13:28–29; 14:15–23). This emphasis comes to expression in the book of Acts, where Luke tells of the spread of the gospel from Jerusalem to Galilee and finally to Rome (see Acts 1:8). The inclusion of appearances of the risen Lord in Galilee would have disturbed that progression, and so they are omitted.

At this point the angels introduce the Lord's prediction of his passion and resurrection: '*The Son of Man must be delivered into the hands of sinful men, be crucified and on the third day be raised again*' (v. 7). On more than one occasion Luke records Jesus as having spoken to his disciples about his forthcoming death and resurrection (see 9:22, 44; 18:31–32). In his account of the resurrection the necessity of Christ's suffering and his subsequent vindication is again highlighted several times (vv. 7, 26, 46).

The fact that Luke records that the women *remembered his words* (v. 8) implies that they too, and not just the disciples, had been told by Jesus of his forthcoming betrayal, crucifixion and resurrection. Indeed, the clear impression is that for Luke the women were as much disciples as the men. Perhaps it is this that accounts for Luke's omission of the command, found in the other Gospels, to go and tell the disciples that Jesus had risen from the dead. As far as Luke was concerned, the women were not errand runners for the disciples – they *were* disciples!

In Acts 11:16 Luke records a similar remembering. On that occasion Peter remembered that Jesus had spoken of the day when his disciples would be 'baptised with the Holy Spirit'. Peter's remembering of what Jesus had said enabled him to make sense of what had been experienced by Cornelius and his friends. Remembering was the key to understanding. This parallel would suggest that the remembering on Easter Day likewise led to understanding. The 'words' of Jesus confirm the words of the angels, so that the empty tomb becomes a sign of resurrection.

Luke broadens the circle of those to whom the news of the resurrection is first taken. It is not only the 'Eleven' but also *all the others* (v. 9) who are told of the empty tomb. The 'others' presumably included the other 'women' who had been with Jesus (Acts 1:14).

Unlike Mark and Matthew, it is only at this point that Luke mentions the names of the women who had been to the empty tomb: *Mary Magdalene, Joanna, Mary the mother of James, and the others with them* (v. 10). As in all the Gospels Mary Magdalene heads the list. As in Mark, Mary the mother of James features. However, instead of mentioning Salome (Mark 16:1) Luke mentions Joanna, presumably the same Joanna who was 'the wife of Chuza, the manager of Herod's household' (8:3). The identity of 'the others' is uncertain. Luke describes those who 'prepared spices and perfumes' as 'the women who had come with Jesus from Galilee' (23:55–56). Maybe they included Susanna and some of the other women who provided economic support for Jesus and his disciples (8:3).

The disciples were not impressed by the testimony of the women (v. 11), whose words seemed like *nonsense* (*lēros*), a word used by

Greek medical writers to denote the babbling of a fevered or insane mind. Unknowingly perhaps, Luke here makes a significant statement, for by implication he strengthens the evidence for the resurrection. The failure of the disciples to 'believe' the women indicates that they too had no expectation of ever seeing Jesus again. They were not looking for an excuse to believe in resurrection. The reverse was the case. They were sceptical.

If verse 12 is to be believed, *Peter . . . ran to the tomb* in order to verify the women's story. This verse is absent in a few important Greek manuscripts, with the result that some have claimed that it was a later insertion made in the light of John 20:6–7. The evidence for the omission of the verse, however, is not compelling. There is no reason why John and Luke should not both have been drawing upon the same source. Whereas in John's Gospel Peter is accompanied by the Beloved Disciple, here in Luke's Gospel only Peter is mentioned. Luke may well have been selective in his material at this point, for the presence of more than one person at the tomb is later implied by the couple on the Emmaus road, who tell Jesus: 'Then some of our companions went to the tomb . . .' (v. 24).

Peter repeats the discovery of the women. He too enters the tomb. He notices *the strips of linen lying by themselves* (v. 12). This piece of evidence was significant, for had anybody wanted to remove the body of Jesus, they would have been unlikely to have left the grave-clothes behind. Rather, they would have carried the body away wrapped in its shroud. Indirectly, therefore, the presence of the grave-clothes was yet another pointer to the resurrection of Jesus. But, in Luke's account, Peter is not yet able to believe – rather *he went away, wondering* (*thaumazōn*) *to himself what had happened* (v. 12). The sight of the empty tomb and of the abandoned grave-clothes caused Peter to be astonished (see 1:63; 8:25; 11:14; 24:41).

a. The message of the empty tomb

First, the empty tomb reveals that the resurrection is not an idea of the mind, but an event in history. Between Good Friday and Easter Sunday God was at work. As Luke records in his second volume, 'But God raised him from the dead, freeing him from the agony of death, because it was impossible for death to keep its hold on him' (Acts 2:24). The Easter gospel unashamedly declares that Jesus is risen from the dead (Luke 24:6). Jesus did not rise, as some theologians would suggest, 'in the hearts of his disciples'. Easter in the first place is not about a change the disciples experienced, but rather a change Jesus experienced. The minds and hearts of the disciples were changed because they discovered that the body of

Jesus had been transformed through resurrection. The initial pointer to the resurrection was the empty tomb.

Secondly, the empty tomb witnesses to the bodily resurrection of Jesus. The *body* was not there (Luke 24:3). The Greeks believed in the immortality of the soul, but Christians believe in the resurrection of the body. When Jesus rose from the dead, he rose with a body that was recognizably his (see Luke 24:37–48). There is a difference between resurrection and resuscitation, however. When Lazarus came back from the dead, his body was the same as before. But when Jesus came back from the dead, his body was transformed.

Thirdly, the empty tomb connects the resurrection with the crucifixion. The body that had disappeared was the body of the crucified (Luke 23:53). It was the body whose brokenness had been symbolized in the broken bread of the upper room (Luke 22:19). In raising his Son from the dead, God was putting his seal of approval on the work of Jesus on the cross.

b. Easter revision

For many people, their minds are made up and they don't want to be confused by the facts. But Easter calls us all to look at the facts and to think again. In particular, Easter calls us to revise our thinking in three areas.

In the first place, Easter calls us to revise our thinking about death. When the women went to the tomb, they expected to find the body of Jesus. Indeed, they went to the tomb to complete the task of anointing the body of Jesus (Luke 24:1). They presumed that death was the end. So too in our culture death is widely seen as the end. Precisely because it is assumed to be the end, it is feared. Death is the last thing we talk about. We spend small fortunes on putting off the evil day by seeking the elixir of youth, but in vain.

In the second place, Easter calls us to revise our thinking about Jesus. The couple on the Emmaus road spoke of Jesus as having been 'a prophet, powerful in word and deed' (Luke 24:19), but at that stage were not able to speak of him as 'Prince and Saviour' (Acts 5:31). It was their discovery of the resurrection that caused the disciples of Jesus to change radically their thinking about Jesus. In our culture many are willing to acknowledge that Jesus may have been 'a prophet' – they speak of him as having been a great religious leader and teacher, but no more. If Jesus is risen from the dead, however, we need to revise our thinking.

In the third place, Easter calls us to revise our thinking about the future in general, and about our future in particular. For the resurrection of Jesus is a pointer to the day when God will wind up all human history and will call humankind to account. As Paul told the Athenians, God 'has set a day when he will judge the world with justice by the man he has appointed. He has given proof of this to all men by raising him from the dead' (Acts 17:31). For Luke, as for the early church in general, the preaching of the resurrection went hand in hand with a call to repentance and an offer of forgiveness (Luke 24:47; Acts 2:36, 38).

c. Easter and the search for truth

Luke wrote his account of the resurrection for the 'most excellent Theophilus' (Luke 1:3; see also Acts 1:1). Bearing in mind that Luke's Gospel is part of a two-volume work, which ends with Paul about to stand trial in Rome, some have suggested that Theophilus was the Roman examining magistrate before whom Paul was due to appear. Others maintain that Theophilus wasn't a particular individual at all, but rather that his name, which means 'friend of God', is a representative term for all who wanted to know about the Christian faith. Whoever Theophilus was, Luke wrote his Gospel to persuade people of the truth that is in Jesus – and not least the truth of the resurrection of Jesus.

In the light of Luke's intention in his introduction, his account of the resurrection can be analysed as follows.

It is an 'eye-witness' account. Luke states that he has drawn upon reports 'handed down to us by those who from the first were eye-witnesses' (1:2). Luke 24 consists of a series of eye-witness reports. The women discover the empty tomb; others (including Peter) go to the empty tomb and find it just as the women had said; Cleopas and his companion encounter Jesus on the Emmaus road; the risen Lord appears first to Peter, and then later eats a piece of broiled fish before all the disciples. These are hard facts. The witnesses do not testify to something they feel, but rather to something they see and somebody they recognize. The resurrection is not to be interpreted in terms that are totally subjective.

It is an 'orderly' account. Luke states that having 'carefully investigated everything from the beginning, it seemed good also to me to write an orderly account' (1:3). Luke was not the first to collect stories of Jesus. Almost certainly Luke had Mark's Gospel before him when he wrote. He also had access to other stories. In writing his Gospel Luke set out to edit and arrange this material in a way that would serve his particular purpose. This explains the orderliness of his accounts of the resurrection – all of which appear to take place on the first Easter Day and all of which take place around Jerusalem. There is no reason to suppose that Luke was unaware of other appearances of Jesus at other times and in other places.

It is a 'reliable' account. Luke states that he wrote his Gospel for Theophilus 'so that you may know the certainty of the things you have been taught' (1:4). In one sense Luke was a propagandist. He did not set out to write an objective biography. Rather, he was concerned to put over the essence of the Christian message. This, however, does not mean that Luke was not concerned for truth. Like Paul in 1 Corinthians 15, Luke would have known that, were anyone able to disprove the historicity of the resurrection, the Christian faith would collapse like a pack of cards. The Christian gospel depends on the fundamental conviction that God raised Jesus from the dead. But, as the Eleven were able to declare to the Emmaus pair, 'It is true! The Lord has risen . . .' (24:34). The Christian gospel does not compromise the truth.

The Christian gospel is about truth – the truth as it is in Jesus (see Eph. 4:21). As Christians we have nothing to fear from the use of the mind on the part of those who are seekers after truth. On the contrary, we should welcome the use of the mind. Sadly, so many of our contemporaries are unwilling to face up to the truth. The words of J. B. Phillips, a Bible translator of a generation or two ago, are even truer today than when he first wrote them:

> Over the years I have had hundreds of conversations with people, many of them of higher intellectual calibre than my own, who quite obviously had no idea of what Christianity is really about. I was in no case trying to catch them out; I was simply and gently trying to find out what they knew about the New Testament. My conclusion was that they knew virtually nothing. This I find pathetic and somewhat horrifying. It means that the most important Event in human history is politely and quietly by-passed. For it is not as though the evidence had been examined and found unconvincing: it had simply never been examined. It is my serious conclusion that here in the New Testament are words that bear the hallmark of reality and the ring of truth.[1]

2. Jesus appears on the road to Emmaus (24:13–35)

Now that same day two of them were going to a village called Emmaus, about seven miles from Jerusalem. [14]*They were talking with each other about everything that had happened.* [15]*As they*

[1] J. B. Phillips, *Ring of Truth: A Translator's Testimony* (Hodder & Stoughton, 1970).

talked and discussed these things with each other, Jesus himself came up and walked along with them; ¹⁶but they were kept from recognising him.

¹⁷He asked them, 'What are you discussing together as you walk along?'

They stood still, their faces downcast. ¹⁸One of them, named Cleopas, asked him, 'Are you only a visitor to Jerusalem and do not know the things that have happened there in these days?'

¹⁹'What things?' he asked.

'About Jesus of Nazareth,' they replied. 'He was a prophet, powerful in word and deed before God and all the people. ²⁰The chief priests and our rulers handed him over to be sentenced to death, and they crucified him; ²¹but we had hoped that he was the one who was going to redeem Israel. And what is more, it is the third day since all this took place. ²²In addition, some of our women amazed us. They went to the tomb early this morning ²³but didn't find his body. They came and told us that they had seen a vision of angels, who said he was alive. ²⁴Then some of our companions went to the tomb and found it just as the women had said, but him they did not see.'

²⁵He said to them, 'How foolish you are, and how slow of heart to believe all that the prophets have spoken! ²⁶Did not the Christ have to suffer these things and then enter his glory?' ²⁷And beginning with Moses and all the Prophets, he explained to them what was said in all the Scriptures concerning himself.

²⁸As they approached the village to which they were going, Jesus acted as if he were going further. ²⁹But they urged him strongly, 'Stay with us, for it is nearly evening; the day is almost over.' So he went in to stay with them.

³⁰When he was at the table with them, he took bread, gave thanks, broke it and began to give it to them. ³¹Then their eyes were opened and they recognised him, and he disappeared from their sight. ³²They asked each other, 'Were not our hearts burning within us while he talked with us on the road and opened the Scriptures to us?'

³³They got up and returned at once to Jerusalem. There they found the Eleven and those with them, assembled together ³⁴and saying, 'It is true! The Lord has risen and has appeared to Simon.' ³⁵Then the two told what had happened on the way, and how Jesus was recognised by them when he broke the bread.

The appearance of the risen Lord to the couple on the road to Emmaus is found only in Luke. However, the longer ending of Mark (16:12–13) probably refers to this story: 'Afterwards Jesus appeared in a different form to two of them while they were walking in the country. These returned and reported it to the rest . . .' Certain parallels to elements in the story can also be found in John's Gospel: for example, the delayed recognition (John 20:14–16) and a meal (John 21:12–13).

The identity of the *village called Emmaus* (v. 13) is uncertain and disputed. The uncertainties arise because Luke describes this village as 'about seven miles from Jerusalem' (literally, 'sixty stadia'). The village that best fits the description was identified by the Crusaders with Kaloniye (today known as El-Qubeibeh), which is indeed just over seven miles from Jerusalem. Unfortunately, this village is known to us only from the Middle Ages, and therefore is unlikely to be the village Luke had in mind. Many scholars therefore opt for the modern Emmaus ('Amwas), mentioned both by Josephus and in 1 Maccabees 3:40, 57; 4:3; etc. The chief snag is that it is almost twenty miles northwest of Jerusalem and thus much further away than suggested by Luke. The two disciples could scarcely have travelled that distance by foot and then returned the same day. The only other likely option is to identify Luke's Emmaus with another village known to Josephus as Emmaus (today called Kuoniyeh), but only some three and a half miles north-west of Jerusalem. If this last suggestion is indeed the Emmaus of Luke 24, then we must assume that Luke meant that this village was a seven-mile round trip from Jerusalem.

Not only is the identity of the village uncertain and disputed, but so also is the identity of the two travellers. The name of one is given as *Cleopas* (v. 18), while the other is unnamed. The latter has often been assumed to be Cleopas's wife, but such an assumption is no more than speculation. Cleopas himself has sometimes been identified with Clopas, the uncle of Jesus (John 19:25). There is no compelling evidence, however, to support that identification. The fact that Luke records Jesus' appearance to these two apparently insignificant disciples is in itself a pointer to the historicity of the account. Had the story been invented, it would have been much more likely to have featured two well-known apostles.

The story begins with the *two of them* (i.e. two of *the others* mentioned in v. 9) setting off on the road to Emmaus later *that same day*, that is, Easter Day (v. 13). We are not given any reason for their making this journey. In the light of the discovery of the empty tomb and of the message of the angels, one might have assumed that all the disciples would have stayed together until the mystery of the 'disappeared body' had been solved. If Emmaus was only three and a half miles away, however, these two may not have been intending to leave the other disciples for any extended period of time. Rather, they may just have been going to their lodgings.

Not surprisingly, on their way they talked about *everything that had happened* (v. 14) – about the crucifixion and their disappointed hopes, and perhaps too about the women's report of the empty tomb. As they talked, *Jesus himself came up and walked along with them* (v. 15). Presumably he overtook them from the rear – he would have appeared to them to have been another pilgrim, returning home from the celebration of Passover in Jerusalem (see v. 18).

Luke continues: . . . *but they were kept from recognising him* (v. 16). The question immediately arises: how was it that these two did not recognize Jesus, the one in whose company they presumably had been for the last three years or so? What prevented them from recognizing him? Perhaps the least acceptable suggestion is that the evening sun was so dazzling that they were unable to see him properly. This would not explain why they did not recognize Jesus when eventually they came into the house for a meal. Certainly their failure to believe the report of the women (v. 11) did not help them. Nor perhaps would their minds, so full of their own loss and disappointment, have been able to focus easily on their new companion. Yet none of these human factors accounts for their non-recognition. Rather, as Luke appears to suggest, some supernatural force was at work: they were actually 'prevented' from seeing it was Jesus. It is unlikely that this was Satan's doing – for if it had been, Luke would surely have been more specific (see 22:31). Rather, we have here another example of a 'divine passive'. God was the cause of their non-recognition (see 9:45; 18:34).

As to why God should have kept them from recognizing Jesus, we can only speculate. Elsewhere in his Gospel Luke states that neither the Father nor the Son can be known except by divine revelation (10:21–22: see also Matt. 16:17 and 1 Cor. 2:6–16). Maybe here we have an instance of the divine refusal to coerce faith. Faith, the story seems to suggest, is best exercised by minds prepared in advance by an understanding of the Scriptures (see vv. 25–27). An attractive thought to those of us living after the cessation of the resurrection appearances is the suggestion that Luke is also wanting to show that we can know the presence of the risen Christ without being able physically to see him. It is above all in the opening of the Scriptures and in the breaking of bread that Jesus is known.

For the time being the Emmaus couple had yet to recognize Jesus. For them Jesus was dead and buried. As their faces indicated, they were filled with sadness and gloom. It was, of course, not Jesus' apparent ignorance that caused them to be *downcast* (v. 17: the adjective, *skythrōpos*, also occurs in Matt. 6:16), but rather his 'ignorance' that brought to the surface their depression.

'*Are you only a visitor to Jerusalem and do not know the things that have happened there in these days?'* (v. 18). The question assumes that the crucifixion of Jesus was the talk of Jerusalem that Passover time. Indeed it is possible that the phrasing of the question reflects Luke's emphasis that the events concerning Jesus were well known and available for public scrutiny (e.g. 4:14; see also Acts 26:26). Unbeknown to Cleopas, there was great irony in his question: it was not Jesus who did *not know*, but rather Cleopas and his companion.

Cleopas seeks to fill in the stranger about Jesus. His description of Jesus as *a prophet, powerful in word and deed before God and all the people* (v. 19; see 4:24; 7:16; 9:19) would in any other context have been high praise. But, as the resurrection so clearly showed, Jesus was far more than a prophet – he was the 'Christ' (v. 26); he was the 'Lord' (v. 34). Or, as Peter later declared at Pentecost, 'God has made this Jesus, whom you crucified, both Lord and Christ' (Acts 2:36).

According to Cleopas, the *chief priests and our rulers* (v. 20) were to be held responsible for the death of Jesus (see 23:13). There is no explicit reference to Pilate and the Roman soldiers and to the part they played in the crucifixion. This fits in with Luke's intention to show Theophilus that the Christian faith was not – and never had been – a threat to Rome (e.g. 23:4, 14–15; Acts 26:30–32).

The disappointment of the two disciples comes to full expression: *'we had hoped that he was the one who was going to redeem Israel'* (v. 21; see also 1:68; 2:38; 21:28). The 'redemption' these two had in mind was first and foremost political. They had looked for one who would free Israel from the Roman occupying power (see Acts 1:6). These hopes had been well and truly dashed by the events of Good Friday. Ironically, they failed to see that it was precisely 'redemption' that Jesus had achieved on his cross. Nor did they see the irony in their reference to *the third day* (v. 21), a phrase whose use in the Old Testament was perceived to be expressive of deliverance. According to the midrash on Genesis 42:17, 'The Holy One, blessed be he, never leaves the righteous in distress more than three days.' They ignored too the fact that Jesus had anticipated not only his suffering and dying, but also his rising on 'the third day' (9:22; 18:33; 20:12).

The disciples then go on to summarize the story of the women's discovery of the empty tomb and confirm the women's story (vv. 22–24; see 24:1–9), and in doing so express their continuing scepticism: *'but him they did not see'* (v. 24). Again we see that the possibility of resurrection was the last thing to come to mind.

Jesus takes the disciples to task: *'How foolish you are, and how slow of heart to believe all that the prophets have spoken!'* (v. 25). Jesus' response is surprisingly forceful. His opening interjection, untranslated in the NIV, indicates strength of feeling: 'Oh (Ō), how foolish you are . . .' (this interjection is found also in 8:41; Acts 13:10; etc.). The word *foolish* (*anoētoi*) literally means 'without intelligence or understanding'; colloquially we might say 'without a brain'. It is the same word with which Paul upbraided the Galatians (Gal. 3:1, 3) for their attempt to add to the work of Christ on the cross by their own human effort. In addition Jesus describes them as slow-witted. Jesus upbraids them in particular for failing to take the Scriptures seriously. If only they had listened to the prophets, they would have believed the report of the women.

Precisely what prophetic passages are in mind is uncertain. Did Jesus point to Isaiah 53, for instance? It may be, however, that the words *all . . . the prophets* (v. 25), *Moses and all the Prophets* (v. 27) and *all the Scriptures* (v. 27) indicate that no particular passage is being referred to. The emphasis may be rather on the Scriptures as a whole, which, with their twin message of the holiness and the love of God, point inevitably to their combining in the cross and resurrection.

The question *'Did not the Christ have to suffer these things and then enter his glory?'* (v. 26) reflects a characteristic theme of Luke's Gospel in which the divine necessity of the cross and resurrection is brought out (see 9:22; 17:25; 24:7; cf. also 22:37; 24:44). As Peter was later to make clear, the death of Jesus was no tragic accident – it was part of 'God's set purpose and foreknowledge' (Acts 2:23; see also 4:28). This is the first time, however, that we find the expression that the 'Christ' must suffer (see 22:46; also Acts 3:18; 17:3; 26:23). In pre-Christian Judaism there was no notion of a suffering Messiah: Isaiah 53, for instance, was not at that stage interpreted as referring to the Messiah. The 'glory' of Luke 24:26 is that of the exalted Son of Man (9:26; 21:27).

Jesus then gave the disciples a lesson in hermeneutics; that is, he *explained* (v. 27) or 'interpreted' (*diermēneusen*) the Scriptures. What an experience that must have been! Philip was later to do the same for the Ethiopian official (Acts 8:35).

With the end of their journey in sight, *Jesus acted as if he were going further* (v. 28). There is no reason to suppose that he was playing games with the two disciples. Had they not invited him into their home, he would have gone on his way. It was not in Jesus' character ever to force himself upon anyone (see Rev. 3:21).

In the ancient world hospitality to strangers counted as a sacred duty (see Heb. 13:2). Luke, however, describes the disciples as being unusually forceful in their invitation to Jesus to stay. *But they urged him strongly, 'Stay with us . . .'* (v. 29; see Acts 16:15). In other contexts the Greek verb (*parabiazomai*) can actually indicate the use of force. Clearly there was something unusually attractive about their companion.

They continue: '. . . *it is nearly evening; the day is almost over*' (v. 29). This accords with the Jewish custom of having the main meal of the day in the late afternoon.

The guest becomes the host. Jesus *took bread, gave thanks, broke it and began to give it to them* (v. 30). In one respect these are the actions familiar at the beginning of any Jewish meal. We are surely right, however, to see here allusions to the Last Supper (see especially 22:19). This may not be a celebration of the Lord's Supper, but it is difficult to believe that Luke did not want to point his readers to the fact that in the preaching of the word and the eucharistic breaking of bread Jesus makes himself known (vv. 30, 32, 35).

Then their eyes were opened . . . (v. 31). A divine passive. It was not the 'fourfold action' or the belated sight of the nail-marked hands that suddenly struck a chord; it was God who enabled them to see. Jesus, however, *disappeared from their sight* (v. 31). Like Mary Magdalene (John 20:17) and the women at the tomb (Matt. 28:9), the disciples were unable to hold on to Jesus.

As the disciples reflected on their experience, they said to one another, '*Were not our hearts burning within us while he talked with us . . .?*' (v. 32). Jesus engaged their minds (see also v. 45), but their hearts too were involved. Here we have a reminder that Christian faith is never just a cerebral experience. It is also an intensely personal relationship of the 'heart', involving our feelings and emotions. Paul describes something of this relationship when speaking of the work of the Spirit in the life of the believer, 'God sent the Spirit of his Son into our hearts, the Spirit who calls out, "*Abba*, Father"' (Gal. 4:6). A parallel may be drawn with John Wesley's experience on 24 May 1738:

> In the evening I went very unwillingly to a society in Aldersgate Street, where one was reading Luther's preface to the Epistle to the Romans. About a quarter before 9, while he was describing the change God works in the heart through faith in Christ, *I felt my heart strangely warmed.* I felt I did trust in Christ, Christ alone, for salvation, and an assurance was given me that He had taken away my sins, even mine, and saved me from the law of sin and death.[2]

Not surprisingly they could not keep to themselves the news of their encounter with the risen Christ. In spite of the argument that

---

[2] *John Wesley's Journal*, ed. R. Backhouse (Hodder & Stoughton, 1993), p. 56 (emphasis mine).

they had used with Jesus about the day being almost over, they *returned at once to Jerusalem* (v. 33). But before they could share their news, the others had news to share: *'It is true! The Lord has risen and has appeared to Simon'* (v. 34). What a day that was!

a. Easter encounter

The story of the Emmaus road is not just a story of a one-off encounter of the risen Lord. Rather, we may see this as a story pointing to how the risen Lord Jesus continues to encounter people – even today.

In the first place, Jesus encounters us *in the darkness of our lives.* As the Emmaus pair trudged along the road, with *downcast* faces (v. 17), they must have been in the depths of depression. As far as they were concerned, they had been let down by God: *'we had hoped that he was the one who was going to redeem Israel'* (v. 21). Yet in their 'darkness' *Jesus came up and walked along with them* (v. 15). Although they did not initially recognize him, Jesus was there. Jesus is there too when we walk through our own particular 'darkness'. The darkness may take the shape of some tragedy or misfortune that hits our lives. We may have experienced loss of one kind or another. We feel let down by God – let down by our faith and maybe let down by his church. As we walk along life's way, we feel crushed, desolate and alone. But the story of the Emmaus road is that God never abandons those who are his. We never walk alone. Jesus, if we will but see, walks alongside us.

Jesus also encounters us *in the exposition of his Word.* Central to the experience of the Emmaus pair was the opening of the Scriptures (v. 27). Indeed, with hindsight they realized that it was precisely in the exposition of the Scriptures that their hearts burned within them (v. 32). The same can be our experience today. The reading of and the preaching from Scripture can be as much of a 'sacrament' as baptism or the Lord's Supper, in the sense that God takes the written and spoken word and uses it to bless our innermost being.

Lastly, Jesus encounters us *in the breaking of the bread.* It was in the breaking of bread that the eyes of the Emmaus pair were opened (v. 31). The Lord's Supper need not be just an occasion to remember the Lord who died for us. It can also be the place where we meet with the Lord who rose from the dead and is now alive for ever. The remembering becomes a means of encountering. Communion is not just with one another, but with the Lord.

b. Openness is the way to truth

If we would discover the truth about Jesus, then we must be open to receive the truth. Such openness involves, first, *open eyes*. The eyes of the Emmaus pair were blind to the presence of the risen Jesus (v. 16), not least because they were blind to all the evidence that pointed to it. No doubt convinced in their own minds that dead people don't rise from the dead, they refused to take the evidence for the empty tomb seriously. They refused to examine the evidence of the women, just as they refused to examine the evidence of Peter. Similarly the blindness of the Emmaus couple is to be found in many of our contemporaries. The evidence for the resurrection of Jesus is compelling for those who are prepared to come and look without prejudice, but too many never make the effort, so sure are they of their position.

Secondly, openness to truth requires *open minds*. The minds of the Emmaus pair were shut to understanding the message of the Scriptures (vv. 25, 45). No doubt they thought they knew the Scriptures, yet they had never studied them to see what they said about the Christ. Their preconceptions of the Christ did not in fact tally with what the Scriptures said of him and of his death and resurrection. Today such ignorance continues. Despite their high level of general education, many in Western society have almost no knowledge of the Scriptures. Yet the evidence of the Gospels regarding the person of Jesus is compelling for those who are prepared to investigate it with an open mind.

Thirdly, openness to truth demands *open hearts*. The hearts of the Emmaus pair were preoccupied with their sense of grief (vv. 17–18). No doubt initially they were more concerned to share their feelings of bewilderment than to be open to what Jesus had to say. But then they listened. The turning point came when they invited Jesus into their homes and allowed him to take charge. Then they experienced the warming of the heart. Finally, they discovered Jesus. If we would experience him, we too must open up our hearts and lives to him. Jesus, however, never forces himself on us – he always waits to be invited.

Open eyes, minds and hearts lead to open mouths. Once the Emmaus pair had discovered Jesus, they could not keep the news to themselves. The good news of Jesus is for telling. In a sense the Christian message is never truly ours until we have opened our mouths and shared it with others.

3. Jesus appears to his disciples (24:36–43)

While they were still talking about this, Jesus himself stood among them and said to them 'Peace be with you.'
³⁷They were startled and frightened, thinking they saw a ghost.
³⁸He said to them, 'Why are you troubled, and why do doubts rise in your minds? ³⁹Look at my hands and my feet. It is I myself! Touch me and see; a ghost does not have flesh and bones, as you see I have.'
⁴⁰When he had said this, he showed them his hands and feet.
⁴¹And while they still did not believe it because of joy and amazement, he asked them, 'Do you have anything here to eat?'
⁴²They gave him a piece of broiled fish, ⁴³and he took it and ate it in their presence.

Suddenly Jesus appears. There the disciples were, talking about him, and *Jesus himself stood among them* (v. 36). By contrast with the parallel passage in John 20:19–23, Luke does not mention that the doors were locked, but nevertheless that is the implication. Throughout this passage, there is a tension. On the one hand, the corporeality of Jesus is emphasized: Jesus has *flesh and bones* (v. 39). On the other hand, Jesus is able to appear (v. 36) and then later to vanish (v. 51) in a way that is not possible for ordinary mortals.

As in John 20:21, Jesus greets his disciples with the words *'Peace be with you'* (v. 36). What could have been but a conventional greeting surely had more force. There is no indication here, however, that Jesus is offering the special kind of peace that he as the Saviour came to bring (see 2:14; 7:50; Acts 10:36). Rather, Jesus is perhaps anticipating the consternation his appearance would cause and seeks to calm their troubled minds. But to no avail: *They were startled and frightened, thinking they saw a ghost* (v. 37). In some ways the reaction of the disciples is quite surprising. For at that very moment they had been talking about Jesus' appearance both to Simon and to the Emmaus pair. They were already coming to terms with the fact of his resurrection. Yet when the risen Jesus appeared to them, instead of welcoming him with warmth, they were scared stiff. In this respect the NIV does not perhaps convey the true force of the Greek. They were 'shocked', if not 'terrified', rather than just 'startled' (the same verb, *ptoeō*, is found in 21:9, where Jesus tells his disciples not to be 'frightened' when in the last days they hear of wars and revolutions). They were well and truly *frightened* (see also 24:5; Acts 10:4). Indeed, they thought they saw a *ghost* or spirit (*pneuma*). They still found it difficult to believe that Jesus had truly risen from the dead. The concept of the 'resurrection of the body' did not come naturally to them; rather, their first inclination was to go for the 'spiritualist' option of believing in some kind of insubstantial apparition. Spirits were considered to be less than real people. Existing in a shadowy world, they were viewed as but empty shells of their previous selves.

In this context Jesus addresses their questions and fears: *'Why are you troubled'* [literally, 'shaken or stirred up', *tetaragmenoi*], *and why do doubts (dialogismoi) rise in your minds?'* (v. 38). The picture here is of an internal discussion or argument going on inside themselves. Various possibilities were 'surfacing' in their thinking as they were trying to work out what this figure before them could actually be. In the light of the appearances to Peter and to the Emmaus pair, the disciples were even more *foolish* and *slow of heart* (v. 25).

As with Thomas (John 20:27), Jesus challenges them not only to *look at* his hands and feet, but also to *touch* him (v. 39). By contrast with John's account of Jesus' appearance to Thomas, nothing is actually said about seeing the marks of the nails (John 20:25), but the thought may nevertheless be present. The Greek (*psēlaphēsate*) indicates that Jesus invites them not just to *touch* him with the tips of their fingers, but actually to 'feel' and 'handle' him (the word occurs again in Acts 17:27, referring to people reaching out for and finding God). According to Ignatius of Antioch, the disciples took up the invitation and 'immediately touched him and believed, being mingled with both his flesh and his spirit'.[3] We have no evidence of this, however, in Luke's account.

'It is I myself!' (v. 39) Jesus could not be more emphatic. He is the same person as before: *'a ghost does not have flesh and bones, as you see I have'* (v. 39). Later the church had to deal with the problem of docetism, the heresy that claimed that Jesus only seemed to be truly man, whereas in fact he never truly assumed 'sinful' flesh (see, e.g., 1 John 4:2). It is highly unlikely, however, that Luke is addressing even incipient docetism here. He is probably seeking primarily to highlight the identity of the risen Lord with the earthly Jesus. The risen Lord is the man of Galilee.

Jesus *showed them his hands and feet* (v. 40). This verse is omitted by some manuscripts. Although it is almost identical with John 20:20, however, there is no strong reason why we should regard it as a later addition imported from the account in John's Gospel. The implication here is that Jesus rolls up his sleeves and perhaps even lifts up the hem of his long-flowing robe. He had nothing to hide! The risen Lord is the crucified Jesus of Calvary.

Yet still the disciples do *not believe it because of joy and*

---

[3] Ignatius, *Letter to the Smyrneans* 3.1.

amazement (v. 41). They are not convinced, but by this stage their unbelief appears to have more to do with the feeling that it is all too good to be true. Their fear has been replaced with *joy* (see also v. 52). They are filled with wonderment (see 1:63; 8:25; 11:14; Acts 4:13). They almost need to pinch themselves to ensure that this is for real. The difficulty they have in believing, however, serves ultimately to emphasize the truth of the resurrection. The disciples were not looking for an excuse to believe in resurrection. No, they needed solid evidence before they could be convinced that Jesus had been raised to life from the dead.

Jesus at this point proceeds to offer that solid evidence. He asks for something to *eat* (v. 41) and *in their presence* (v. 43) eats *a piece of broiled fish* (v. 42), possibly left over from their evening meal. If ever proof of resurrection was needed, this was it. This truly was Jesus, risen from the dead.

Parallels have been drawn with the meal Jesus had with the Emmaus pair (v. 30). Indeed, some have seen here an allusion to the Last Supper, but that is fanciful. Equally fanciful is the suggestion that the offering of *fish* indicates that originally this appearance must have taken place in Galilee, for fish was in fact readily available in Jerusalem (see, e.g., Neh. 3:3; 13:16).[4]

Some have objected to this particular story and have argued that the so-called crass materialism present is a creation of the early church, and speaks not so much of resurrection as of resuscitation. The fact is, however, that throughout all the resurrection narratives the physical nature of the resurrection of Jesus is to the fore. Above all the story of the empty tomb is such an evidence (Matt. 28:1–8; Mark 16:1–8; Luke 24:1–10; John 20:1–10). Matthew tells us that the disciples 'clasped his feet' (Matt. 28:9). In Luke's Gospel Jesus breaks bread (Luke 24:30) and eats fish (Luke 24:43). In John's Gospel Mary has to be told not to cling on to Jesus (John 20:17); Jesus shows the disciples his hands and side (John 20:20) and encourages Thomas to feel the nail marks with his finger and to put his hand into the wound in his side (John 20:27), and later on gives his disciples bread and fish to eat (21:13). Significantly the two Gospels that most emphasize the physical aspects of the resurrection body of Jesus, namely those of Luke and John, are also the two that most stress the 'spiritual' aspects of his body. For example, in Luke's Gospel Jesus *disappeared from sight* (Luke 24:31) and in John's Gospel Jesus appeared in spite of the fact that the doors were 'locked' (John 20:19, 26). As far as Luke and John were concerned, they were able to hold together in their minds an understanding of

---

[4] See also J. Jeremias, *Jerusalem in the Time of Jesus* (SCM, 1969), p. 20.

the resurrection body of Jesus which unified both physical and spiritual motifs.

The truth is that there is no simple way of resolving the tension between the apparent 'materialistic' and 'non-materialistic' appearances of Jesus. It will not do to maintain the former over against the latter.[5] A helpful explanation is offered by Murray Harris:

> The resurrection of Jesus was not his transformation into an immaterial body, but his acquisition of a 'spiritual body' which could materialise or dematerialise at will. When, on occasion, Jesus chose to appear to various persons in material form, this was just as really the 'spiritual body' of Jesus as when he was not visible . . . In his risen state Jesus transcended the normal laws of physical existence. He was no longer bound by material or spatial limitations.[6]

a. A ghost story? Fact or fiction?

Did the risen Jesus really appear to his disciples or was it just some kind of a *ghost* (vv. 37, 39)? Were the appearances of Jesus to Peter and to the other disciples more akin to the kind of hallucination often experienced by the recently bereaved? Are we to think of the appearances more in terms of subjective visions than of objective events? Such questions are inevitably raised by the resurrection stories, and none more so than by the appearance recorded here in Luke 24:36–43.

First, the resurrection appearances of Jesus came as a genuine surprise to the disciples. Their fear and fright (v. 37), their initial doubt (v. 38) and disbelief (v. 41), can be paralleled in the other resurrection stories. The disciples did not expect to see Jesus again, and so the appearances can scarcely be regarded as a product of their wishful thinking.

Secondly, the resurrection appearances of Jesus involved not simply individuals – not even just a couple like the two on the Emmaus road – but also large groups of people. On this particular occasion Luke records that the Eleven and others were present (v. 33). The others almost certainly included *Mary Magdalene, Joanna,*

---

[5] Wayne Grudem's attempt to stress the material or physical aspect of all the resurrection appearances of Jesus involves a good deal of special pleading: for example, 'The fact that Jesus appeared in a room when the doors had been shut or locked (Jn. 20:19–20) may not mean that he passed through a wall or door . . . it is possible that the door miraculously opened for Jesus' (*Systematic Theology: An Introduction to Biblical Theology* [IVP, 1994], p. 612).

[6] M. J. Harris, *From Grave to Glory: Resurrection in the New Testament* (Zondervan, 1990), pp. 142–143.

Mary the mother of James and other women (v. 10), as well as Cleopas and his companion (v. 35). In other words, there could well have been as many as twenty of them present, if not more. Paul even speaks of a group of more than five hundred seeing Jesus at the same time (1 Cor. 15:6). Hallucinations come to individuals, not to groups. People in a group never see the same thing unless there is an objective basis to what they see.

Thirdly, the resurrection appearances of Jesus involved a wide cross-section of individuals. The women (v. 10) might have been regarded as neurotic, and Peter (v. 34) as somewhat excitable, but the disciples themselves included fishermen like James and John, who elsewhere appear to be pretty down to earth, and Matthew the tax collector who in his former life was almost certainly not a 'soft touch'. And then there was Thomas, who with his doubts must have taken some convincing.

Fourthly, the resurrection appearances of Jesus took place at different times and in different places. Here in Luke we have an afternoon walk in the country (vv. 13–32) and an evening gathering in Jerusalem (vv. 36–43). We do not know where Peter was when he saw the Lord first, but on another occasion it was during the morning by the Lake of Galilee (John 21). By contrast, psychic experiences are normally limited to particular times and places.

The appearance in Luke 24:13–32 provides solid evidence of the corporeality of the risen Jesus. This was no mere *ghost*. But if the whole story is an invention, either by Luke or by the Christian community he represents, how are we to explain the change that takes place in the disciples as recorded in Acts? Where did their boldness come from? If the book of Acts itself is regarded as suspect (how sceptical some sceptics can be!), how are we to explain the emergence of the Christian church? Something momentous must have happened, for, as the Jewish religious leader Gamaliel observed, the crucifixion of a leader normally brings any movement to an end (Acts 5:34–39). The resurrection is the only logical, and indeed credible, explanation.

4. Jesus instructs his disciples (24:44–49)

He said to them, 'This is what I told you while I was still with you: Everything must be fulfilled that is written about me in the Law of Moses, the Prophets and the Psalms.'
⁴⁵Then he opened their minds so they could understand the Scriptures. ⁴⁶He told them, 'This is what is written: The Christ will suffer and rise from the dead on the third day, ⁴⁷and repentance and forgiveness of sins will be preached in his name to all nations, beginning at Jerusalem. ⁴⁸You are witnesses of these things. ⁴⁹I am

*going to send you what my Father has promised; but stay in the
city until you have been clothed with power from on high.'*

Jesus now begins to recapitulate the teaching he has already given
to the couple on the Emmaus road. As he talked to his disciples, he
opened their minds (v. 45) by opening to them *the Scriptures* (v. 45;
see vv. 27, 32). On the basis of *the Law of Moses, the Prophets and
the Psalms* (v. 44), the three parts of the Jewish Scriptures, he again
pointed to the necessity that his suffering should precede his glory
(vv. 44–45; see v. 26). Later the apostles were to use the Scriptures
in presenting their faith to their contemporaries (see, e.g., Acts 10:43;
26:22–23) and in this way emphasize that the Christian gospel was
no innovation, but rather the fulfilment of the Scriptures.

But then Jesus turns from the events of the immediate past to the
future: *'repentance and forgiveness of sins will be preached in his
name'* (v. 47). Literally, it is 'on *(epi)* his name', that is, 'on the basis
of the name', on the basis of the crucified and risen Lord (v. 46), that
repentance and forgiveness can be preached. It is because of what
God achieved in the cross and through the resurrection that there
is any good news to be preached. The good news, however, is not
unconditional: the promise of forgiveness is only for those who
repent. Repentance in the Scriptures is always more than feeling
sorry: it involves a turning away from sin. We cannot be forgiven if
we persist in clinging to our sins. Furthermore, the good news is to
be taken *to all nations* (v. 47). This is an emphasis dear to Luke's
heart, for Luke more than any other Gospel writer brings out the
universal scope of the gospel (e.g. 2:1; 2:32; 3:1; 4:16–30; etc.).

Within a matter of weeks all this became a reality. It was in 'the
name of . . . Jesus' (see Acts 4:30) that repentance and forgiveness
of sins were preached (e.g. Acts 2:38). The book of Acts tells how
the mission of the church spread from Jerusalem to Rome, to
encompass all nations (see Acts 1:8; 2:7–11; etc.).

'You are witnesses of these things' (v. 48). Here we have Luke's
version of the Great Commission. The disciples are instructed not
so much to 'make disciples' (Matt. 28:19) as to be witnesses to the
gospel. Here Luke anticipates the book of Acts, where he shows in
particular that the disciples were witnesses to the resurrection (e.g.
Acts 1:21–22; 2:32; 3:15; 10:39–41; 13:30–31).

In order to enable them to fulfil this commission Jesus tells his
disciples to *'stay in the city until you have been clothed with power
from on high'* (see Luke 24:49; see also Acts 1:4, 5). This *power* is
the power of the Holy Spirit (Acts 1:9), the promise of the Father
(see Is. 32:15; 44:3; Ezek. 39:29; Joel 2:28–29), whom Jesus himself
sent on the day of Pentecost (Acts 2:33). In the early church the

Spirit was not a doctrine to be believed and confessed, but rather a power to be received and experienced.

a. Go and witness!

Here in a nutshell is the Great Commission as we find it in Luke. Although the commission was first addressed to those who had been with him during the three eventful years of his earthly ministry, it is applicable to any who claim to be disciples of Jesus. *'You are witnesses'* (v. 48), says Jesus. Witnessing is not an option as far as any disciple is concerned. It is for all Christians. Furthermore, important as is the witness of a life, in Luke's writings a Christian's witness is always verbalized (e.g. Acts 8:25; 10:39–43; 13:30–31, 38; 18:15; 20:24–25). We may not have to preach, but we most certainly have to speak.

Secondly, our witness is to focus on the good news of Jesus. When Jesus said, *'You are witnesses of these things'* (v. 48), he was referring to the 'repentance and forgiveness of sin' that were available as a result of his death and his resurrection. In other words, the task of every disciple – and not just of every preacher – is to interpret the significance of the life, death and resurrection of Jesus for others, and in doing so to spell out the gospel offer of forgiveness and the gospel demand for repentance. There is, no doubt, a place for talking about the church we attend and all the interesting activities our church has to offer, just as there is a place for discussing subjects as diverse as creation, suffering and biblical inspiration, but primarily we are to witness to Jesus.

Thirdly, important though our friends and neighbours are – those who may well form our 'Jerusalems' – we are also to witness to *all nations* (v. 47). This term, however, cannot be limited to people living in distant lands. Some of the traditional mission fields are today more 'Christian' than the countries from which missionaries initially came. 'All nations' today refers to those who have yet to become part of God's people. Those furthest from Christ may well include groups in our neighbourhood and not just those in some distant place. They – including increasingly the children and young people of our nation – need to hear our witness.

Witnessing has never been easy. It is perhaps no accident that the English word 'martyr' is derived from the Greek word for 'witness' (*martys*). Not everybody will welcome us when we seek to share our faith in Jesus. Thank God, Jesus has not left us on our own! He has promised his Spirit. As Luke in the book of Acts makes clear, the secret of the expansion of the early church lay not in the gifts that any of the apostles had, but rather in the Holy Spirit who worked through them. Here is hope for us too!

4. The witness of John to the resurrection

1. The empty tomb (20:1–10)

Early on the first day of the week, while it was still dark, Mary Magdalene went to the tomb and saw that the stone had been removed from the entrance. *²So she came running to Simon Peter and the other disciple, the one Jesus loved, and said, "They have taken the Lord out of the tomb, and we don't know where they have put him!"*

³So Peter and the other disciple started for the tomb. *⁴Both were running, but the other disciple outran Peter and reached the tomb first.* *⁵He bent over and looked in at the strips of linen lying there but did not go in.* *⁶Then Simon Peter, who was behind him, arrived and went into the tomb. He saw the strips of linen lying there,* *⁷as well as the burial cloth that had been around Jesus' head. The cloth was folded up by itself, separate from the linen.* *⁸Finally the other disciple, who had reached the tomb first, also went inside. He saw and believed.* *⁹(They still did not understand from Scripture that Jesus had to rise from the dead.)* *¹⁰Then the disciples went back to their homes . . .*

Like the other three Gospels, John's account of the discovery of the empty tomb begins *Early on the first day of the week* (v. 1). In John's account it is *still dark* (v. 1), and not surprisingly so, since it is within the fourth watch of the night (*early, prōi*), some time between three and six o'clock. But the implication is that by the time Mary Magdalene arrives at the tomb, it is already light. Otherwise, unless she had had a torch of some kind, she would have had dificulties in seeing that the Lord's body had been taken away (v. 2).

One key difference between John's account and the Synoptic Gospels is that only *Mary Magdalene* features. This Mary is always identified by her village of Magdala, a village on the west shore of the sea of Tiberias. Except for Luke 8:2, where Mary appears as one of the women helping Jesus during his ministry in Galilee and where she is described as one 'from whom seven demons had come out' (see also Mark 16:9), in all the Gospels she features only in relation to the crucifixion and the empty tomb. Later tradition identified Mary Magdalene with the sinful woman who anointed Jesus in the house of the Pharisee (Luke 7:36–50), but this identification cannot be proved.

There is no direct mention of any other women with her (see 19:25). However, Mary's report to the two disciples indicates that John was not unaware that others were present: *'They have taken the Lord out of the tomb, and we* (note the plural) *don't know where they have put him!'* (v. 2). The plural normally requires that more than one person be present. If a singular is required, then the singular is used (see v. 11). A further indication that others were present is that a woman would have been unlikely to have ventured out on her own while it was *still dark*.

We know from Mark and Luke that Mary and the women came to anoint the body of Jesus. There is no mention, however, of this motive in John. Nor is there mention of any concern as to how the stone might be rolled away. Instead, John immediately gets to the point: she *saw that the stone had been removed from the entrance* (v. 1).

Palestinian archaeology shows that the entrance to such rock tombs, of which there were many around the city of Jerusalem, was on ground level through a small doorway, usually less than a yard high, so that adults had almost to crawl in to get into the burial chamber itself. To prevent the tomb being disturbed by wild animals and by curious passers-by, such tombs were sealed by rolling a heavy boulder across the entrance. The more elaborate tombs had a wheel-shaped slab of stone that rolled in a track across the entrance, rather like a sliding door.

When Mary saw *the stone* rolled to one side and then presumably stooped down and peeped in, to discover that the tomb was empty, her immediate reaction was to believe that the body of Jesus had been removed by some person or persons unknown. *'They'*, whoever 'they' might be, *'have taken the Lord out of the tomb'* (v. 2). It is highly significant that Mary did not jump to the conclusion that Jesus had risen from the dead. Mary came to the tomb expecting to find a body. As John's account and indeed the other Gospel accounts make clear, neither Mary nor any of the disciples ever expected to see Jesus again. No doubt, like any good Jew, she believed in the resurrection of the dead, but this resurrection of the dead was to take place on the Last Day, at the end of time, not in the here and now (see John 11:24).

Mary *came running* first to Peter, and then to John, *the other disciple* (v. 2). The Greek phrasing implies that the two disciples were not together. They ran to the tomb in turn (v. 4), presumably to check out Mary's story. In John, Easter begins with running legs. A race appears to have developed between the two. John, the Beloved Disciple, *outran Peter and reached the tomb first* (v. 4). Was it because he was the younger of the two? The suggestion that his greater love for the Lord spurred him on is surely a little fanciful.

For one reason or another initially *he did not go in* (v. 5). Was it that he wanted to avoid the ritual contamination that came from touching a dead body? We don't know. Instead, he just *looked in* (v. 5).

Peter, ever impulsive, showed no reticence about entering, but immediately 'went into the tomb' (v. 6). There he *saw the strips of linen lying there, as well as the burial cloth that had been around Jesus' head. The cloth was folded up by itself, separate from the linen* (vv. 6–7). According to John, Jesus' body was wrapped in *strips of linen* (*othonioi*) (also 19:40), whereas the other evangelists state that Jesus was wrapped in a 'linen cloth' (Mark 15:46; Matt. 28:59; Luke 23:53), a 'shroud' (*sindōn*). The traditional harmonization is that the body was first wrapped in a large sheet of cloth after being taken down from the cross; but the shroud was torn into strips which were used to bind the body, limb by limb, between layers of 'myrrh and aloes' (John 19:9, 40). Alternatively strips of cloth were wound around the shrouded body. In addition, reflecting normal first-century Jewish practice (*Shabbat.* 23.5), the head was wrapped in an all-embracing turban, which would have supported the chin.

The sight of the grave-clothes without the body must have seemed very strange. For had Mary been right and the corpse had been removed, then this would have meant that the grave robbers had undressed the corpse. But who in their right mind would go around with a naked corpse? It beggared belief.

Peter himself, however, failed to make sense of what he saw. According to Luke *he went away, wondering to himself what had happened* (Luke 24:12). The empty tomb by itself did not convince. It took an appearance of the risen Lord to convince him of the truth of the resurrection.

The reaction of John, the *other disciple*, however, was very different. When he eventually went inside the tomb, he *saw and believed* (v. 8). Why should John have believed? Did he believe simply on the basis that the grave-clothes had not been removed? Or did he believe on the basis that the grave-clothes had not been left in an untidy heap, but rather that the shroud was in one place, and the head-covering in another place? John Chrysostom, the fourth-century bishop of Constantinople, commented: 'If anyone had removed the body, he would not have stripped it first, nor would he have taken the trouble to remove and roll up the napkin and put it in a place by itself.'[1] No robber is ever concerned with tidying up! Or did the *strips of linen* and the burial head-cloth (*soudarion*) lying on one side remind John of the raising of Lazarus and in turn trigger his faith? For when John describes Lazarus coming out of the tomb, he uses precisely the same terms: 'his hands and feet [were] wrapped with strips of linen, and a cloth [was] around his face' (John 11:44).

There is another possibility. It may have been the evangelist's intention to suggest that John saw the grave-clothes lying like a chrysalis out of which the risen body of the Lord had emerged. Something happened to the body of Jesus, giving it new and marvellous powers. The body emerged from the grave-clothes without disturbing them, leaving them intact. It is possible that the linen grave-clothes around the body of Jesus remained firm on account of the aromatic oils and spices wrapped in them.

The empty tomb by itself may not have convinced. However, the arrangement of the grave-clothes together with the empty tomb may have caused John to believe. This was for him a 'sign' from the Lord. The fact that Peter did not see the significance of the shape of the grave-clothes is no argument against the 'chrysalis' theory. In this Gospel's account, Peter is depicted as a little obtuse!

Like Peter, John still did not understand the Scripture that pointed to the resurrection of Jesus (v. 9). The *Scripture* (the singular form is used, as distinct from Luke's expression, 'according to the Scriptures') probably refers to the Old Testament as a whole rather than to individual texts such as Psalm 16:10; Hosea 6:2; or Jonah 1:17, 21. In spite of this lack of understanding, it would seem that for John the penny had dropped – the earlier predictions of Jesus about suffering, dying and rising suddenly began to make sense. *He saw and believed* (v. 8). The fact that John lacked full understanding as far as the Scripture was concerned is no reason for questioning the genuineness of his belief. Faith never fully understands! Furthermore, in John's Gospel, when the underlying Greek verb 'to believe' (*pisteuō*) is used absolutely, it always means genuine faith (e.g. 5:44; 6:47; 19:35; 20:29).

The final verse of this section is something of an anticlimax: *Then the disciples went back to their homes* (v. 10). Strangely, in spite of the relative brevity of the account, there is no mention of their sharing the news of their discovery with peers. It is possible that in

---

[1] Chrysostom, *Homiliae in Ioannis Evangelium* 85.4.

this way John was seeking to underline the scepticism of the disciples, who found it difficult to believe even when the Lord appeared to them (see Luke 24:36–43). Instead, it is left to Mary Magdalene to be the bearer of the news, not just of the empty tomb, but that Jesus is alive (v. 18).

a. Seeing and believing

John tells of three different people 'seeing' the empty tomb – but only one of these actually realizes its significance and believes in the resurrection. Mary Magdalene, for instance, saw that the stone had been removed from the entrance (v. 1), but jumped to the wrong conclusion. *'They have taken the Lord out of the tomb'* (v. 2), she cried. Since Mary, there have been many others who likewise have jumped to the wrong conclusion. For example, it has been suggested that on finding the tomb to be empty, the disciples wrongly concluded that resurrection had taken place. Among others, the prize for the silliest explanation for the empty tomb must probably go to the theory that the corpse decomposed with unique speed, so that when Mary Magdalene (and the others) arrived on the third day there were simply no remains to be found. It was only later, when the risen Lord actually appeared to Mary Magdalene, that she came to realize how wrong she was.

Peter also saw the empty tomb, and the strips of linen lying there (v. 6), but he did not know what to think. The evidence for the resurrection was before his eyes, but he could not believe his eyes! Amazed though he was (see Luke 24:12), Peter at that stage was an 'agnostic'. He just didn't know what to make of it. There have been many others since like Peter. They have heard the Easter story time and again, but they have yet to arrive at a conclusion. Maybe they need to examine the evidence more carefully!

John, however, saw – and believed (v. 8). He saw the implications of the empty tomb. He saw the significance too of the grave-clothes, if not of their arrangement. He allowed the evidence to speak for itself.

Today we are no longer able to see the empty tomb – nor are we able to see physically the arrangement of the grave-clothes. The evidence, however, is still before us.

The question is, will we see and believe? George Bernard Shaw maintained that 'belief is literally a matter of taste'. But he was wrong. There is nothing whimsical about belief – or certainly nothing whimsical about Christian belief. Christian belief is rooted in history. We do not have to give up our intellectual faculties to believe. As *The Times* said in one of its leaders for Easter Eve, 'Our reasoning powers intact, our grasp of science and philosophy unshaken, we can possess the truth of the Resurrection – or rather, be possessed by it – by means of the gift of faith which is freely given to all who seek it. None needs make apology for accepting that gift, which enhances and does not diminish all that is human, the intellect included.'[2] Seeing can lead to believing.

2. Jesus appears to Mary Magdalene (20:11–18)

But Mary stood outside the tomb crying. As she wept, she bent over to look into the tomb [12]*and saw two angels in white, seated where Jesus' body had been, one at the head and the other at the foot.*

[13]*They asked her, 'Woman, why are you crying?'*

'They have taken my Lord away,' she said, 'and I don't know where they have put him.' [14]*At this, she turned round and saw Jesus standing there, but she did not realise that it was Jesus.*

[15]*'Woman,' he said, 'why are you crying? Who is it you are looking for?'*

Thinking he was the gardener, she said, 'Sir, if you have carried him away, tell me where you have put him, and I will get him.'

[16]*Jesus said to her, 'Mary.'*

She turned towards him and cried out in Aramaic, 'Rabboni!' (which means Teacher).

[17]*Jesus said, 'Do not hold on to me, for I have not yet returned to the Father. Go instead to my brothers and tell them, "I am returning to my Father and your Father, to my God and your God."'*

[18]*Mary Magdalene went to the disciples with the news: 'I have seen the Lord!' And she told them that he had said these things to her.*

Mary remained on her own at the tomb. As the story develops, it would seem that not only the two disciples but also the other women, whose presence is implied in verse 2, have left (see v. 13). She *stood outside the tomb crying* (v. 11). Her tears were not just because Jesus was dead, but rather because his body had disappeared. The removal of a body from the tomb was a form of desecration; it was an outrageous abuse of the dead (see 1 Sam. 31:9–13). In this context Mary's tears are understandable; they are not to be portrayed as the tears of some 'hysterical' woman, but are rather the tears of a woman who truly loved Jesus.

[2] *The Times*, 6 April 1985.

In the midst of her crying she stooped to *look into the tomb* (v. 11). There, like the women in Luke's account (Luke 24:4) *she saw two angels in white, seated where Jesus' body had been* (v. 12) But John goes into further detail: *one at the head and the other at the foot*, guarding as it were the place where Jesus had lain. If Mary could but realize it, the angels are witnesses that God has been at work. But she does not seem to take particular note of their heavenly origin. In response to their question, *'Woman, why are you crying?'* (v. 13), she replies, *'They have taken my Lord away . . . and I don't know where they have put him'* (v. 13). The thought of God's intervention does not cross her mind. Instead, she is overwhelmed by her sense of loss. The Lord to whom she was so attached (*my Lord*) is missing.

Suddenly *she turned round* (v. 14). She became aware that there was someone else present. Turning, *she saw Jesus standing there* (v. 14). Like the pair on the Emmaus road (Luke 24:13–31) and like the disciples out fishing (John 21:1–14), she too fails to *realise that it was Jesus* (v. 14). Was she blinded by her tears? Was she over-absorbed in her own grief? True, the tomb must have been gloomy, but not only does she fail to recognize the features of Jesus, she also fails to recognize his voice. For when Jesus repeats the question of the angels, *'Woman, why are you crying?'*, and then goes on further to ask, *'Who is it you are looking for?'*, she still fails to know it is Jesus. Instead, she mistakes him for *the gardener. 'Sir, if you have carried him away, tell me where you have put him, and I will get him'* (v. 15). How much more confused could Mary get!

Only when Jesus calls her by name (see 10:3), *'Mary'*, does reality strike home. It would seem that until now Mary has not given Jesus her full attention. She has 'seen' Jesus, but not really looked at him. The calling of her name, however, makes all the difference. She turns round and addresses him respectfully but affectionately: *'Rabboni!' (which means Teacher)* (v. 16). The significance of this term has been a matter of some discussion. The Aramaic word *Rabboni* was certainly not a form of address reserved for God, and therefore Mary's cry of recognition cannot be compared with Thomas's confession of faith (20:28). Nor is there any evidence to suggest that Mary reaches a new level of 'owned' understanding, if not of 'personal' faith, by addressing Jesus as 'my teacher' (*Rabboni*) rather than just as 'teacher' (*Rabbi*). Mary may well be simply addressing Jesus by the term she had always used of him. Indeed, this form of address may indicate that she thinks life can now go back to how it always was. She fails to recognize that Jesus is now the risen Lord.

Not unnaturally Mary embraces Jesus. We are surely not reading too much into the story to see Mary throwing her arms around Jesus with great joy and relief. But Jesus stops her. *'Do not hold on to me'* (v. 17). Comparisons are often made with the invitation of Jesus to Thomas to feel with his finger where the nails were and to put his hand into Jesus' side (20:27). Why is Mary not allowed to 'touch', while Thomas is encouraged to 'touch'? Two things need to be noted. First, in John 20:24–29 there is no word for 'touching'. Secondly, the rendering of the Authorized Version, 'Touch me not', is misleading, for although the underlying Greek verb (*haptō*) can mean just to 'touch' (e.g. Mark 3:10; 6:56; etc.) it can also have much stronger overtones and mean to 'have sexual intercourse' (e.g. 1 Cor. 7:1), or to 'eat' (Col. 2:1). Here in verse 17, almost certainly more than mere 'touching' – 'clinging to' or 'holding on to' – is meant. Furthermore, the command here is a present imperative, 'Stop holding on to me.'

The explanation Jesus gives for his command is that *'I have not yet returned to the Father'* (v. 17). Literally, 'I have not yet ascended' (*anabebēka*) (see 3:13; 6:62). He has yet to return to the Father (14:12, 28; 16:5, 10, 17, 28). Jesus is speaking about the completion of his earthly mission, not of the ascension as described by Luke, which is an acted parable of Jesus' final return to his Father and so the end of his resurrection appearances (e.g. Acts 1:9–11). Mary fails to realize that there can be no return to the old way of life. There can be no holding Jesus back. In future Jesus is to be present with her by his Spirit.

Jesus goes on to give Mary a message for his *brothers*, that is, his disciples (see Matt. 28:10): *'tell them, "I am returning to my Father and your Father, to my God and your God"'* (v. 17). The message Mary has to share is not about geography (there is no reference to 'Galilee'), but about a new relationship. The Father of Jesus is now their Father; his God is their God. The fact that Jesus does not speak of 'Our Father and our God' has caused commentators in the past to believe that Jesus was making a careful distinction between his disciples and himself, 'since what Jesus is by nature, his disciples are by grace' (Augustine). However, the emphasis may well in fact be the opposite – Jesus is drawing attention not so much to the difference as to the likeness. See Ruth 1:16, where Ruth says to Naomi, 'Your people will be my people and your God my God.'

a. Tears on Easter Day

Mary shed tears of unbelief. The empty tomb, which has been a source of joy and assurance to Christians down through the centuries, was to Mary a cause of grief. In her bewilderment only one explanation came to mind: some enemies of Jesus must have stolen the body. If only she had reflected a little more deeply! If only she had looked a little more closely! But Mary wept, presenting a picture of all who believe only in a dead Christ. Where there is no belief in the risen Christ, there is no joy. Nor is there any hope (see 1 Thess. 4:13), only tears.

Mary shed tears of love. She wept because she loved her Lord (v. 13) so dearly. Why was the Lord so special to Mary? Luke 8:2 and Mark 16:9 give the clue. Jesus had freed her from 'seven demons' and in doing so had brought an end to what must have been a hell-on-earth existence. Jesus had restored to her her own personality and made her whole. No wonder she loved him. She owed her all to him. Mary presents a picture of true love for Jesus; a love not to be confused with sentimentalism or emotionalism. Her love challenges us all. How much do we love Jesus? We may not have been freed from demon possession, but we have been freed from the iron grip of sin and death. Jesus went through hell that we might go to heaven. How much do we love Jesus in return?

Mary eventually shed tears of joy. For as she wept in her grief, Jesus came to her. Mary may have found the empty tomb, but Jesus found her. He called her by name. The tears of grief were replaced by tears of joy. For Mary the words of the psalmist came true:

> . . . weeping may remain for a night,
>   but rejoicing comes in the morning.
>   (Ps. 30:5; see also Ps. 126:5)

Mary presents a picture of the joy that can be known by those who encounter the risen Lord. For the Lord who rose is the Lord who is with us. The life he offered he offers still today:

> he will swallow up death for ever.
> The Sovereign LORD will wipe away the tears from all faces;
>
> . . . In that day they will say,
>
> 'Surely this is our God;
>   we trusted in him, and he saved us.
>   . . . let us rejoice and be glad in his salvation.'
>   (Is. 25:8–9)

b. No holding Jesus back

Mary's first discovery that Easter Sunday morning was that death could not hold Jesus back. In the words of Peter at Pentecost, 'it was impossible for death to keep its hold on him' (Acts 2:24). The consequence is, of course, that because death could not hold Jesus back, neither can death hold on to us (Heb. 2:14). Because he lives, we too may live (John 14:19).

But Mary made a second discovery that Easter Sunday morning: neither death nor earth could hold Jesus back. Heaven beckoned. The risen Lord was to become the ascended Lord. The ascension was not a matter of aerodynamics; it was an 'acted' parable, in which Jesus demonstrated that he was going to the Father. This no doubt was why Gothic and Byzantine painters painted heaven gold – not blue. Heaven is not a place beyond the bright blue sky. Heaven is where God is, beyond all space and time. 'I am going', said Jesus in the upper room, 'to prepare a place for you . . . that you also may be where I am' (John 14:2–3).

Thank God that earth could not hold him back. Thank God that Jesus has gone on ahead, blazing a trail for us to follow on by faith.

But there is another discovery Mary had to make: heaven cannot hold Jesus back. Mary wanted to cling to his feet; she wanted to see his face; she wanted to hear his voice call her by name. She wanted to express her love for him and in turn bask in his love for her. It was, however, for her good and for the good of us all that Jesus left her and ascended to his Father, for only so could the Spirit come (John 16:7). Now Jesus can be present by his Spirit wherever we are. In his earthly life, Jesus was limited by space and time. He could be in only one place at any given time. But by his Spirit he can be present wherever and whenever he wills. In this sense heaven cannot hold Jesus back. Through his Spirit, Jesus remains our ever-present friend.

All this Mary failed to understand. She wanted to hold on to him. She wanted him to stay with her. She thought that life could return to how it was before Jesus was crucified. But Mary had another discovery to make. She could not hold Jesus back. Neither can we hold Jesus back. Our life with him has to move on. We may long, for instance, for the good old days of doing church, but we cannot hold Jesus in a time warp of our own making. He is the risen Lord.

Mary could not hold on to Jesus. She had to go and tell others that Jesus was ascending to his Father. A new age of mission was dawning. We too cannot keep Jesus to ourselves. Sometimes we prefer to keep busy doing things in church, rather than moving out into the big wide world. It's more comfortable to hold on to Jesus than to share him with others. But others must know the good news of Jesus risen, ascended, and ever-present by his Spirit. Let's not hold Jesus back!

3. Jesus appears to his disciples (20:19–23)

On the evening of that first day of the week, when the disciples were together, with the doors locked for fear of the Jews, Jesus came and stood among them and said, 'Peace be with you!' [20]*After he said this, he showed them his hands and side. The disciples were overjoyed when they saw the Lord.*

[21]*Again Jesus said, 'Peace be with you! As the Father has sent me, I am sending you.'* [22]*And with that he breathed on them and said, 'Receive the Holy Spirit.* [23]*If you forgive anyone his sins, they are forgiven; if you do not forgive them, they are not forgiven.'*

If ever there was a group of frightened people, these were they. Wicked men had already crucified their Master. Would they be next on the list? Here they were on Easter Sunday evening, meeting *with the doors locked for fear of the Jews* (v. 19), fearing some heavy-handed pounding on the door, dreading that they too would be arrested.

Into this tense atmosphere *Jesus came and stood among them* (v. 19). Although John later stresses the corporeality of the risen Lord – the wounds to his hands and side are still evident (v. 20) – Jesus is not hindered by physical barriers such as locked doors. His body possesses strange, non-physical powers. No doubt this ability to 'materialize' apparently from nowhere must have caused the disciples further *fear*. Although by this stage the disciples were aware of the empty tomb, and would have received the news from Mary Magdalene of her having seen the risen Lord, they were surely still wrestling with the implications of these unexpected events.

It was in such a context that Jesus greeted his disciples with the words *'Peace be with you!'* (v. 19). 'Shalom' (*Eirēnē*) was a customary Eastern greeting and as such normally would not have had the deepest of meanings. The fact that Jesus repeated the greeting (v. 21) suggests, however, that on this occasion his greeting had more than usual significance.

That his greeting had particular significance is indicated by John's addition, *After he said this, he showed them his hands and side* (v. 20). At the most basic level, by drawing attention to the marks of the nails and the wound to his side, Jesus could have been seeking to reassure his disciples that it was indeed he; that it was no phantom, but it truly was their old friend, crucified but risen from the dead (see Luke 24:4, 37–39).

Jesus, however, may have had deeper concerns to address. Prior to his arrival, his disciples may have been reflecting on the events of Good Friday, and in so doing blaming one another for having failed to stand by him. The very sight of Jesus therefore must have intensified that sense of guilt. What a difference it must have made that the first words of Jesus were *'Peace be with you'*. Indeed, by stating that Jesus then *showed them his hands and side*, John may have been trying to imply that Jesus is able to offer peace to the guilty precisely because of his death on the cross. At that stage the disciples could not have understood the full significance of what Jesus was doing. But later, in his first letter, John was able to work out more fully the implications of the cross: 'the blood of Jesus, his Son, purifies us from all sin' (1 John 1:7); 'If anybody does sin, we have one who speaks to the Father in our defence – Jesus Christ, the Righteous One. He is the atoning sacrifice for our sins, and not only for ours but also for the sins of the whole world' (1 John 2:1–2).

The disciples may have remembered the words of Jesus spoken in the upper room, 'Peace I leave with you; my peace I give you. I do not give to you as the world gives. Do not let your hearts be troubled and do not be afraid' (14:27). Precisely because Jesus had 'overcome the world' (16:33), he could offer peace. No wonder *the disciples were overjoyed when they saw the Lord* (20:20). The words of Jesus in the upper room, 'I will see you again and you will rejoice, and no-one will take away your joy' (John 16:22), had been fulfilled.

Once more Jesus repeats his greeting, *'Peace be with you!'* (v. 21). But instead of again showing them his hands and side, he gives them a new task. *'As the Father has sent me, I am sending you'* (v. 21). Just as there was significance in the initial greeting's being followed by the display of his wounds, so too there may well be significance in the repeated greeting's being followed by a new commission. It is those who have experienced his *peace* that Jesus sends out to do his work in the world.

The implications of the parallelism are important. Jesus himself was 'sent' by the Father to do the Father's work (5:36; see also 4:34). In all he said and did, Jesus was the Father's representative, so much so that he could say, 'it is the Father, living in me, who is doing his work' (14:10). To encounter Jesus was therefore to encounter the Father (1:18; 14:9). The disciples in turn are sent out by Jesus to do his work. In all they say and do they act as his representatives. To encounter them is in a very real sense to encounter Jesus. The continuity of the mission of Jesus in the church is underlined by John's use of the Greek perfect tense to describe the sending of Jesus: *'As the Father has sent (apestalken) me. . .'* The Greek perfect describes a past action reaching into the present. The implication is that the disciples are commissioned to carry on the mission of Jesus, and not to begin a new work. In the original Greek text two different verbs for 'sending' are used: *'As the Father has sent* (*apestalken*) *me, I am sending* (*pempō*) *you.*' There appears, however, to be no intended distinction of meaning. The choice of the two verbs is to be accounted for by John's love of synonyms.

The words of Jesus, in the first place, are prescriptive. They are a command: '*I am sending you.*' Here we have the Johannine form of the Great Commission. By definition disciples of Jesus are people who are 'sent' to fulfil the 'mission' of Jesus. The English word 'mission' is in fact derived from the Latin verb for 'to send' (*mitto, mittere, misi, misum*). Mission is the activity of the church. The implications are of great importance for today. The church does not send out missionaries, for the church by definition is a missionary body, composed entirely of missionaries. A missionary congregation may send out some on special assignment, but it can never delegate mission to others.

The words of Jesus are also descriptive, in the sense that they give a pattern for mission: '*As* (note that word) *the Father has sent me.*' This same pattern is found in the 'high-priestly' prayer: 'As you sent me into the world, I have sent them into the world' (17:18). The phrase 'into the world' is missing here in John 20, but is surely presupposed. Just as the Word 'became flesh and made his dwelling among us' (1:14), so too Jesus' disciples are to identify themselves with others in their need. Jesus defines the mission of his disciples in terms of his mission. The Greek conjunction *kagō*, unfortunately not translated by the NIV, may perhaps best be rendered, 'So I also'. '*As the Father has sent me, so I also* (*kagō*) *am sending you*' (v. 21). Within the Christian church there has often been a debate as to the meaning of 'mission'. Some have defined it in terms of evangelism, whereas others have defined it in terms of service and of social action. But that is a sterile and false debate, once it is recognized that Jesus is the pattern of the church's mission. Because Jesus is the pattern, Christian mission must involve both telling and caring, both evangelism and social action. For in the life of Jesus, words and works went together. Jesus was both a preacher and a healer. He was concerned not just for people's souls, but also for their bodies. Jesus set a pattern of comprehensive mission – 'holistic' mission – that reflects God's love and concern for every aspect of people's lives.

In order to enable his disciples to carry out their mission Jesus *breathed on them and said, 'Receive the Holy Spirit*' (v. 22). There is an intimate link between verses 21 and 22. Just as the Father had sent out Jesus in the power of the Spirit, so now Jesus sends out his disciples in the power of the Spirit. Indeed, we can infer from this link that a primary purpose for which the Spirit is given is that the mission of Jesus may be furthered (see Acts 1:8). The link between the two verses also testifies to the implicit trinitarianism present in

Scripture: the church's mission is modelled on the Father's sending of the Son and empowered by the Son's sending of the Spirit.

Jesus breathed on them. This action is rich in symbolism. John may have had in mind an allusion to Genesis 2:7, where 'the LORD God formed the man from the dust of the ground and breathed into his nostrils the breath of life, and the man became a living being'. As the Spirit was active in creation, so God is active through his Spirit in the new creation (John 3:5–8). There may also be an allusion to Ezekiel 37, where Ezekiel is called to 'breathe into' the men of Israel 'that they may live' (v. 9). 'So I prophesied . . . and breath entered them; they came to life and stood up on their feet – a vast army' (v. 10). The symbolism of Jesus mobilizing a new army, and not just a new people, as he breathed on his disciples, is an attractive one.

But was Jesus engaging in more than symbolism? Did the disciples actually receive the Holy Spirit that Easter Sunday evening, or did they receive the Spirit forty days later, at Pentecost (Acts 2)? Many believe that John's and Luke's accounts of the sending of the Spirit cannot be harmonized. Yet, although the actual chronology is different, the theological perspective is very similar. In Luke's account, for instance, the outpouring of the Spirit on the day of Pentecost is an act of the risen Lord (Acts 2:32–33). John, by setting the sending of the Spirit on Easter Day, may have deliberately accommodated chronology to theology in order to make the same theological point. Alternatively, it may be that John intended his readers to see here an acted parable, which was only later fulfilled at Pentecost. The footwashing in John (13:1–17), like the Last Supper in the Synoptic Gospels, are acted parables: the cleansing of the former and the breaking of the bread in the latter point to the cross. Likewise, the invitation to come and drink at the Feast of Tabernacles is another acted parable, which points to the subsequent gift of the Spirit (7:37–39).

Jesus went on, *'If you forgive anyone his sins, they are forgiven; if you do not forgive them, they are not forgiven'* (v. 23). The grammatical construction of the Greek is of interest. In the first clause, a simple past (aorist) subjunctive (*aphēte*) is used, which implies a specific action that brings about a state of forgiveness (a Greek perfect tense is used): *they are forgiven (apheōntai)*, their sins are no more. In the second clause, a present subjunctive (*kratēte*) is used, which implies an ongoing action of not forgiving, which in turn does not bring about a state of forgiveness (*kekratēntai*). It will be seen that again John uses two different verbs to convey the meaning of forgiveness: the former (*aphiēmi*) refers primarily to the 'letting go' of sins, the latter (*krateō*) to the retaining of sins. There does not appear, however, to be any intended distinction here, and again the choice of the two different verbs is to be accounted for by John's love of synonyms.

To what exactly is John referring? The wording is strange, not least because, as the Jews themselves rightly recognized, 'God alone' can forgive sins (see Mark 2:7). Traditionally, Roman Catholics have regarded this verse, along with Matthew 16:19 and 18:18, as a proof text for the priestly practice of 'absolving sins'. Nowhere in the life of the early church as depicted in the Acts and the Letters, however, do we read of anybody requiring the private confession of sins or the giving of absolution to sinners. Yet others, on the basis of the longer ending of Mark, detect a reference to baptism: by conferring or not conferring baptism, the church opens or closes the door of the redeemed community (Mark 16:16). Yet, the prime determinative factor in interpretation should surely be the context in which the words are found. If these words are linked with the mission of the disciples, then the reference must be to the way in which people respond to the disciples and their mission activities. As Jesus proclaimed the message of the kingdom by his words and deeds, so too are his disciples to proclaim by their words and deeds that in Jesus the kingdom has come. On the basis of their response, people will be either forgiven or not forgiven. There is no sitting on the fence, as far as Jesus is concerned: 'For judgment I have come into this world, so that the blind will see and those who see will become blind' (9:39). As John himself comments, 'Whoever believes in him [Jesus] is not condemned, but whoever does not believe stands condemned already because he has not believed in the name of God's one and only Son' (3:18). It is important to note that the withholding of forgiveness is not ultimately dependent upon the disciples, but rather upon those to whom they go: some will turn to the light and receive forgiveness, others will turn away from the light and will not be forgiven (3:19–21). If there is a parallel with Matthew 16:19, it is this: the 'keys of the kingdom' given to Peter related to knowledge (Luke 11:52; Matt. 23:23) enabling others to enter the kingdom. Peter's power to 'bind' and 'loose' sins involved the admission or exclusion of people from the kingdom of God. This power was exercised in his preaching: it was, for instance, as a result of Peter's preaching that on the day of Pentecost over three thousand were admitted to the kingdom (Acts 2:41), and that a little later on, the Roman centurion Cornelius and his Gentile friends were accepted into the kingdom too (Acts 10:47–48). Here, however, the emphasis is upon the response to the preached word; in John the emphasis is upon the response to the preached and embodied word.

a. The many-faceted peace of Jesus

As the crucified Saviour, Jesus offers peace to the guilty. When Jesus declared peace to his disciples, he showed them his hands and his side, indicating that he had dealt with their sin and guilt precisely because of his death on the cross. Here is good news today. To those who know that they too have let Jesus down, Jesus says, 'Peace be with you!' Jesus is still able to deal with our sin and guilt. In him there is always a new beginning (1 John 1:9). Through Jesus we may have 'peace with God' (Rom. 5:1).

To those who feel battered by life's storms Jesus offers peace as the risen Lord. When Jesus showed his hands and side, he was also indicating that he had risen from the dead. He had conquered the world, and therefore was able to offer peace to his fearful disciples (John 16:33). We may not be meeting behind locked doors, but there are times when everything seems to go wrong and we are fearful of the future. What a difference it is to know that with Jesus, we can face even the worst that life delivers!

There is yet another facet to the peace Jesus has to offer, a facet perhaps not present in John's mind as he wrote his Gospel, but a truth none the less present as with the Spirit's aid we reflect on that incident long ago (see John 16:13). When Jesus rose victorious from the grave, the marks of the wounds were still with him. Is it too much to believe that the ascended Lord in glory still bears the marks of those wounds? If so, then in rising from the dead and ascending to the Father Jesus did not become oblivious to the hardships of life. He knows; he understands (Heb. 4:15–16). Indeed, the Father knows. In the words of Cleverley Ford, the wound marks 'tell us, as no words could tell us more plainly, that the sufferings of this world, the cries of the distressed since the world began and until it ends, are echoed always in the very heart of God in heaven itself. God suffers because we suffer. He is a compassionate God, he suffers with us (this is what the word means). So the cross of Christ is not only an event in history, it is a proclamation of what God is like for all eternity.'[3] We may be misunderstood by others, but by Jesus never. Jesus, the risen but marred Lord, offers peace to the hurting.

b. Going the Jesus way

We have a mission to fulfil. The risen Lord Jesus sends his disciples out to continue his work. Mission is no optional extra; it is of the essence of the church. Christians are not in the business of self-improvement; they are in the business of reaching out to others with

[3] C. Ford, *Preaching the Risen Christ* (Mowbray, 1988), p. 21.

the love of God in Christ. There is something wrong with a church whose programmes and activities, whether intentionally or not, are geared primarily to the needs of its members rather than to the needs of the unchurched. There is also something wrong with a church whose programmes and activities are so time-demanding that its members have little or no time to give to their unchurched neighbours and friends.

We have a pattern to follow: Jesus set a pattern of mission in which evangelism and compassionate service were inextricably bound. These two strands of Jesus' mission were in fact one. From beginning to end, Jesus embodied the message he preached. There is something wrong with a church whose programmes and activities do not include meaningful evangelism; there is also something wrong with a church whose programmes do not include meaningful social action. There is, however, also something wrong with a church whose programmes of evangelism and social action are not meaningfully interrelated. John Stott was right when he wrote: 'Words remain abstract until they are made concrete in deeds of love, while works remain ambiguous until they are interpreted by the proclamation of the gospel. Words without works lack credibility; works without words lack clarity. So Jesus' works made his words visible; his words made his works intelligible.'[4]

We have a message to communicate. Our message, expressed in word and deed, centres on Jesus, crucified and risen, and the forgiveness he offers. In order to communicate this message, we cannot shout from a distance; rather, we must go 'into the world' to where people are. Just as Jesus left the security and splendours of eternity to come into our world, so we in turn must leave the security and the certainties of our church life to enter into the world of those who need to know that in Jesus life can begin again. Effective communication does not involve a preacher and a pulpit, but rather people who live out God's love in the world. In this respect Michael Green draws attention to a story told about St Vincent, who wanted to reach the slaves in the Roman galleys with the gospel. He was notably unsuccessful – until he himself became a galley slave and was able to proclaim the good news when he was one of them, sharing their situation and conditions. Michael Green adds, 'You can, as one wise man put it – almost truly – only evangelise friends.'[5]

We have a power to receive. The task before us is immense. In the West, at least, where churches for the most part are in retreat, and

---

[4] J. R. W. Stott, *The Contemporary Christian* (IVP, 1992), p. 345.
[5] M. Green, *Evangelism through the Local Church* (Hodder & Stoughton, 1990), p. 16.

where church growth is mainly church transfer, the task of effectively communicating the good news of Jesus to our world as a whole appears to be beyond our resources. The truth is that the task *is* beyond our means – but not beyond God's. Where there is God's Spirit, there is hope; even the deadest of churches can arise as an army. For God's Spirit is the Spirit of resurrection. God's Spirit brings life; God's Spirit brings power. The good news for the church is that God gives life and power through his Spirit to his church as its members go out into the world to fulfil the mission of Jesus.

4. Jesus appears to Thomas (20:24–29)

> *Now Thomas (called Didymus), one of the Twelve, was not with the disciples when Jesus came.* ²⁵*So the other disciples told him, 'We have seen the Lord!'*
>
> *But he said to them, 'Unless I see the nail marks in his hands and put my finger where the nails were, and put my hand into his side, I will not believe it.'*
>
> ²⁶*A week later his disciples were in the house again, and Thomas was with them. Though the doors were locked, Jesus came and stood among them and said, 'Peace be with you!'* ²⁷*Then he said to Thomas, 'Put your finger here; see my hands. Reach out your hand and put it into my side. Stop doubting and believe.'*
>
> ²⁸*Thomas said to him, 'My Lord and my God!'*
>
> ²⁹*Then Jesus told him, 'Because you have seen me, you have believed; blessed are those who have not seen and yet have believed.'*

Thomas, also called *Didymus*, the 'Twin' (see also 11:16 and 21:2), had missed the visit of the risen Lord that had turned the sorrow of the ten into rapturous joy, and *was not with the disciples when Jesus came* (v. 24). Why he was absent, we don't know. Was he a loner, who found the company of others difficult? Whatever the reason, he could not believe his fellow-disciples when they *told him, 'We have seen the Lord!'* (v. 25). Literally, 'they kept on telling him': John uses a Greek imperfect (*elegon*), which indicates an ongoing process; indeed, the use of this tense could have the sense of 'they kept on trying to tell him'. Their efforts had no success. Thomas could, as it were, only shake his head and say, *'Unless I see the nail marks in his hands, and put my finger where the nails were, and put my hand into his side, I will not believe it'* (v. 25). For Thomas at this stage it was not enough to see. Unlike the disciples the previous week, for whom seeing was believing (v. 20), for him more was required:

feeling was believing. Thomas wanted tangible evidence of the resurrection of Jesus.[6]

In some respects Thomas's reaction was thoroughly reasonable. Dead people do not rise. In one sense the disciples' talk of resurrection was unreasonable. Yet, as his attitude in the Lazarus story (11:14–16) showed, there was a streak within Thomas that tended to look on the gloomy side of things. Thomas had before him two of the strongest of pieces of evidence for the resurrection: namely the witness of the empty tomb and the witness of Mary Magdalene and his fellow-disciples to having seen the risen Lord. It is strange that Thomas did not believe, for the evidence was so compelling. He would have known, for instance, that the last person the disciples expected to see was Jesus. But when they claimed to have seen the Lord, Thomas did not believe. What was missing for him was the element of personal experience.

A week later, on the first Sunday after Easter, *the disciples were in the house again* and this time Thomas was present (v. 26). Strangely, *the doors were locked* (v. 26) again. Although there is no reference to *fear of the Jews* (see v. 19), it is clear that the disciples had still to work through the implications of the resurrection. In words that parallel John's description of Jesus' first Easter appearance to the disciples, *Jesus came and stood among them and said, 'Peace be with you!'* (v. 26). The very mention of the locked doors may indicate that this greeting was again more than an ordinary greeting. It contained a message of peace the disciples needed to hear.

Jesus' concern on this occasion, however, was not with the disciples in general, but with Thomas in particular. Jesus turned to Thomas: *'Put your finger here; see my hands. Reach out your hand and put it into my side. Stop doubting and believe'* (v. 27). Was Jesus rebuking Thomas, or was he appealing to him? The final imperative is quite strong. John uses a present imperative, literally, 'Do not keep on being (*ginou*) unbelieving, but become believing.' Jesus was calling upon Thomas to change his attitude.

Suddenly Thomas's doubts were removed: he became convinced of the resurrection of Jesus. His earlier need for tangible evidence disappeared, for he too had seen the Lord. In a wonderful act of

---

[6] There is an interesting relationship between 'seeing' and 'believing' in John 20. Mary sees, but does not believe (vv. 1–2); the Beloved Disciple sees and believes (v. 8); Mary eventually sees and believes (vv. 11–18); the disciples' joy is faith's response to seeing (v. 20); Thomas eventually sees and believes (vv. 24–29). Unfortunately this relationship is less clear in the original Greek, where various words for 'seeing' are employed.

surrender Thomas cries out, *'My Lord and my God!'* (v. 28). Indeed, it is more than an act of surrender; it is an act of worship. For Thomas is the first man to worship Jesus as God. There is no need to distinguish between the two terms, as if 'my Lord' referred to the Jesus of history, and 'my God' were a theological evaluation of this Jesus. Both terms are an affirmation of Jesus' divinity, and represent the two Hebrew terms for God: 'Lord' (*kyrios*) represents the Hebrew *yahweh*, and 'God' (*theos*) the Hebrew *'lōhîm*. Like the psalmist who cried out to his 'God and Lord' (Ps. 35:23), Thomas personalized his faith, but in doing so he dared to say what for any Jew would have been unthinkable, for he addressed his confession to one who had lived a fully human life. From the furnace of his doubt emerges the finest confession of faith in Jesus found in the New Testament.

But Jesus told him, *'Because you have seen me, you have believed; blessed are those who have not seen and yet have believed'* (v. 29). The blessing of Jesus on those who see, yet have not believed, is reminiscent of an observation of Rabbi Simeon ben Lakish: 'The proselyte is dearer to God than all the Israelites who were at Sinai. For if these people had not witnessed thunder, flames, lightning, the quaking mountain and the trumpet blasts, they would not have accepted the rule of God. Yet the proselyte who has seen none of these things comes and gives himself to God and accepts the rule of God. Is there anyone who is dearer than this man?''[7]

Whereas for Thomas seeing was believing, for subsequent Christians believing is seeing. Today it is through faith that we encounter the risen Lord Jesus and enter into a personal relationship with him. Our experience is that of those to whom Peter wrote his first letter: 'Though you have not seen him, you love him; and even though you do not see him now, you believe in him and are filled with an inexpressible and glorious joy, for you are receiving the goal of your faith, the salvation of your souls' (1 Pet. 1:8–9). Whether or not one sees, the important thing is that one believes!

John goes on to make it clear that the kind of faith called for is not faith for faith's sake. Rather, it is faith rooted in the witness of the apostles. John's final word at the end of this chapter is not just apposite to his Gospel as a whole, but is particularly apposite to the story of Thomas: this account, as indeed the Gospel as a whole, has been written 'that you may believe that Jesus is the Christ, the Son of God, and that by believing you may have life in his name' (v. 31).

---

[7] *Midrash Tanḥuma* 6.32a.

a. Hope for the doubters

Thomas has had an unfair press, for down through the centuries he has all too often been termed 'Doubting Thomas'. We do not refer to Peter as 'Peter the Denier', but somehow we cannot forgive Thomas his doubt. That he ended up confessing his faith in Jesus so gloriously is strangely forgotten. The fact is, however, that there is nothing wrong in doubting. For many, doubt is the pathway to belief. Indeed, faith is often the stronger because of the doubt. For those who are struggling with their faith, Thomas is a sign of hope. The most perplexed of unbelievers can become the most exultant Christians of all. Doubts can be overcome – they can turn to faith – provided three factors are present.

First, *doubt must be honest doubt*. Not all doubters have any desire to believe. Some doubters are simply sceptics who seek to 'protect' themselves from Christian commitment through their scepticism. They are dishonest doubters, in the sense that they are not willing to 'doubt their doubts'. The fact is that those whose doubt is simply an excuse to escape from the disciplines of religion will never find God. But those who doubt sincerely, who long for certitude, will eventually emerge into the bright sunlight of full faith. According to Jeremiah, the Lord says, 'You will seek me and find me when you seek me with all your heart' (Jer. 29:13). Although in some ways Thomas was a natural doubter, there is no reason to suppose he enjoyed his doubts. The very strength of his protestations when the disciples claimed to have seen the Lord may well indicate that he had a strong desire to believe. But what he regarded as 'common sense', and perhaps too a fear of disillusionment, held him back from believing.

Secondly, *doubt must be prepared to face up to the evidence*. Doubt that simply buries its head in the sand will get nobody anywhere. The honest doubter must be prepared to look into the story of Jesus – and in particular to examine the Gospel narratives of the resurrection. It is significant that immediately after the story of Thomas's coming to believe in the risen Lord, John wrote: 'Jesus did many other miraculous signs in the presence of his disciples, which are not recorded in this book. But these are written that you may believe that Jesus is the Christ, the Son of God, and that by believing you may have life in his name' (vv. 30–31). Sometimes doubt is simply an excuse for intellectual laziness. Doubt that is honest must be prepared to go to the trouble of examining the evidence. The encouragement for the doubter is that the evidence is so strong and so compelling that in many ways it takes more faith to disbelieve than to believe.

Thirdly, *doubt must be exposed to the test of faith.* Jesus said, 'blessed are those who have not seen and yet have believed' (v. 29). Strange as it may sound, it is in believing that we see the risen Lord. Certainty comes only as we take the leap of faith. It is not until we jump that we truly know the reality of the risen Lord Jesus. In the words of the psalmist, 'Taste and see that the LORD is good' (Ps. 34:8). It has been said that it is not that Christianity has been tried and found wanting: rather, it has not been tried. If this call to faith sounds unreasonable, we need to consider that the exercise of faith is not peculiar to the Christian religion, but is a constant feature of everyday life. Every couple who get married, for instance, embark on an act of faith: however much they may think they know about one another, it is still a risk. Furthermore, the exercise of faith in the risen Lord Jesus is not unreasonable. In this respect it is not to be compared to a blind leap into the dark, for there are good grounds for believing in the resurrection. When Jesus said, *'blessed are those who have not seen and yet have believed'*, he was not promoting credulity or gullibility; he was not endorsing a belief without enquiry or consideration.

The story of Thomas gives hope to the doubters. Doubts can be resolved. This is well brought out by Sheldon Vanauken's description of the dilemma he faced as he struggled to decide whether to believe the Christian faith or not:

There is a gap between the probable and the proved. How was I to cross it? If I were to stake my whole life on the risen Christ, I wanted proof, I wanted certainty. I wanted to see him eat a bit of fish. I wanted letters of fire across the sky. I got none of these . . . It was a question of whether I was to accept him – or reject him. My God! There was a gap behind me as well! Perhaps the leap to acceptance was a horrifying gamble – but what of the leap to rejection? There might be no certainty that Christ was God – but by God, there was no certainty that he was not. This was not to be borne. I could not reject Jesus. There was only one thing to do once I had seen the gap behind me. I turned away from it, and flung myself over the gap towards Jesus.[8]

Those who honestly work at their doubts will discover that Jesus of Nazareth is no ordinary figure of history, but is the Lord who died and rose again and is alive for evermore.

---

[8] S. Vanauken, *Severe Mercy* (Hodder & Stoughton, 1977), p. 98.

5. Jesus appears to seven of his disciples (21:1–14)

Afterwards Jesus appeared again to his disciples, by the Sea of Tiberias. It happened this way: ²Simon Peter, Thomas (called Didymus), Nathanael from Cana in Galilee, the sons of Zebedee, and two other disciples were together. ³'I'm going out to fish,' Simon Peter told them, and they said, 'We'll go with you.' So they went out and got into the boat, but that night they caught nothing.

⁴Early in the morning, Jesus stood on the shore, but the disciples did not realise that it was Jesus.

⁵He called out to them, 'Friends, haven't you any fish?'

'No,' they answered.

⁶He said, 'Throw your net on the right side of the boat and you will find some.' When they did, they were unable to haul the net in because of the large number of fish.

⁷Then the disciple whom Jesus loved said to Peter, 'It is the Lord!' As soon as Simon Peter heard him say, 'It is the Lord,' he wrapped his outer garment around him (for he had taken it off) and jumped into the water. ⁸The other disciples followed in the boat, towing the net full of fish, for they were not far from shore, about a hundred yards. ⁹When they landed, they saw a fire of burning coals there with fish on it, and some bread.

¹⁰Jesus said to them, 'Bring some of the fish you have just caught.'

¹¹Simon Peter climbed aboard and dragged the net ashore. It was full of large fish, 153, but even with so many the net was not torn. ¹²Jesus said to them, 'Come and have breakfast.' None of the disciples dared ask him, 'Who are you?' They knew it was the Lord. ¹³Jesus came, took the bread and gave it to them, and did the same with the fish. ¹⁴This was now the third time Jesus appeared to his disciples after he was raised from the dead.

The evangelist begins his account of this appearance of the risen Lord with the words, *Afterwards Jesus appeared again to his disciples, by the Sea of Tiberias* (v. 1; see also v. 14). Lake Galilee (Matt. 4:18; Mark 1:16), known to the Jews as the Lake of Gennesaret (Luke 5:1) was also known as the 'Sea of Tiberias' (6:1), so named because of Tiberias, a city on the west shore of the lake. It was here that Jesus took the initiative in making himself known. Literally, he 'revealed' (*ephanerōsen*) himself: see also 1:31; 2:11; 17:6. It is significant that nowhere in the New Testament accounts of Easter do people go looking for Jesus. On this occasion the disciples had not gone to look for Jesus; they had gone to look for fish. The fact that Jesus appeared to them – when and where they least expected it – again reinforces the truth of the resurrection stories.

It happened this way (v. 1). Easter Sunday had come and gone. The eight-day Passover festival was over and the disciples, like hundreds of other pilgrims, had returned home to Galilee (see Matt. 28:7, 10; Mark 16:7). It must have been a strange feeling for them to be back home – yet without Jesus. What were they now to do? They knew that Jesus had risen from the dead: his tomb was empty. Furthermore, he had appeared to them on at least two occasions. Nevertheless, the disciples do not seem to have been much the wiser. So there they were, seven of the disciples, back in their old haunts, perhaps wandering along the shore of Lake Galilee. Peter suddenly said to his friends, *'I'm going out to fish'* (v. 3). Not surprisingly the other six replied, *'We'll go with you'* (v. 3).

Why did Peter decide to go on a fishing trip? It has been suggested that he decided he had had enough of Jesus and of being one of his disciples. Peter wanted security. In going fishing he was signalling that he was giving up and returning to his old life and occupation. Peter and his friends, it is argued, were in effect fulfilling the prediction of Jesus, 'A time is coming . . . when you will be scattered, each to his own home. You will all leave me alone' (16:32). A psychological variation on this suggestion speculates that by going fishing Peter was seeking to suppress the memories of his past failure to stand by Jesus at the time of trial and crucifixion. His reversion to his former way of life was in effect an expression of his current state of 'denial'. The fact is, however, that we don't know why Peter went fishing. In all probability he was not trying to achieve anything more than simply having a night out fishing. If there was any deeper motive, it may have been an issue of economics. Peter and his friends had to live – and instead of being dependent on friends they decided to go and get some fish for themselves.

So the evangelist tells us that *they went out and got into the boat, but that night they caught nothing* (v. 3). Night was traditionally the best time for fishing on Lake Galilee, but that night the fish refused to co-operate. The fishing expedition was proving to be a waste of time.

But as daybreak came, Jesus appeared on the beach. He must have sensed that the fishing trip had been futile, for he called out, *'Friends, haven't you any fish?'* (v. 5). Literally, the Greek text indicates that Jesus calls the disciples 'children' (*paidia*). Perhaps a better translation might be 'lads'. The term implies familiarity and intimacy (see, e.g., 1 John 2:18).

The evangelist records that at that stage *the disciples did not realise that it was Jesus* (v. 4) who was shouting out to them. Was there a bit of a sea mist around? For it was after all still early morning. Or had the distance something to do with the lack of recognition, although in fact they were only *about a hundred yards* from the shore (v. 8)? Furthermore, not only did the disciples fail to recognize his face; they also appeared initially not to recognize his voice (v. 5). The lack of recognition is all the stranger in that the disciples had already encountered the risen Lord (20:19–29). Furthermore, if Mark and Matthew are to be believed, there must have been at least a partial expectation on the part of the disciples that they might meet with the risen Lord in Galilee (Mark 16:7; Matt. 28:7, 10). Or are we here dealing with the fact that there was indeed something mysterious and unfamiliar about the body of the risen one? For this was not the first time Jesus was not immediately recognized (for instance, Mary Magdalene initially failed to realize that it was Jesus who was with her; 20:14).

The apparent stranger commands the disciples, *'Throw your net on the right side of the boat and you will find some'* (v. 6). The fact that the *right side* was considered the 'favoured' or 'lucky' side in the ancient world is an irrelevant detail. The evangelist records that on doing so, they ended up with a massive catch: *they were unable to haul the net in because of the large number of fish* (v. 6). How did Jesus know there were fish to be caught? Was this supernatural knowledge on his part? Was the size of the catch a miracle of Jesus' making? Or are we to assume that from his position on the shore, Jesus was able to spot a shoal of fish that had escaped the disciples' notice? We do not know.

At this point most commentators draw attention to the similarities between John's account and Luke's story of a much earlier fishing trip (Luke 5:1–11). On that occasion too, Peter and his friends had had a fruitless night's fishing (Luke 5:5). Then too the disciples were told to 'let down the nets for a catch', although instead of being told to throw their net 'to the right side', they were urged to 'put out into the deep' (Luke 5:4). Finally, on that occasion they too caught a 'large number' of fish (Luke 5:6). The similarities are striking. This has led some to speculate that we have in fact two versions of one event. Yet there are a number of major differences between the two accounts (for instance, in Luke the context is totally different, the disciples know all along that it is Jesus who is addressing them, and the nets begin to break). It may well be that the fourth evangelist is alluding to the story as found in Luke, but this does not mean that he is deliberately creating a new story.

The massive catch proves the catalyst to recognition. John, the Beloved Disciple, says to Peter, *'It is the Lord'* (v. 7). Whereupon Peter, ever impulsive (see 20:6), *wrapped his outer garment around him (for he had taken it off) and jumped into the water* (v. 7). The traditional interpretation is that Peter, who had stripped to fish and was 'naked' apart perhaps from a loincloth, for modesty's sake put on his *outer garment* before he swam to the shore to meet Jesus. The Greek text, however, is open to another possibility. The underlying Greek verb (*diazōnnymi*) although it can mean to 'put on clothes', normally has the meaning of to 'tie around' (see 13:4). Furthermore, the Greek text does not actually say that Peter *had taken it off*, but simply that he was 'naked' (*gymnos*). The text may mean that Peter, who was wearing nothing but an *outer garment*, tucked up this loosely flowing 'smock' into his belt, so that he could swim more easily to the shore. Of greater significance is that Peter does not doubt his fellow-disciple's identification. Does this confirm that he has already met with the risen Lord?

On landing *they saw a fire of burning coals* (v. 9). This was in fact a 'charcoal fire' (*anthrakia*), the same kind of fire that had been burning in the courtyard of the high priest (18:18) when Peter had denied Jesus. One interesting suggestion is that Jesus lit such a fire to enable Peter to face up to the memories of his recent shameful past. The evangelist records that there was but one *fish* (the singular, *opsarion*, is used) on it, together with a loaf of *bread*, apparently insufficient food for them all. Hence perhaps the request of Jesus, *'Bring some of the fish you have just caught'* (v. 10).

Simon Peter returned to help his fellow-disciples to drag the net ashore. *It was full of large fish, 153, but even with so many the net was not torn* (v. 11). The obvious point the evangelist wishes to make is that in spite of the size of catch, the net was not torn (in contrast to Luke 5:6). That in itself may perhaps have been a small miracle. The interest of commentators, however, has centred on the number of fish. Is the number simply a sign of an eye-witness account? Or is it more than simply factual? Is it also symbolic? At this point a large number of suggestions have been made, none of which is compelling, and most of which are positively abstruse. Augustine, for instance, had the following ingenious explanation: ten represents the Ten Commandments of the law; seven is the number of the sevenfold Spirit (Rev. 1:4). Now 7 + 10 = 17; and 153 is the sum of all the figures up to 17! The most attractive suggestion goes back to Jerome. In his commentary on Ezekiel 47 he links the miracle of the fish with the prophet's vision of the stream of living water that flows from the temple and which begins to teem with life: 'Writers on the nature and properties of animals who have learned "fishing" in either Latin or Greek (one of whom is the most learned poet Oppianus Cilix) say that there are 153 species.'[9] If this is behind the Gospel's 153, then we have

[9] Jerome, *Commentary on Ezekiel* 15: 47.

here an acted parable of the mission of the church. As Jesus himself said, 'I, when I am lifted up from the earth, will draw all people to myself' (12:32). The miracle of the catch points to the universality of the gospel. Unfortunately, Jerome's reference to 'writers' in the plural is a generalization from Oppian's writings. Oppian himself apparently lists 157 fish! Whatever the symbolism John may have intended, therefore, remains unclear to us today.[10]

Jesus invites the disciples to *'Come and have breakfast'* (v. 12). This invitation may show that Jesus is concerned with the whole person: after a night's fishing the disciples must have been in need of some food. In so far as the sharing together in a meal is also a sign of fellowship, however, it is probable that this is also a reference to the willingness of Jesus to accept and forgive his disciples, even after they have let him down.

The disciples were strangely reticent. *None of the disciples dared ask him, 'Who are you?' They knew it was the Lord* (v. 12). Unlike Mary Magdalene, who came and flung her arms around the Lord (20:17), the disciples appear to have remained at a distance. Does this distance signal uncertainty? Or does it signal a sense of awe (see Mark 16:8)? Jesus, however, continues to take the initiative: he *came* to them (v. 13).

Jesus then *took the bread and gave it to them, and did the same with the fish* (v. 13). In early Christian art the meal of bread and fish is often treated as an alternative expression of the Lord's Supper. Although there are strong verbal parallels with the feeding of the five thousand (John 5:11), which leads on to a later discourse with distinctive eucharistic overtones (6:25–59), however, here in John 21 there are no hints of an allusion to the Lord's Supper. It is but a fellowship meal. Furthermore, unlike Luke 24:41–43, there is no mention of Jesus' own eating: Jesus is not trying to prove he is not a ghost; rather, he is seeking to meet the needs of his disciples.

The evangelist ends his account of the fishing trip: *This was now the third time Jesus appeared to his disciples after he was raised from the dead* (v. 14). In his numbering, the evangelist ignores appearances recorded in the other Gospels. He also ignores the appearance of Jesus to Mary Magdalene.

a. Let's go fishing!

At first sight this 'third appearance' seems to be just a story about catching fish. However, as with so many of his stories, John may

---

[10] See R. M. Grant, 'One Hundred Fifty-Three Large Fishes', *Harvard Theological Review* 42 (1949), pp. 273–275.

have seen a deeper significance: this may have been a story about winning the world for Jesus. Mark and Matthew, in their Gospels, record that when Jesus called Peter and his brother to follow him, he said, 'Come, follow me . . . and I will make you fishers of men' (Mark 1:17; Matt. 4:19). Here in John 21 the risen Lord may be reminding Peter, and in turn us, of this calling. The clue to the story is possibly found in the number of fish caught. The evangelist records that *Simon Peter . . . dragged the net ashore. It was full of large fish, 153* (21:11). Almost certainly we are dealing here with an 'acted' parable.

Whether or not Jerome was right in linking the number of fish with the number of known species of fish, it was a massive catch. This massive catch of fish points to the later mission of the church. Peter and his friends are called not so much to fish as to win the world for Christ. Read in this light, three things stand out.

First, the risen Lord calls us to go out fishing. In this regard the timing of the call is significant. When he first called Peter to follow him and become a fisher of people, Jesus was at the beginning of his ministry. But here the cross and the resurrection are behind him. He is no longer the Galilean teacher, but the crucified and risen Lord. Now there is added impetus to the call to fish for people. For Jesus died that all might be forgiven; he rose that all might have life. In the words of John 3:16, 'For God so loved the world that he gave his one and only Son, that whoever believes in him shall not perish but have eternal life.' But if we are to share this good news, then we cannot just stand at the water's edge – we must get into our boats and go fishing. We must 'Put out into deep water, and let down the nets for a catch' (Luke 5:4). All too often we just dabble at the water's edge and fool ourselves that we are evangelizing. In reality we may only be tickling minnows. We need to become adventurous and actually go fishing.

Secondly, to those of us who have been unsuccessful in our 'fishing', the risen Lord calls us to try again. Jesus didn't just sympathize with his disciples' bad luck – rather, he encouraged them to have another shot, but this time to do it differently: *'Throw your net on the right side of the boat, and you will find some'* (v. 6). It must have been very tempting for Peter and his friends to ignore the advice of Jesus. After all, they must have been exhausted – they had been fishing all night. If fish don't bite at night, they almost certainly don't bite in the daytime. But the disciples gave it one further try and, to their great surprise, ended up with an enormous catch. Here are lessons for us to learn. We need, for instance, to learn to persevere. Successful fishermen are patient fishermen. By and large it takes time before fish begin to bite. Conversion tends to be a process: in an increasingly pagan world, Damascus-road experiences are rare; people need to be given time to make their way to Christ. We also need to be prepared to change our tactics. Fish no longer bite in the way they used to! The good news may remain unchanged, but methods of communicating the good news may need to change.

Thirdly, the risen Lord promises a large catch. That is a message many churches need to hear, especially churches that have not been effective in their evangelism. There are many reasons why evangelism today is difficult. One reason is that the world has changed: people may be religious, but they no longer want to take part in organized religion. Another reason is that churches have *not* changed: many operate with methods no longer appropriate for the world in which they live: their buildings tend to speak of a God who belongs to the past rather than the present. There is no room, however, for pessimism. The catch of the 153 fish speaks of a world being won for Christ. Indeed, Jesus said, 'But I, when I am lifted up from the earth, will draw all men to myself' (12:32). Not everything depends on us. It is God who gives the catch. There was something supernatural about the catch that morning – it happened not just because the fish were there, but because Jesus was there.

6. Jesus and Peter (21:15–25)

When they had finished eating, Jesus said to Simon Peter, 'Simon son of John, do you truly love me more than these?'

'Yes, Lord,' he said, 'you know that I love you.'

Jesus said, 'Feed my lambs.'

[16]Again Jesus said, 'Simon son of John, do you truly love me?' He answered, 'Yes, Lord, you know that I love you.'

Jesus said, 'Take care of my sheep.'

[17]The third time he said to him, 'Simon son of John, do you love me?'

Peter was hurt because Jesus asked him the third time, 'Do you love me?' He said, 'Lord, you know all things; you know that I love you.'

Jesus said, 'Feed my sheep. [18]I tell you the truth, when you were younger you dressed yourself and went where you wanted; but when you are old you will stretch out your hands, and someone else will dress you and lead you where you do not want to go.'

[19]Jesus said this to indicate the kind of death by which Peter would glorify God. Then he said to him, 'Follow me!'

[20]Peter turned and saw that the disciple whom Jesus loved was following them. (This was the one who had leaned back against

Jesus at the supper and had said, 'Lord, who is going to betray you?') [21]When Peter saw him, he asked, 'Lord, what about him?'

[22]Jesus answered, 'If I want him to remain alive until I return, what is that to you? You must follow me.' [23]Because of this, the rumour spread among the brothers that this disciple would not die. But Jesus did not say that he would not die; he only said, 'If I want him to remain alive until I return, what is that to you?'

[24]This is the disciple who testifies to these things and who wrote them down. We know that his testimony is true.

[25]Jesus did many other things as well. If every one of them were written down, I suppose that even the whole world would not have room for the books that would be written.

Peter failed to stand by his Lord. Three times in the courtyard of the high priest he had denied that he had anything to do with Jesus (18:17, 25, 27). Peter, like the hired hand, had run away when danger loomed (10:12). It is this incident that lies behind Jesus' presumably private conversation with Peter after breakfast. The threefold questioning of Peter is designed to recall his threefold denial of Jesus. Jesus was concerned, however, not to shame Peter, but rather to rehabilitate him. Yet rehabilitation was possible only as Peter faced up to his past.

The very way in which Jesus addresses Peter is significant. Three times Jesus calls him *Simon son of John* (vv. 15, 16, 17). Jesus does not address him as 'Peter', the name given to him at Caesarea Philippi, when Peter had confessed Jesus to be the Christ, the Son of the living God. To him then Jesus had said, 'you are Peter, and on this rock I will build my church' (Matt. 16:18). The implication now is that the Lord can build his church only on those who confess his name, not on those who deny him. True, John does not record this incident at Caesarea Philippi. Nevertheless, he does record an occasion when Jesus looked ahead and gave the apostle the new name of 'Cephas' or 'Peter' (1:42). The evangelist would have been aware that by using Peter's old name of *Simon son of John*, Jesus was in effect challenging his friendship: 'Where do you stand with me now, Simon son of John?'

The first time the question is put, Jesus goes on to ask, *'Do you truly love me more than these?'* (v. 15). It has been suggested that Jesus pointed to the boat and the fishing gear, as if Jesus was challenging Peter to give his life from now on to caring for the flock. It is much more probable, however, that the *these* were the other disciples. Jesus was asking Peter whether he loved him more than his fellow-disciples loved him. The form of the question is accounted for by Peter's earlier brash assertions of loyalty to Jesus. For Peter had boldly declared, 'I will lay my life down for you' (13:37; see also Matt. 26:35; Mark 14:31; Luke 22:33). Indeed, according to Matthew and Mark, when Jesus had told the disciples in the Garden of Gethsemane that they would all desert him that night, Peter had gone so far as to say, 'Even if all fall away on account of you, I never will' (Matt. 26:33; see also Mark 14:29). Ironically, it was Peter who let Jesus down more than the others.

Twice more Jesus asks, *'Do you love me?'* (vv. 16, 17). The NIV translation suggests a special intensity in the Lord's questioning on the first two occasions: 'Do you truly love me?' as distinct from 'Do you love me?' The difference in translation reflects the fact that in the first two instances the evangelist uses the Greek verb normally associated with self-giving love (*agapaō*), whereas on the third occasion he uses the Greek verb associated more with friendship (*phileō*). As we have already noticed, however, John has a love for synonyms and almost certainly does not intend to distinguish between the threefold questioning. The difference is purely stylistic. Indeed, were there to be any distinction, one would have expected the final question to reflect a higher degree of intensity. Certainly, as far as Jesus himself was concerned, there would have been no opportunity for him to have made such a subtle distinction, since in Aramaic, as in Hebrew, there is only one basic verb for expressing the various types of love. That the difference is stylistic is confirmed by the fact that in his reply Peter always uses the Greek verb expressing friendship (*phileō*).

Three times Peter replies, *'you know that I love you'* (vv. 15, 16, 17). The only difference is that on the final occasion, Peter, understandably 'hurt' by this constant questioning, gives an even fuller reply: *'Lord, you know all things; you know that I love you'* (v. 17). The suggestion has been made that Peter's additional statement, *'Lord, you know all things'* is an indication of growing maturity on Peter's part. There is nothing else in the context, however, to suggest that he is now a little wiser. Rather, this admission of Jesus' superior knowledge underlines both his sense of frustration and his desire to convince. Although it was early morning, one can even imagine the sweat pouring down his face. Jesus, by reminding him of his past failure, was well and truly twisting the knife. As a result, Peter was deeply 'pained' (*elypēthē*) by this experience. John uses the same word of a woman in childbirth experiencing 'pain' (16:21). But out of Peter's anguish Jesus was seeking to bring something positive to birth.

In response to Peter's declaration of love, three times Jesus entrusts him with the task of caring for his sheep. The threefold challenge followed by the threefold confession is now followed by a threefold commission. Peter's declared love for Jesus needs to be translated into action. Jesus says, 'Feed my lambs... Take care of my sheep... Feed my sheep' (vv. 15, 16, 17). The fisherman now becomes a shepherd. The imagery has to change, for fish die when they are caught, but sheep must be fed and cared for. The task is ongoing.

The picture of a shepherd caring for the sheep is a familiar New Testament metaphor for the exercise of Christian leadership, (e.g. Acts 20:28; Eph. 4:11; 1 Pet. 2:25; 5:2–3). This metaphor has its roots in the Old Testament, where 'shepherds' are the leaders of God's people (e.g. 2 Sam. 5:2; Jer. 23:1; 50:6; Ezek. 34:2–10), just as, in the ancient world as a whole, kings were often likened to shepherds.

Roman Catholics have traditionally seen Jesus' commissioning of Peter to care for the flock as the moment when Jesus designated Peter as his 'Vicar upon earth' and as the 'Supreme Pontiff' of his church. Although, in his new role as shepherd, Peter is clearly entrusted with authority, however, there is nothing to suggest exclusive authority. Absolute authority belongs to Jesus, the model shepherd (John 10). The sheep are 'his' sheep and not Peter's! The emphasis here is not on status, but on function. Verbs rather than nouns are used. Peter is not primarily appointed a shepherd; rather, he is commissioned to act as a shepherd in caring for the flock.

There has been much discussion as to whether or not there is any significant difference between these tasks of 'feeding the lambs', 'taking care of the sheep' and 'feeding the sheep' – or whether they are all variations on the same theme. To 'take care of sheep' (poimainō), for instance, clearly involves more than 'feeding' (boskō): it also involves guarding and guiding. Likewise, there is a distinction between 'lambs' (arnia) and 'sheep' (probata). It has, for instance, been suggested that there is a gradation in caring. Classic expression of such a gradation was given by William Temple, who commented:

'Feed my lambs': the first charge is to supply the needs of the young of the flock – a task of infinite responsibility, but not, as spiritual work is reckoned, conspicuously difficult, for the lambs are ready to accept the sustenance offered to them. 'Tend my sheep': the second charge is to exercise general guidance of the flock, including its mature members, a task for one of greater experience than the first. 'Feed my sheep': the third charge is the hardest – to supply the needs of the mature members of the flock; for it is less easy to discern their needs than those of the 'lambs', and they often have no knowledge of what their own needs are, or, still worse, suppose that they know when in fact they do not.[11]

[11] W. Temple, Readings in St John's Gospel, first and second series (Macmillan, 1961), p. 386.

Temple is right in so far as the pastoral task is indeed multifaceted (see Ezek. 34:16). These insights into the pastoral task, however, are not actually present in John. As we have continued to note, John is partial to the use of synonyms. Any difference in the threefold commission is therefore purely stylistic.

Jesus' conversation with Peter is not over. He has a serious and solemn word to say: *'I tell you the truth'* (literally Amēn, Amēn, a favourite expression of Jesus to strengthen what he is about to say: see, e.g., 1:51; 3:3, 5, 11; 5:19, 24, 25; etc.). For having commissioned Peter to care for his sheep, Jesus now looks ahead to the day when Peter will die for him. In the course of fulfilling his commission, Peter, like the good shepherd, will lay down his life for the sheep (10:14): *'when you were younger you dressed yourself and went where you wanted; but when you are old you will stretch out your hands, and someone else will dress you and lead you where you do not want to go'* (v. 18). At first sight it may appear that Jesus is talking about the limitations and difficulties of old age, as if Peter will glorify God through a long life lived in obedience to God. It is much more likely, however, that Jesus is in fact alluding to the day when Peter would die on a cross. Objection to this reference to death by crucifixion has been taken on the ground that it is contrary to the text order, which places the stretching out of the hands prior to being dressed and led away. This objection loses its force, however, once it is recognized that the phrase 'to stretch out one's hands' was an expression used of a condemned man being tied to the cross-beam before carrying it out to the place of crucifixion. According to Eusebius, the church historian, in AD 61 the day came when, in Rome, Peter did indeed die for his Lord. Peter too went to the cross and, when he was being nailed to it, asked to be nailed head downwards, for he said he was not worthy to die as his Lord had died. Jesus, however, sees Peter's death as an occasion when Peter would, like his Lord, *glorify God* (v. 19; see 11:27).

In this sobering context, Jesus reminds Peter of his even more basic call to *follow* him (v. 19; see 1:40–43). To go the way of Jesus is to go the way of the cross. John, unlike the Synoptic Gospels, may not specifically equate following Jesus with cross-bearing (see, e.g., Mark 8:34). He does, however, include the words of Jesus, 'The man who loves his life will lose it, while the man who hates his life in this world will keep it for eternal life'; to which Jesus adds, 'Whoever serves me must follow me' (12:25–26). In following Jesus, Peter was to fulfil the declaration of Jesus in the upper room, 'Where I am going, you cannot follow now, but you will follow later' (13:36).

Not surprisingly, Peter wanted to know whether the Beloved Disciple would share a similar fate: *'Lord, what about him?'* (v. 21).

A constant temptation in the Christian life is to compare ourselves with others. Jesus, however, highlights the need of Peter to follow him: *'You must follow me'* (v. 22). The pronoun here is emphatic: literally, Jesus says, 'You yourself (*sy*) follow me.' To 'follow' Jesus is to take our eyes off others and instead focus on Jesus alone. Jesus said, *'If I want him to remain alive until I return, what is that to you? You must follow me'* (v. 22). The evangelist goes on to clarify what exactly Jesus had said: *But Jesus did not say that he would not die; he only said, 'If I want him to remain alive until I return, what is that to you?'* (v. 23). Clearly these words of Jesus had been responsible for a good deal of speculation. Tradition has it that John lived to a great old age and eventually died in his sleep. Initially exiled to the island of Patmos, he was eventually released and went to Ephesus, where he became a leading figure in the church.

The evangelist closes the Gospel first by affirming the truth of what he has written (v. 24), and secondly by making it clear that what has been written has been only a selection of the *many other things* Jesus did (v. 25). Both these statements are important as far as the message of the resurrection is concerned. In the first place, the resurrection narratives are eye-witness accounts, which seek to give 'testimony' (*martyria*) to the truth of the resurrection. Right from the start the first Christians were concerned for truth. When, for example, they came to replace Judas Iscariot and bring the apostolic team up to strength, nominations were restricted to 'those who have been with us the whole time the Lord Jesus went in and out among us . . . one of these must become a witness (*martys*) to the resurrection' (Acts 1:21, 22). In other words, the Gospels may be theological tracts with a point to hammer home, but the evangelists will not pervert the truth to make their point. Secondly, the resurrection narratives include but a selection of stories relating to the risen Lord Jesus. It is this process of selection that in part accounts for the differences between the Gospels. Each evangelist has included material best suited to his purpose. The fact that a story of an appearance of the risen Jesus may appear in only one Gospel does not reduce its credibility. The authors of the Gospels did not set out to write a comprehensive account of the resurrection of Jesus, just as they did not set out to write a comprehensive account of the life of Jesus.

a. Beginning again with Jesus

The good news of the gospel is that in Jesus there is always a new beginning. It doesn't matter who we are or what we have done – in Jesus we can always begin again. This basic message is reinforced by the encounter of the risen Lord with Peter. From a human point of view Jesus' behaviour toward Peter is utterly mind-blowing. If we had been Jesus, we would have wanted to have nothing more to do with Peter after those denials in the courtyard of the high priest. The friendship would have been well and truly over. If we had been Jesus, the last thing we would have done would have been to have invited Peter to come and have breakfast with us, let alone entrust him with fresh responsibility. But then this just illustrates the massive gulf between us and Jesus. For Jesus never gives up on anybody, not even on close friends who have let him down. In spite of our failure, Jesus never turns his back on us. We may give up on him, but he never gives up on us. But if we would begin again with Jesus, then action is called for on our part too.

First, beginning again with Jesus involves *facing up to our past*. That morning, Peter was made to face up to his past in a number of ways. There was, for instance, the charcoal fire, which Jesus may have built to remind Peter of what happened when he had warmed himself by a similar charcoal fire a week or so previously (18:18). There was the threefold questioning of Peter designed to help him recall his threefold denial of Jesus. There was the formal use of his old name, *Simon son of John*, which in turn challenged his friendship. All this was exceedingly painful (v. 17). But as they say, 'no pain, no gain'. The painful business of facing up to his past failure was essential if Peter were to make a new beginning. As David Runcorn helpfully puts it: 'Until there is a remembering there can be no forgiveness. To re-member means to put back together something that has been broken and disconnected . . . To truly remember requires that we turn back to past actions and relationships and recognise our own place within what happened – only then can reconciliation be offered and received.'[12] Forgiveness becomes complete only as we face up to our past failures. As John was to write in his first letter, 'If we confess our sins, he is faithful and just and will forgive us our sins and purify us from all unrighteousness' (1 John 1:9).

Secondly, beginning again with Jesus involves *falling in love again with Jesus*. Peter was not simply reminded of his past failure. Peter was also given an opportunity to obliterate this threefold failure by reaffirming his love for Jesus again and again and again. Jesus did not ask, 'Simon son of John, are you sorry for what you did? From now on will you be more faithful?' Jesus asked if he loved him. This is the essential religious question. Of course, there is more to faith than

---

[12] D. Runcorn, *Rumours of Life: Reflections on the Resurrection Appearances* (Darton, Longman & Todd, 1996), p. 115.

loving. Faith has an intellectual side, as well as an emotional side. The determinative point in our religious pilgrimage, however, is not when we say, 'Yes, I understand,' but rather, 'Yes, Lord, I do love you.' Nor is it enough to believe, for even demons 'believe . . . and shudder' (Jas. 2:19). Christian faith begins when we respond to the love of God in Jesus and, in the words of St John the Divine, open our 'heart' to the Lord Jesus (Rev. 3:20).

Thirdly, beginning again with Jesus involves *fulfilling a task*. Love for Jesus always brings a task. In particular, we prove our love for Jesus by loving others. Self-centred worship of Jesus is a contradiction in terms: if we truly love Jesus, we shall love others. For Peter that task involved caring for the sheep. We too are called to care for one another (1 Cor. 12:25). Caring is not the exclusive preserve of pastors. Such caring may be costly. For Peter it involved a cross. Love that costs nothing is not love, but sentiment.

b. Called to lead?

This passage in John 21 has been the inspiration of many an ordination sermon. Indeed, it has been suggested that the threefold question and answer actually reflect an ancient liturgical form, such as would be used in an ordination service. For those called to lead, and in particular for those called to follow in Peter's steps as pastors of the flock of Jesus, this conversation between Jesus and Peter contains a number of important lessons.

In the first place, those who are called to lead are *called to love the Lord Jesus*. Such a statement may appear to be simplistic, but if the grace of God expressed in Jesus is essential for ministry, so too is our love for God and for his Son, the Lord Jesus. It is not so much that our love for Jesus will prove infectious (although that ought to be true), as that it will be our love for Jesus, above all, that will sustain our ministry. The fact is that there are times when Christian ministry is hard and apparently unrewarding. Hopes will be dashed; people will go their selfish way. Then we shall be sustained not by our love for the ministry, for the ministry itself will be unattractive; instead it will be only our love for Jesus, and his love for us, that will keep us going.

In the second place, those who are called to lead are *called to care for the flock*. Christian ministry is primarily not about the management of an institution, but about the care of people. Christian ministry can never just be task-centred; it must always be people-focused. Christian ministry is not about the development of a career, but about the development of people. It is because we care for people that we will pray for them, visit them, teach them, and even lead them. Nor must we forget that there are 'other sheep' who do not belong to the flock (10:16). Ministry that is truly Christian is never mere 'chaplaincy', for it may never be confined to the church.

In the third place, those who are called to lead are also *called to follow*. They are called to follow Jesus, the crucified, albeit risen, Lord. Christian ministry is always a costly business. There are times when we feel (and indeed are!) misunderstood, rejected and even crucified, not (as was Peter's case) by those outside the church, but by those within. Our call, however, is to follow Jesus, whatever the cost. Furthermore, our call is to follow wherever Jesus may lead. This means resisting the temptation to compare ourselves with others in ministry. Our eyes must be on Jesus, and on Jesus alone. As Peter discovered, Jesus has a distinctive plan for each of our lives. The only pattern common to Christian ministry is the pattern of the crucified and risen Lord.

5. The witness of Paul to the resurrection

Dubbed by J. B. Phillips 'the most important chapter in the Bible', 1 Corinthians 15 is the key text in which Paul elaborates on the resurrection of Christ and its consequences for us. Not surprisingly, never a Christian funeral passes without verses from this chapter being read. Here there are great words of hope to be found. Because 1 Corinthians 15 deals with the resurrection hope, this chapter is of permanent relevance. For death never goes away. This portion of Scripture has always contained good news for men and women whose condition is terminal. In today's death-denying and death-fearing culture, 1 Corinthians 15 is perhaps of even more good news: death can be defied – for in Jesus God has given us the victory (v. 57)!

At first sight the context in which Paul first penned this chapter appears to be similar to the circumstances in which we find ourselves today. People were denying that there was such a thing as resurrection from the dead. On closer examination, however, the context was very different. For the people who were denying resurrection from the dead were members of the church at Corinth; furthermore, they were the 'enthusiasts' in the church. A careful reading of 1 Corinthians reveals that there were some members of the church who assumed that they were already sharing in the resurrection life of Jesus, so much so that there was nothing more to anticipate than the final ridding of the body itself. In one sense those Christians were right to stress their new life in Christ, for as Paul himself elsewhere makes clear, by our faith expressed in baptism we have already begun to share something of the resurrection life of Jesus (see Rom. 6:1–8; Col. 2:12; 3:1–4). Whereas we know that this life in the Spirit is but a foretaste of more to come (2 Cor. 5:5; Eph. 1:13–14), however, some of the Corinthians appear to have been convinced that they already had all there was to have (see 4:8). For them the gifts of the Spirit, and especially the gift of tongues, were a sign of their present angelic existence (13:1). They would have agreed with Hymenaeus and Philetus that 'the resurrection has already taken place' (2 Tim. 2:18).

To us today such an 'over-realized eschatology' seems strange. Yet perhaps the triumphalistic 'prosperity' teaching of certain charismatic groups, with its emphasis on the present blessings of health, wealth and success, is not so far removed from the Corinthian way of thinking. Indeed, such thinking is not confined to these groups. It is amazing how easy it is for the cross to disappear from Christian living (as distinct from Christian believing) in mainline churches too. The fact is that we follow both a crucified and risen Lord.

In terms of structure, 1 Corinthians 15 divides into three basic sections. In the first section (vv. 1–11), Paul deals with the resurrection of Christ himself. In the second section (vv. 12–34), Paul writes of the resurrection of the dead, which is consequent upon Christ's resurrection. In the third section (vv. 35–58), Paul elaborates on the nature of the resurrection body before he concludes with an assurance of the victory that is ours in Christ.

1. The resurrection of Jesus (1 Cor. 15:1–11)

Now, brothers, I want to remind you of the gospel I preached to you, which you received and on which you have taken your stand. [2]By this gospel you are saved, if you hold firmly to the word I preached to you. Otherwise, you have believed in vain.

[3]For what I received I passed on to you as of first importance: that Christ died for our sins according to the Scriptures, [4]that he was buried, that he was raised on the third day according to the Scriptures, [5]and that he appeared to Peter, and then to the Twelve. [6]After that, he appeared to more than five hundred of the brothers at the same time, most of whom are still living, though some have fallen asleep. [7]Then he appeared to James, then to all the apostles, [8]and last of all he appeared to me also, as to one abnormally born.

[9]For I am the least of the apostles and do not even deserve to be called an apostle, because I persecuted the church of God. [10]But by the grace of God I am what I am, and his grace to me was not without effect. No, I worked harder than all of them – yet not I, but the grace of God that was with me. [11]Whether, then, it was I or they, this is what we preach, and this is what you believed.

In this first section Paul is probably not trying to prove the resurrection of Christ. Rather, he is reminding the Corinthians of the beliefs he and they have in common. On the basis of these commonly held beliefs in the second section he will argue for the resurrection of the dead.

The gospel Paul *preached* is that which the Corinthians not only 'received' in the past, but also that on which they have taken their *stand* (v. 1). Paul uses a Greek perfect (*hestēkate*) to convey the fact that their past stance is in fact their present stance. Salvation is a present process, with roots in the past, and one that will be completed only in the future. Paul, therefore, uses the present tense: 'By this gospel you are *being* saved.' Salvation depends on their continuing to *hold firmly to the word . . . preached* (v. 2). Otherwise their believing will have been 'futile' (see vv. 14, 17).

Paul proceeds to define the gospel he preached (vv. 3–5): *For what I received I passed on to you as of first importance: that Christ died for our sins according to the Scriptures, that he was buried, that he was raised on the third day according to the Scriptures, and that he appeared to Peter, and then to the Twelve.*

Paul's definition of the gospel is not his own; rather, he quotes an early Christian creed, which he first *received* and then *passed on* to the Corinthians. Paul is using technical language to describe the official reception and transmission of what is termed 'oral tradition'. We find the same kind of language in 1 Corinthians 11:23, where Paul introduces his account of the Last Supper with the words 'For I received from the Lord what I also passed on to you . . .' In days before the invention of the printing press, teachers made pupils learn information by heart. This was particularly true of the Jews, who learnt off by heart not just the Torah but also the 'traditions of the elders' (see Mark 7:1–13). It was also true of the first Christians, who learnt by rote the stories of Jesus 'handed on' to them.

It is generally agreed that 1 Corinthians was written some time in AD 54, that is, around some twenty to twenty-five years after the death of Jesus. The creed Paul quotes is even earlier. The fact, for instance, that Paul speaks of Jesus' appearing to Cephas (the Aramaic form of 'Peter', which is the term used by the NIV) may indicate that we have here a form of words possibly formulated in the Jerusalem church within a few years of the death of Jesus. Paul was possibly taught the words of this creed by Ananias. Certainly, what we have here is the earliest evidence for the death and resurrection of Jesus.

It is this creed that Paul taught the Corinthians as being *of first importance* (v. 3). Here was the essence of the Christian faith. Here were the 'basics'.

At first sight there appear to be four propositions: (1) Christ died for our sins according to the Scriptures; (2) Christ was buried; (3) Christ was raised on the third day according to the Scriptures; and

(4) Christ appeared to Peter, then to the Twelve. On closer examination, however, these four affirmations can be reduced to two propositions: 'Christ died' and 'Christ was raised'. The 'being buried' and 'appearing to Peter and the Twelve' simply strengthen these two basic propositions.

First, *Christ died for our sins according to the Scriptures* (v. 3). The Greek preposition (*hyper*), here translated 'for', normally means 'on behalf of' and as such is usually used of persons: for example, 'But God demonstrates his own love for us in this: While we were still sinners, Christ died for us' (Rom. 5:8). What we have here is probably a form of shorthand, indicating that Christ died 'on our behalf to deal with' our sins. Although there is no developed theory of the atonement present, the concept of 'substitution' is surely to be found: Jesus took our place.

The 'Scripture' that comes immediately to mind is Isaiah 53, with its emphasis on the Servant of the Lord being 'pierced for our transgressions . . . crushed for our iniquities' (Is. 53:5). This identification of Jesus with the Servant is made repeatedly in the early speeches of Acts (e.g. 3:13ff.; 8:32ff.), an identification that would appear to go back to Jesus himself. The plural form, *Scriptures*, however, probably indicates the belief that the Scriptures in general point to the death of Christ. The death of Jesus is best interpreted within the scriptural categories of sacrifice and atonement. Because this death was *according to the Scriptures*, Peter and the early church proclaimed that the death of Christ was no accident of history – it was part of God's plan and purpose (see Acts 2:23).

That Christ really *died* (and did not simply faint on the cross) was confirmed by the fact that *he was buried* (v. 4; see Acts 2:29). Almost certainly this line anticipates the next, and in so doing alludes to the 'empty tomb'. Contrary to what some suggest, the tradition of the empty tomb was not a later development, but was known to the early church from the very beginning.

The second main proposition is that *he was raised on the third day according to the Scriptures* (v. 4). The passive mood, *he was raised*, indicates that God is the implied subject: it is not so much that Jesus rose as that God raised him, and in doing so vindicated his death on the cross. The tense is even more significant. In the other three lines of this creed a simple Greek past (aorist) is used, namely he *died*, *was buried* and *appeared*; but in this line the verb is in the Greek perfect (*egēgertai*), a tense expressing a past action with consequences in the present. The implication is that Christ was raised to life and lives for ever. Christ is alive! This Greek perfect is repeated throughout the chapter when Paul is referring to Christ (vv. 12, 13, 14, 16, 17, 20).

The reference to *the third day* is in one sense a simple fact of history. Jesus was crucified on a Friday. Yet when the women went to the tomb early on the morning of the first day of the week (Sunday), he had risen. What happened was an event, not just an experience. This phrase may also underline the reality of Christ's death: his body lay in a tomb for more than two days, and no doubt in that time began to decompose. By implication, this fact of decomposition offers hope to us: for if God could transform Jesus' decomposing body when he raised his Son from the dead, he can do the same for us.

All this was *according to the Scriptures*. Which scriptures does the creed have in mind? Is the emphasis on the third day, or on resurrection? If the former, then there could well be an allusion to Hosea 6:2, a verse the rabbis themselves interpreted of the resurrection. Other texts that have been suggested include Jonah 1:17 (Jonah was inside the fish 'three days and three nights': see Matt. 12:40) and 2 Kings 20:5 (the promise of restoration to Hezekiah: 'on the third day from now you will go up to the temple of the LORD'); also Exodus 19:10–11 (the Lord comes down on Mount Sinai on 'the third day') and Leviticus 23:10, 11, 15 (the firstfruits of the harvest are to be waved 'on the day after the Sabbath': see 1 Cor. 15:20). However, nowhere in the New Testament are any of these texts cited to support the resurrection. If the emphasis is on resurrection and consequent vindication, texts such as Psalms 110:1 and 16:10 (see Acts 2:25–36) come to mind, as also Isaiah 53:11–12. In the light of the parallelism with the first line of the creed, however, it may be that the emphasis is on the witness of the Old Testament as a whole to the resurrection on the third day. Whatever the scripture, almost certainly the main thrust of the phrase is this: the resurrection was not just an afterthought; it was part and parcel of the divine plan.

Christ *appeared to Peter* (Cephas), *and then to the Twelve* (v. 5). Just as the phrase *he was buried* underlines the reality of Christ's death, so this corresponding phrase underlines the objective reality of his resurrection. Jesus *appeared to* (literally, he 'let himself be seen by', *ōphthē*) a number of witnesses. The list of witnesses is not exhaustive. Significantly, there is no reference to the women – probably because in Jewish courts the testimony of women was not admissible as public evidence.

Within the creed itself only two appearances are singled out. First, the appearance to *Peter*. The only reference to such an appearance within the Gospels is found in Luke 24:34. Secondly, the appearance to *the Twelve*. This term, not found elsewhere in Paul (an indication of the pre-Pauline nature of the creed) refers to the twelve apostles as a group: clearly it will not have included Judas Iscariot, and on one occasion it did not include Thomas (John 20:19–23). The Gospels include a number of such appearances: for example, Matthew 28:16–17; Luke 24:33–51 (with others present); and John 20:26–29.

At this point Paul adds to the creed a number of further appearances known to him from other sources, but interestingly not known to us. Here we have a reminder that the New Testament does not give us a complete record of the life of Jesus, but only a selection of things he did and said (see John 21:25).

After that, he appeared to more than five hundred of the brothers at the same time, most of whom are still living, though some have fallen asleep (v. 6). It has been suggested that the account of the day of Pentecost in Acts 2 is Luke's rewriting of what was originally a resurrection appearance. Such an explanation fails to convince, however, if the historicity of the New Testament documents is to be taken at all seriously. The expression *at the same time* emphasizes the reality of the appearance. Visions may come to individuals, but certainly not to large groups. Synchronized ecstasy on this scale is out of the question! The phrase *most of whom are still living* may actually form an invitation to the Corinthians to make enquiries themselves of those who saw the Lord. Some, however, *have fallen asleep*. In the ancient world, death was often likened to sleep. Jesus, for instance, uses this euphemism (John 11:11, 13), as does Paul, not least in this letter (e.g. 7:39; 11:30; 15:18, 20, 51).

Then he appeared to James (v. 7). An appearance to James is recorded in the apocryphal *Gospel of the Hebrews*. This James is the Lord's brother, who, along with his other brothers, 'did not believe' in Jesus (John 7:5) during the course of his earthly ministry. Was this appearance of the risen Christ instrumental in his conversion? We can only speculate.

Then he appeared *to all the apostles* (v. 7). Probably this is not just another way of speaking of *the Twelve*, but rather refers to a larger group, more limited no doubt than the five hundred, who along with the Twelve saw the risen Lord Jesus and were sent out by him to preach the gospel.

To this list of appearances of the risen Lord Paul adds his own experience: *and last of all he appeared to me also, as to one abnormally born* (v. 8). The fact that Paul includes this experience within the list of the Lord's appearances shows that as far as he was concerned his encounter with the risen Christ on the Damascus road was not some kind of subjective vision to be placed on a par with his other 'visions and revelations' (see 2 Cor. 12:1). The Lord *appeared* to him. As he mentions earlier in the letter, he too is an 'apostle' because he had actually 'seen Jesus' (1 Cor. 9:1). Paul recognizes that this appearance was outside the 'normal' process. Hence he uses the unusual expression *as to one abnormally born.* The Greek word (*to ektrōma*) described any kind of premature birth, whether a miscarriage, a stillbirth or an abortion. The fact that in the Greek the definite article is present suggests that Paul is in fact taking up a term of abuse used of him by some of his Corinthian opponents. Perhaps some called him a 'foetus-like freak' and in doing so referred to the fact that physically speaking Paul was not the most attractive of people (see 2 Cor. 10:10). Alternatively, there may have been a play on his name, 'Paulus' (literally, 'the little one'): some may have dismissed him as a 'half-formed dwarf' (this might explain the digression in vv. 9–10 where he talks of himself as the 'least of the apostles').

I (literally, 'I in particular', *Egō gar eimi*) *am the least of the apostles* (v. 9). Paul never forgot that at one stage he had 'persecuted the church of God'. Nevertheless, *by the grace of God I am what I am* (v. 10). God's grace was at work in his conversion (see Rom. 6:14), but came to particular expression in his calling to be an apostle (3:10). In his role as an apostle Paul *worked harder than all* the other apostles (v. 11). Paul is probably referring not just to the greater hardships he had experienced (2 Cor. 11:23–27), but to his greater achievements in planting new churches in places where the gospel had not been preached (Rom. 15:20; 2 Cor. 10:12–16). Yet Paul was conscious that the credit for all this belonged to God: *yet not I, but the grace of God that was with me* (v. 10).

Paul ends the section by returning to where he began: *Whether, then, it was I or they, this is what we preach, and this is what you believed* (v. 11). Christ crucified and risen was at the heart of the apostolic preaching. This too the Corinthians claimed to believe.

a. Back to basics

Christian 'agnosticism' in many areas is inevitable. There are all kinds of issues of faith that belong to the sphere of question and debate. Christian faith can never be totally systematized, for we are dealing with a God who is beyond all systematization. Because God's ways and thoughts are not our ways and thoughts (see Is. 55:8), there will always be areas of uncertainty. We cannot dot all the i's and cross the t's of faith. There will be times when we just don't know. There are basic issues, however, on which certainty is not only possible, but necessary. Here in 1 Corinthians 15 Paul touches upon three basic issues, three matters 'of first importance' (v. 3).

Of first and basic importance is that the gospel centres on a death, namely the death of Christ. At the very beginning of his letter Paul talks of the 'message of the cross' (1 Cor. 1:18), but the uniqueness of the death of Christ does not lie in the manner of his death. Thousands had been crucified before Christ died, just as thousands would be crucified after his death. Indeed, when Emperor Titus subdued a Jewish revolt, Josephus tells us that 'there was no space left for crosses, and insufficient crosses for all the bodies'. The uniqueness of Christ's death lay in its purpose: *Christ died for our sins according to the Scriptures* (v. 3). We die because of our sins. As Paul later wrote to the Romans, 'the wages of sin is death' (Rom. 6:23). But Jesus died *for our sins*. In other words, the death of Jesus was no mere act of heroic or exemplary love. Something actually happened when Jesus died. Jesus died to make an 'atonement' for our sins – he died to make us 'at one' with God. As such the death of Jesus is the only hope for sinful men and women.

Of first and basic importance is that the gospel centres on a life, namely the risen life of Christ. Without the resurrection of Jesus the death of Jesus would have no meaning and the cross would be devoid of its power. The crucified Christ whom Paul preached is the crucified and risen Lord. The uniqueness of the resurrection of Jesus does not lie just in his coming back to life, miraculous as that was. Jesus was no Lazarus, who came back to life only to die again. No, the uniqueness of the resurrection of Jesus lies in his having been raised to life and being alive for ever. Jesus is alive, and will be for all eternity. Because he is alive, not only sin but also death have been dealt with for ever. The resurrection of Jesus is the only hope for mortal men and women.

Of first and basic importance is that the gospel deals in matters of life and death, namely our lives and death. Paul is quite clear that it is not enough to 'receive' the gospel. We need to continue to *hold firmly to the word . . . preached* (v. 2). We must never lose our grip on the Christ crucified and risen. The adage 'Once saved, always saved' is misleading. We can never take our salvation for granted. Salvation in the New Testament comes in three tenses: past, present and future. We have been saved, we are being saved, and we will be saved. Salvation is a process (see 1 Cor. 1:18), which will be completed only on some future day (see Rom. 5:9; 1 Thess. 5:9–10) when the Lord returns (see also 2 Thess. 1:7; 1 John 3:2). All this lies behind Paul's exhortation to the Corinthians to continue to take their stand on the basics of the gospel. Our eternal destiny depends on it, *Otherwise, you have believed in vain* (v. 2). Origen, the early church father, rightly commented, 'Those who believe for a time, and in time of trial turn away, believe to no purpose.' Some 'traditions' prove redundant with the passing of time. But not the tradition enshrined in the creed of 1 Corinthians 15:3–5. To throw such beliefs away is to throw our very future away.

2. The resurrection of the dead (1 Cor. 15:12–34)

But if it is preached that Christ has been raised from the dead, how can some of you say that there is no resurrection of the dead? [13]*If there is no resurrection of the dead, then not even Christ has been raised.* [14]*And if Christ has not been raised, our preaching is useless and so is your faith.* [15]*More than that, we are then found to be false witnesses about God, for we have testified about God that he raised Christ from the dead. But he did not raise him if in fact the dead are not raised.* [16]*For if the dead are not raised, then Christ has not been raised either.* [17]*And if Christ has not been raised, your faith is futile; you are still in your sins.* [18]*Then those also who have fallen asleep in Christ are lost.* [19]*If only for this life we have hope in Christ, we are to be pitied more than all men.*

[20]*But Christ has indeed been raised from the dead, the firstfruits of those who have fallen asleep.* [21]*For since death came through a man, the resurrection of the dead comes also through a man.* [22]*For as in Adam all die, so in Christ all will be made alive.* [23]*But each in his own turn: Christ, the firstfruits; then, when he comes, those who belong to him.* [24]*Then the end will come, when he hands over the kingdom to God the Father after he has destroyed all dominion, authority and power.* [25]*For he must reign until he has put all his enemies under his feet.* [26]*The last enemy to be destroyed is death.* [27]*For he 'has put everything under his feet'. Now when it says that 'everything' has been put under him, it is clear that this does not include God himself, who put everything under Christ.* [28]*When he has done this, then the Son himself will be made subject to him who put everything under him, so that God may be all in all.*

[29]*Now if there is no resurrection, what will those do who are baptised for the dead? If the dead are not raised at all, why are people baptised for them?* [30]*And as for us, why do we endanger ourselves every hour?* [31]*I die every day – I mean that, brothers – just as surely as I glory over you in Christ Jesus our Lord.* [32]*If I fought wild beasts in Ephesus for merely human reasons, what have I gained? If the dead are not raised,*

> *'Let us eat and drink,*
> *for tomorrow we die.'*

[33]*Do not be misled: 'Bad company corrupts good character.'* [34]*Come back to your senses as you ought, and stop sinning; for there are some who are ignorant of God – I say this to your shame.*

From the resurrection of Christ Paul now turns to the resurrection of the dead. From having established the certainty of the resurrection of Christ, Paul now seeks to establish the certainty of the resurrection of the dead. To do this, he develops his argument in three different ways. First of all, he looks at the negative implications if Christ has not been raised from the dead (vv. 12–19); then he looks at the positive implications if Christ has been raised from the dead (vv. 20–28); finally, he returns to the negative implications and lists three immediate consequences in the present if Christ has not been raised from the dead (vv. 29–34).

a. The negative implications (vv. 12–19)

In this section Paul, for argument's sake, assumes the Corinthian position: 'there is no resurrection of the dead' (v. 12). If that is true, *then not even Christ has been raised* (v. 13). If that is also true, then there are a number of inevitable corollaries.

First, *our preaching is useless* (v. 14). Paul has already spelt out the content of his preaching (vv. 3–7). Take away the resurrection of Christ and there is nothing left: literally, it is 'empty' (*kenon*). So-called Christian preaching which denies the reality of the resurrection of Christ has no content, no substance. Here indeed are strong words!

Secondly, God has been discredited: *we are then found to be false witnesses about God* (v. 15). There is nothing worse than Christian preachers' bringing God in to support what is essentially an untenable position. Apart from anything else, it ultimately makes it difficult for people to take God himself seriously. Sadly, many people have not only given up on church, they have also given up on God himself, because of the way in which he has been brought into an argument.

Thirdly, *faith is futile* (v. 17). It, like preaching, is *useless*. When faith has lost touch with reality, it may be likened to the attempts of someone to sew a fabric without a knot at the end of the thread. In particular, if the cross has the last word and Christ has not been raised, then there is no forgiveness: *you are still in your sins.* Preaching that lacks the note of resurrection is not gospel preaching, as there is no longer any good news.

Fourthly, *those also who have fallen asleep in Christ are lost* (v. 18). In a sense this is but an elaboration on the third point. Without faith in a risen Christ, not only can the gospel no longer deal with our past; it can no longer offer any hope for the future. The Corinthians may have believed that all was well with their dead: they had simply shed their bodies and entered into some kind of final 'spiritual' existence. No, says Paul, they are *lost*; they have perished for ever!

Finally, *we are to be pitied more than all men* (v. 19). There is some scholarly debate as to where the adverb *only* belongs: does it modify the verb ('if we only hoped in Christ') or the phrase 'in this life' (so NIV: *If only for this life we have hope in Christ* . . .). The difference is negligible, however, for the overall thrust is more or less the same: those who believe that Christ is risen from the dead may be likened to people who have put all their eggs into the wrong basket. A partial parallel may be found in *2 Baruch* 21:13: 'If there were this life only, which belongs to all men, nothing could be more bitter than this.'

Paul does not pull his punches. If the tomb were not empty and Christ not risen from the dead, then Christian believing has nothing to offer. The Christian gospel stands or falls with the resurrection of Christ from the dead. Here is a warning so-called radicals in the church need to heed. Preaching that lacks the dimension of the resurrection has no power to change lives, either now or in the future. It is no longer Christian preaching. It is not just radicals, however, who need to hear this word of warning. There are also so-called Bible-believing Christians who may assent with their minds to the truth of resurrection, but for whom the resurrection of Christ is not at the heart of their preaching and believing. If the content of their worship and of their preaching be examined, the truth may well be that their Easter faith is limited to Easter Day. To all intents and purposes they celebrate a crucified Saviour but not a risen Lord. Of course, preaching the resurrection without the cross leads to false triumphalism; but preaching the cross without the resurrection leads nowhere: it is a 'dead' end.

b. The positive implications (vv. 20–28)

Thank God, there is no need to major on the negatives. For, with great certainty Paul declares, *But Christ has indeed been raised from the dead* (v. 20). The two little Greek words translated 'but . . . indeed' (*Nyni de*) convey the sense 'The truth of the matter, however, is . . .' The resurrection of Christ is the great reality on which the whole future of the world depends. Paul spells out the positive implications of the resurrection, which may be summed up in a series of Christological statements.

First, Christ is *the firstfruits of those who have fallen asleep* (v. 20; see also v. 23). The expression *the firstfruits* recalls the first sheaf of the grain harvest being 'waved' at the Jewish Feast of Weeks as a token of a greater harvest to come (see Lev. 23:9–14). This Feast of Weeks actually coincided with the Passover. In using this metaphor, therefore, Paul may have been conscious that Christ rose from the dead about the time when the sheaf of the *firstfruits* was being offered in the temple on 16 Nisan, the day after the Sabbath following the Passover. As the *firstfruits*, Jesus is the guarantee of a harvest of life to come. Our hope of resurrection from the dead is anchored in Christ's resurrection.

Secondly, he is a 'second Adam' in whose resurrection from the dead there is life for all. Like the first Adam, Christ is a representative figure: but whereas the first Adam brought death, the second Adam brought life (v. 21): *For as in Adam all die, so in Christ all will be made alive* (v. 22). There has been a good deal of debate as to the precise meaning of this second phrase, *so in Christ all will be made alive.* Does it refer simply to the resurrection of believers? If so, then those who are *in Christ* are those who 'depend on Christ'. Or, in so far as verse 22b is perfectly balanced by verse 22a, is Paul also referring to a general resurrection, in which *all* without exception will be raised to life? Much depends on the interpretation of verses 23–24.

The NIV translates verses 23–24, *But each in his own turn: Christ, the firstfruits; then, when he comes, those who belong to him. Then the end will come* . . . The difficulty here is that the normal meaning of the Greek word translated by the NIV as 'turn' (*tagma*) does not mean 'turn' at all, but rather 'group'. Yet if the translation 'group' be adopted, a problem immediately arises: the phrase 'each in his own group' implies more than one 'group', yet Christ cannot very well be included in a group. Other versions adopt the meaning 'order' (e.g. REB, 'each in proper order'; NRSV, 'each in his own order'), but this is not the primary meaning of *tagma*. Furthermore, if such a meaning be adopted, then the Greek construction is strained almost to breaking point.[1] The logical consequence is in fact to see Paul here alluding to yet another group, the group formed by the 'wicked' or 'unrighteous' dead, who, according to Luke's account of Paul in his defence before Felix, are also to share in a 'resurrection', that is, a resurrection for judgment (see Acts 24:15). The arguments involved here in 1 Corinthians 15 are extraordinarily complex. Certainly, Paul's primary concern here is the resurrection of believers. Yet if Paul had not believed in a resurrection of the unrighteous for judgment, he would have been consciously disassociating himself from the general Christian tradition (see, e.g., Matt. 25:46; John 5:28–29; Rev. 20:5, 12–13), as well as from most of the Jewish apocalyptic writers.

---

[1] If *tagma* were to bear this proposed sense, we should expect to read *kata tagma*, and not *en tagmati*.

Thirdly, Jesus is Lord. The actual term 'Lord' is not used, but the thought is most certainly present. *He must reign* (v. 25) is the overall message of a very closely argued passage. In summary, Paul states that Jesus is not only Lord of all humankind (vv. 22–24a), but also Lord of the whole universe (vv. 24b–28). Every hostile power must submit to his rule (v. 24) – even death will be brought to heel (v. 26). When that moment arrives, it will be the time of the end, when Jesus hands over the kingdom to the Father (v. 28).

It has sometimes been supposed that Christ's rule over the world, depicted in verses 24–28, was understood by Paul to take place in the interval between the resurrection of the righteous and the resurrection of the unrighteous. That is, Paul is said to be foreshadowing John's millennial understanding of Christ's kingdom here (see Rev. 20). However, Paul nowhere explicitly mentions such a kingdom, not even in 1 Corinthians 15:50–57, where such a reference might have been expected. Furthermore, if the evil powers are to be conquered before the parousia, there is little reason for the battle to start all over again in this messianic kingdom. Indeed, the early church's understanding of the reign of Christ was not that it was to come, but rather that it has already come. Jesus became Lord of all at the moment of resurrection (see, e.g., Acts 2:36; Rom. 1:3–4; 10:9; Phil. 2:9–11).

Paul proceeds to justify this present reign of Christ from the Scriptures. He is to reign *until he has put all his enemies under his feet* (v. 25). In view of the fact that Paul is quoting from Psalm 110:1, where God is the subject, and that God is also the subject in verses 26–27, where Paul is quoting from Psalm 8:7, God is probably the subject here too. When death, *the last enemy*, sustains its complete defeat (v. 26), then resurrection will take place. Whether death will actually be 'destroyed' (so NIV) or simply 'robbed of its power' is debatable. The Greek verb (*katargeō*) can have the meaning to 'annihilate' (e.g. 2 Thess. 2:8; 1 Cor. 6:13), but its primary meaning is to 'render ineffective'. If the latter meaning be adopted, death may still continue to exist, but no longer as an effective enemy to God. Rather, it is an instrument in his hand that may be used against those whom he sees fit to punish (see Rom. 6:21–23; 1 Cor. 1:18ff.; 2 Cor. 2:16; 4:3–4; Phil. 1:28). Interestingly, Paul uses a present tense here: literally, death is being 'destroyed' or 'rendered ineffective' (*katargeitai*). This may indicate that death is already in the process of losing its power. Alternatively, we have here a 'prophetic' present – after all, death is the *last enemy* (v. 26).

Fourthly, Jesus is 'the Son', who *himself will be made subject to him who put everything under him* (v. 28). The 'subordination' of the Son to the Father has caused a good deal of comment. Was there a Corinthian belief that at his exaltation Christ became the one supreme God? It may be that the subordination of the Son to the Father is to be explained, in part at least, by the quotation from Psalm 8:5, where the son of man exercised his appointed lordship over the rest of creation as one made 'a little lower than the heavenly beings'. With the subjection of all things to him, Christ's mandate comes to an end – his mission is fulfilled. The outcome is that God the Father becomes *all in all* (v. 28). In the words of the Jewish Targum on Zechariah 14:9, 'the kingly rule of God will be revealed over all the inhabitants of the earth'. God alone will be King!

c. Present consequences (vv. 29–34)

From somewhat high-flying eschatology, Paul comes down to earth with three very practical consequences for the present *if there is no resurrection* (v. 29).

First, if there is no resurrection, why do the Corinthians bother to baptize *for the dead* (v. 29)? The clear implication is that there is no point. The number of interpretations of this custom of baptizing *for the dead* are legion. Were converts at Corinth baptized 'with death before their eyes', so recognizing their mortality and the fact that they too would be among the dead shortly? Or were people at Corinth baptized 'out of respect for the dead', in this way expressing hope of some kind of reunion with loved ones who had died before them? Or were they being baptized 'with a view to becoming united with the dead' in the resurrection? The general consensus is that the most likely interpretation involves some kind of 'vicarious' baptism – baptism 'on behalf of' (*hyper*) those who had died. It is just possible that Paul is referring here to a group of Christians who practised baptism on behalf of those who had died believing, but before they had been baptized.[2] If this last suggestion is indeed so, then this goes against Paul's understanding of baptism articulated elsewhere (e.g. Rom. 6:1–10). Alternatively, Paul's mention of this practice may not necessarily give evidence of his approval: he could just have been arguing hypothetically. Frankly, we don't know what Paul had in mind. The only thing that is clear is that this practice would not have made sense if there were no resurrection.

Secondly, if there is no resurrection, why should Paul and anyone

---

[2] Chrysostom, for instance, describes a similar practice of the Marcionites: 'When a catechumen among them dies, they hide a living man under the dead man's bed, approach the dead man, speak with him, and ask if he wishes to receive baptism; then when he makes no answer the man who is hidden underneath says instead of him that he wishes to be baptized, and so they baptize him instead of the departed' (Homily 40 in *1 Cor.* 2).

else bother to 'endanger' themselves for the cause of Christ (vv. 30–32a)? *I die every day* (v. 31). A slight exaggeration, but nevertheless it is manifest that Paul constantly risked his life and in so doing repeatedly faced the reality of death. Paul's life as a Christian missionary was always marked by hardship (see 2 Cor. 6:4–10; 11:23–28). It would appear, however, that his stay in Ephesus, from where he was writing this letter (1 Cor. 16:19), was particularly dangerous. Indeed, Paul goes on to speak of fighting *wild beasts in Ephesus* (v. 32). If he had literally fought with wild beasts, the odds are that he would not have survived. He is in fact employing a metaphor, however, which was later used by Ignatius: 'From Syria to Rome, by land and sea, I am fighting with wild beasts . . . being bound to leopards, by which I mean a detachment of soldiers.'[3] The actual occasion to which Paul is referring may have been the riot recorded by Luke in Acts 19:23–40. If there were no resurrection, then such fighting 'for merely human reasons' (NIV) – or rather 'on a merely human level' (see 1 Cor. 3:3) – would have no point.

Thirdly, if there is no resurrection, why bother to live a moral life? For if there is no resurrection, there will be no day of judgment. To support his argument Paul cites Isaiah 22:13: *'Let us eat and drink, for tomorrow we die'* (v. 32). Similar sentiments were to be found in the pagan world generally. Herodotus, for instance, tells of a custom of the Egyptians: 'In the social meetings among the rich, when the banquet is ended, a servant carries round to the several guests a coffin, in which there is a wooden image of a corpse . . . As he shows it to each guest in turn, the servant says, "Gaze here, and drink and be merry, for when you die, such you will be."'[4] The fact of the matter, however, is that there is a basis for morality, for there will be a resurrection. So, *Do not be misled* (v. 33). Paul cites a line from *Thais*, the lost comedy of Menander: *'Bad company corrupts good character.'* Unfortunately, some of the bad company appears to have been inside the church! Paul, ever the pastor, pleads with the Corinthians: *Come back to your senses as you ought* (v. 34), literally, 'Sober up, as is right' (*eknēpsate dikaiōs*). *Stop sinning* (v. 34): Paul uses the present tense, 'Do not keep on sinning'. Whereas some of the Corinthians thought they knew it all (see, e.g., 1 Cor. 13:2), Paul seeks to shame them (see 1 Cor. 6:5) by declaring that some of them are no better then pagans, for they *are ignorant of God* (v. 34). Belief in the resurrection affects how we live.

---

[3] Ignatius, *Letter to the Romans* 5.1.
[4] Herodotus, *Alcestis* 781–789.

d. Death the last enemy?

Paul was not exaggerating when he described death as the last enemy
(v. 26). Death is final. In one of his soliloquies Job put it this way:

> At least there is hope for a tree:
> If it is cut down, it will sprout again . . .
> But man dies and is laid low;
> he breathes his last and is no more.
>
> (Job 14:7, 10)

Death is the end. In pessimistic vein, Gustav Mahler, in *Das Lied von
der Erde* put to music a Chinese drinking song:

> So strike the lute and drain the glasses,
> These are the things that go together.
> A full goblet of wine at the right time,
> Is worth more than all the kingdoms of the earth.
> Dark is life, dark is death.

In the past, people have sought to defeat death by trying to
preserve themselves. The Egyptian Pharaohs built their pyramids
and arranged to have themselves embalmed, so that their mummies
would last through the ages. But in the end the mighty Pharaohs
ended up just as dead as their poorest subjects buried in the sand.
By and large, we now realize the folly of trying to preserve
ourselves. In the USA, however, there are those who indulge in
cryonics, a procedure that involves freezing a body at the point of
death until a cure is found for whatever caused the death. Today, we
more often seek to defeat death by avoiding all talk of it. Death has
become the great unmentionable. People often spend their last days
surrounded by a great conspiracy of silence, in which both family
and medical staff seek to protect the dying from the harsh reality of
death. The American way of death is increasingly becoming the
Western way of death, where euphemisms turn death into 'negative
patient care outcome', the funeral parlour into a 'turnstile to
eternity', and the cremation oven into a 'slumber chamber'. But
death is a destructive enemy, the greatest 'adulterer', destroying
relationships, tearing apart husband and wife, parent and child,
friends, and lovers. It is a ruthless enemy, cutting down not just the
old, but also the young. Death is not so bad when we have reached
our allotted span of three-score years and ten (Ps. 90:10), but it can
be appallingly cruel when it strikes a little child, or deprives children
of a parent. Death is also a terrifying enemy. Job described it as the
'the king of terrors' (Job 18:14). The psalmist wrote that when the

'terrors of death' assailed him and 'fear and trembling' beset him and 'horror' overwhelmed him (Ps. 55:4–5). The fear of death is in many ways what distinguishes humans from animals. In no way is death something to be made light of.

The good news of the resurrection is that death is a defeated enemy (v. 25). Jesus has risen from the dead, and in rising has broken death's icy grip on humankind. The resurrection of Christ is 'the guarantee that those who sleep in death will also be raised' (v. 20, GNB). The resurrection of Christ is not just another incredible feat to be entered in the *Guinness Book of Records*, something to be admired but not emulated. Jesus is the *firstfruits* – his resurrection is a sign to all the world of a great harvest of life to come. Alternatively, we can liken the resurrection of Christ to a breach in a North Sea dyke – just as, once a hole has been made in the sea defences, the sea comes rushing in, so once a hole has been blown through death's defences, life comes flooding into the world's wide graveyard. *For as in Adam all die, so in Christ all will be made alive* (v. 22). Easter is Adam's Easter in the sense that in Christ, God's representative human being, there is life for all. In the words of Paul to Timothy, Christ 'has destroyed death and has brought life and immortality to light through the gospel' (2 Tim. 1:10). The dream of 'immortality' has in Jesus become real.

But to share in Christ's victory we have to die. We cannot experience the fullness of Christ's victory over death in the here and now. It is only as we ourselves pass through the gates of death that we can truly begin to experience life. In the words of the German theologian Dietrich Bonhoeffer, just before he was martyred for his faith by the Nazis on 8 April 1945: 'This is the end, but for me the beginning of life.'[5] There is nothing automatic, however, about entering into the life of heaven. We do not share in the risen life of Christ as of right. This life is for those who belong to him – to those who are *in Christ* (v. 22). In other words, if we are to experience life in the world to come, then in this world we need to identify ourselves through faith with the Christ who died and rose for us; we need to die to self and to begin to live for Christ (Rom. 6:3–4). Over against the enemy of death, the Christian message is not 'All will now be well' – but rather 'All will now be well for those who share in Christ's victory by putting their trust in the crucified and risen Lord.' Or, in the words with which George Carey concluded his 'millennium message', 'The future has no terrors if we know the person who holds the key to the future.'[6]

[5] E. Robertson, *The Shame and the Sacrifice: The Life of Dietrich Bonhoeffer* (Hodder & Stoughton, 1987).
[6] G. Carey, *Jesus 2000* (HarperCollins, 1999), p. 54.

3. The resurrection of the body (1 Cor. 15:35–58)

But someone may ask, 'How are the dead raised? With what kind of body will they come?' [36]*How foolish! What you sow does not come to life unless it dies.* [37]*When you sow, you do not plant the body that will be, but just a seed, perhaps of wheat or of something else.* [38]*But God gives it a body as he has determined, and to each kind of seed he gives its own body.* [39]*All flesh is not the same: Men have one kind of flesh, animals have another, birds another and fish another.* [40]*There are also heavenly bodies and there are earthly bodies; but the splendour of the heavenly bodies is one kind, and the splendour of the earthly bodies is another.* [41]*The sun has one kind of splendour, the moon another and the stars another; and star differs from star in splendour.*

[42]*So will it be with the resurrection of the dead. The body that is sown is perishable, it is raised imperishable;* [43]*it is sown in dishonour, it is raised in glory; it is sown in weakness, it is raised in power;* [44]*it is sown a natural body, it is raised a spiritual body.*

If there is a natural body, there is also a spiritual body. [45]*So it is written: 'The first man Adam became a living being'; the last Adam, a life-giving spirit.* [46]*The spiritual did not come first, but the natural, and after that the spiritual.* [47]*The first man was of the dust of the earth, the second man from heaven.* [48]*As was the earthly man, so are those who are of the earth; and as is the man from heaven, so also are those who are of heaven.* [49]*And just as we have borne the likeness of the earthly man, so shall we bear the likeness of the man from heaven.*

[50]*I declare to you, brothers, that flesh and blood cannot inherit the kingdom of God, nor does the perishable inherit the imperishable.* [51]*Listen, I tell you a mystery: We will not all sleep, but we will all be changed –* [52]*in a flash, in the twinkling of an eye, at the last trumpet. For the trumpet will sound, the dead will be raised imperishable, and we will be changed.* [53]*For the perishable must clothe itself with the imperishable, and the mortal with immortality.* [54]*When the perishable has been clothed with the imperishable, and the mortal with immortality, then the saying that is written will come true: 'Death has been swallowed up in victory.'*

[55]*'Where, O death, is your victory?*
Where, O death, is your sting?'

[56]*The sting of death is sin, and the power of sin is the law.* [57]*But thanks be to God! He gives us the victory through our Lord Jesus Christ.*

⁵⁸Therefore, my dear brothers, stand firm. Let nothing move you. Always give yourselves fully to the work of the Lord, because you know that your labour in the Lord is not in vain.

Having sought to argue the certainty of the resurrection of the dead, Paul now turns to deal with the resurrection of the body and, in particular, its nature. This final section of 1 Corinthians 15 can be divided into three subsections. First of all, Paul seeks to illustrate the nature of the resurrection of the body by analogy with *seeds* and with various kinds of *bodies* (vv. 35–44); then, again with the nature of the resurrection of the body in mind, he develops the analogy of Christ and Adam (vv. 45–49); he concludes with a third section in which he principally links the victory of Christ with the transformation of the body (vv. 50–58).

a. Analogies of seeds and bodies (vv. 35–44)

The underlying issue is spelt out in verse 35: *How are the dead raised? With what kind of body will they come?* These were no hypothetical questions at Corinth. Strictly speaking, Paul does not write, *But someone may ask*, but rather, 'But someone *will* ask'. To be fair, this was an issue that concerned not just the Corinthians. The Jews themselves were much concerned not just with the issue of the nature of the body. Some Jewish teachers held that the resurrection body will be identical with the mortal earthly body (2 Macc. 14:46); others that the same earthly body would be raised and only later transformed (2 *Baruch* 50:2). Down through the centuries Christians too have been concerned with this issue. They have asked questions such as: what if a Christian dies at sea and his body is eaten by various fishes who then scatter to the seven seas? What if another Christian is eaten by cannibals, so that some of the material of his body becomes the material of their bodies? In more recent times people have asked: what happens to the body of a Christian who is blown to bits by a bomb? Ultimately, the Christian answer must be that if God created the world *ex nihilo*, then in the light of that supreme miracle, everything is possible. To an all-powerful God the resurrection of the body creates no difficulties. Indeed, is this not what Paul is to all intents and purposes stating right at the beginning of his argument when he describes such questions as *foolish* (v. 36)? A fool in the Bible is a person who fails to take God into account (see Ps. 14:1; 53:1; 92:6; Luke 12:16–21). The objection raised is not a sign of ignorance, but rather a sign of a godless attitude. In the words of Jesus, 'with God all things are possible' (Matt. 19:26; Mark 10:27). Paul goes on to answer the questioner through the use of several analogies.

First, the analogy of the seed: *What you sow does not come to life unless it dies. When you sow, you do not plant the body that will be* . . . (vv. 36–37). The analogy of the seed illustrates that one living thing, through death, can have two modes of existence. Unlike Jesus' use of the figure of a seed in John 12:24, Paul is concerned to bring out not the necessity of death, but rather the fact of transformation. Death is not the end; death simply means change. In other words, the resurrection will involve continuity, but also discontinuity. In the words of C. S. Lewis, 'The old field of space, time, matter, and the senses is to be weeded, dug and sown for a new crop. We may be tired of that old field: God is not.'[7] Furthermore, this process of change or transformation is in God's hands. The divine passive (*zōopoietai*) in verse 37 (literally, 'what is sown') is clarified in verse 38: *But God gives it a body . . . to each kind of seed he gives its own body* (v. 38).

Secondly, the analogy of different kinds of bodies, each given by God to enable it to adapt to its particular existence: *All flesh is not the same . . . There are also heavenly bodies and there are earthly bodies* (vv. 39–40). On the one hand, there are different kinds of 'animal' life (humans, beasts, birds and fish); on the other hand, there are different kinds of 'heavenly' bodies (sun, moon and stars). God is not locked into giving his creatures one kind of body. He is a God of infinite creativity and variety.

So will it be with the resurrection of the dead (v. 42). The resurrection will involve transformation into a new kind of body suitable for its new form of existence. In four clauses, each repeating the verbs *it is sown . . . it is raised,* Paul contrasts the old with the new (vv. 42–44). The first three clauses clearly go together and are to be distinguished from one another only with difficulty. First, the new body will be *imperishable* (v. 42), and as such will no longer be characterized by physical decay. Secondly, the new body will be *glorious* (literally, 'raised in glory'), and as such will not be marked by the indignities (*dishonour*) associated with our present existence (v. 43). Thirdly, the new body will be *powerful* (literally, 'raised in power') in contrast with the *weakness* of our present existence (v. 43). Although the distinction between each of these first three clauses is not always certain, the overall thrust is clear. In the resurrection that is to come there will be an end to all the limitations, frustrations and disabilities we experience in this life.

Instead, what *is sown a natural (psychikos) body will be raised a spiritual (pneumatikos) body* (v. 44). The Greek words have no

---

[7] C. S. Lewis, *Miracles*, in *Selected Works of C. S. Lewis* (HarperCollins, 1999), p. 1213.

equivalent terms in English and are therefore difficult to translate. The NIV uses the terms 'natural' and 'spiritual'; the RSV and NRSV 'physical' and 'spiritual' – possibly 'natural' and 'supernatural' are better. Paul is not saying that one body is made up of *psychē* (the Greek word for 'life' or' soul'), and the other of *pneuma* (the Greek word for 'spirit'). The adjectives carry a functional rather than a material sense. The old body is animated by the 'soul', God's life-force in this world, while the other is animated by the Spirit of God, God's life-force particularly in the new resurrection world to come.

b. Analogy of Christ and Adam (vv. 45–49)

In this next analogy Paul links the resurrection with Jesus as being the pattern of the new body. Since in our present life we have borne the *likeness* of the first Adam, 'the earthly man', in the life to come we shall bear the *likeness* of the last Adam, 'the heavenly man'.

So it is written: 'The first man Adam became a living being (psychē)'; the last Adam a life-giving (zōopoioun) spirit (pneuma) (v. 45). The Scripture in question, which underlies the first half of the sentence, is part of the LXX version of Genesis 2:7; the second half of the sentence is not a quotation, but nevertheless reflects the immediately prior clause in Genesis 2:7: 'and [God] breathed into his nostrils the breath of life (*pnoēn zōēs*)'. Here again we have the contrast between the *psychē* of the first Adam, representing the animating power of the present 'natural' form of existence, and the *pneuma* of the last Adam, representing the animating power of the 'supernatural' form of existence to come.

From this exposition of Genesis 2:7 Paul establishes that the *natural* (*psychikon*) precedes the *spiritual* (*pneumatikon*) or 'supernatural' (v. 46): the 'natural' form of existence precedes the 'supernatural' form of existence. The implication is that those Corinthians who believed that they were already experiencing a 'spiritual' or 'supernatural' form of existence were wrong – they were still very much part of this present 'natural' age. This is the point that Paul seems to wish to emphasize: *The first man was of the dust of the earth*, literally, 'a man of earth, made of dust'; *the second man* was *from heaven*, better, 'a man of heaven' (v. 47). The emphasis here appears to be not so much on origin as on destination. Until now *we have borne the likeness* (literally, 'image', *eikōn*) *of the earthly man* (see Gen. 5:3). According to the NIV Paul goes on to state that in the future we shall *bear the likeness of the man from heaven* (literally, 'the heavenly man', *tou epouraniou*) (v. 49). Another and better attested manuscript reading, however, indicates that we have here a subjective: 'let us bear the likeness of the heavenly man'. Paul the theologian is also Paul the ethicist. Paul is concerned for how the Corinthians live. He wants them to prepare for the future in the here and now by patterning their lives on the life of the 'man of heaven'.

From our point of view today, the analogy between Christ and Adam appears highly convoluted. The chief point of relevance for us is that our resurrection is totally dependent on Christ. Furthermore, Christ provides the pattern for the body we shall have in the resurrection.

c. Final victory (vv. 50–58)

Paul now switches tack and returns to the more general theme of transformation: *flesh and blood cannot inherit the kingdom of God, nor does the perishable inherit the imperishable* (v. 50). Some believe that Paul refers in the first instance to the living (*flesh and blood*) and then to those who have died (*the perishable*). Alternatively, both expressions may be synonyms. In any case, the overall thrust is clear: we cannot enter the resurrection life as we are; instead, *we will all be changed* (v. 51). The *mystery*, once hidden but now revealed, is that while not all will *sleep* – some will be alive at the time of the Lord's return – both the living and the dead *will all be changed*. The moment of transformation will be instantaneous: *in a flash* (literally, 'in a moment of time that cannot be divided', *atom ō*), *in the twinkling of an eye* (i.e. 'before an eye can blink') the *trumpet* of the end time (see Is. 27:13; Jer. 51:27; Zech. 9:14) *will sound*, and *the dead will be raised imperishable* (v. 52). For the Christian, here is music to the ears. No wonder this passage formed the basis for one of the most moving passages in Brahms's *German Requiem*. But Paul is not finished. He continues to underline the fact that *we will be changed* (v. 52): *the perishable must clothe itself with the imperishable, and the mortal with immortality* (v. 53). Is Paul just piling synonym upon synonym, or does the first clause refer to the deceased, whose bodies have long since perished, and the second clause to the living, who have yet to exchange their 'mortal' bodies to share in the resurrection? Again, the details are unclear, but there is no doubt concerning Paul's overall point: transformation will be the order of the day.

As the apostle comes towards the end of his argument, he breaks out on a tremendous note of triumph. As he looks to the future he declares, *'Death has been swallowed up in victory'* (v. 54; see 2 Cor. 5:4). The *saying* he here quotes is Isaiah 25:8, which actually reads, 'he will swallow up death for ever'. A subtle change has occurred: *in victory* has replaced 'for ever', a change helped by the fact that in the LXX the former is a common idiom for the latter. Paul has adopted this change because he wishes to highlight the victory that is ours in Christ. Significantly the word *victory* (*nikos*) is found only three times in all of Paul's letters, and these three occurrences are here in 1 Corinthians 15:54–57.

Paul pursues the theme of *victory* as he loosely quotes from Hosea 13:14 (v. 55):

'Where, O death, is your victory?
Where, O death, is your sting'?

Again the Old Testament Scripture has been modified, above all to bring out the note of victory. For whereas the LXX version refers to the 'penalty' of the 'grave', Paul now speaks of the victory of death. These slight changes, however, should not cause us concern. Paul is not grounding his argument in the Old Testament; rather, his argument is grounded in the victory Christ has already gained in his resurrection. The words of Hosea are illustrative rather than foundational. Already the *sting* of death has been removed. This sting (*kentron*) is not some mild irritant, but is like a scorpion's sting (see Rev. 9:10) that results in death. Christ has drawn out the poison, however, by drawing it, as it were, into himself. To use the language of Hebrews, in 'tasting death' he has destroyed 'him who holds the power of death' (see Heb. 2:9, 14). The final 'victory' in which we shall share is therefore not simply limited to the future. Rather, the future has already invaded the present; the beginning of the end has already set in. Death can already be mocked in the here and now as a defeated enemy.

Not only death has been overcome; so too have *sin* and the *law* (v. 56). According to the rabbis, 'The law is the power of God.' For Paul, however, 'sin sprang to life' through the law (see Rom. 7:7–12). Death has had its deadly power (*sting*) precisely because of sin and the law. Sin and the law are the root cause of death. But, *thanks be to God*, sin and death do not have the last word. Christ has dealt with this 'root infection'. The victory is indeed already ours *through our Lord Jesus Christ* (v. 57).

In the light of this victory new meaning and purpose are given to our lives. *Therefore . . . stand firm. Let nothing move you* (see also Col. 1:23). Instead, *Always give yourselves fully to the work of the Lord, because you know that your labour in the Lord is not in vain* (v. 58). Paul concludes the chapter on the same note with which he began: when the risen Christ is the focus of our believing (v. 2) and of our working (v. 58), life is not *in vain*.

d. Life in tomorrow's world

The Christian faith is a resurrection faith. There is life after death. There is a world to come. The Christian hope of life in the world to come, however, is not to be confused with the Greek conception of the immortality of the soul. The Christian hope is altogether different and involves the resurrection of the body. The difference is well illustrated by some words of Oscar Cullmann: 'Belief in the immortality of the soul is not belief in a revolutionary event. Immortality, in fact, is only a negative assertion: the soul does not die, but simply lives on. Resurrection is a positive assertion: the whole man, who has really died, is recalled to life by a new act of creation by God.'[8]

The resurrection of the body is not the same as the 'resuscitation' of a body. 'Bodily' resurrection is not 'physical' resurrection, as *flesh and blood cannot inherit the kingdom of God* (v. 50). Tertullian, therefore, was wrong when he used the sayings of Jesus that 'the very hairs of your head are all numbered' (Luke 12:7) and that 'there will be weeping and gnashing of teeth' (e.g. Matt. 13:50) to prove that both hair and teeth will be present in the resurrection.[9] At the end of time both the living and the dead will be transformed: *we will all be changed* (v. 51). The *natural* order of things will be changed into a *spiritual* or supernatural way of life (v. 44). This resurrection of the body will inevitably be a superior form of existence. The limitations of this present life, with all its indignities and weaknesses, will be left behind; instead, God will raise us to a life of *glory* and of *power* (v. 43). The life to come will not be a pale imitation of this life, but rather the new order of things will be more real and more vibrant. In the life to come we shall not be maimed ghosts tapping out pathetic messages at the behest of mediums. We shall be more alive than ever.

The resurrection of the body expresses continuity. Along with change, there will be continuity. In one sense our bodies experience change already in this life. Biochemists, for instance, inform us that during a seven-year cycle the molecular composition of our bodies is completely changed. In one sense there is no relationship between our bodies as children and our bodies as young people, let alone our bodies as old people. And yet there is continuity. This continuity is expressed through personality. At death, however, our bodies undergo far more radical change. The *seed* of our earthly bodies dissolves. And yet the new life God gives has a relationship with the

---

[8] O. Cullmann, *Immortality of the Soul or Resurrection of the Dead?* (Epworth, 1958).

[9] See Tertullian, *De Resurrectione Carnis* 35.

old. It is a 'fruit' of the old. In spite of all the changes, it is still the same person. In the Bible the body represents the whole person. Whereas the Greeks would say a man or a woman 'has' a body, from a biblical perspective a man or a woman 'is' a body. It is through the body that we communicate personality. Changes to the body, however, do not affect the essential personality. Just as a message is the same whether spoken in words or transmitted by e-mail or flashed in Morse Code, so we shall be the same persons, whatever the 'material' form in which our personalities are expressed.

The resurrection of the body also expresses community. For the body is a way in which we communicate with others. If life in the world to come were to be just a solitary existence, then maybe a 'soul' would have been sufficient. But life in the world to come is life together. True, it will be a new way of living together. There will, for instance, be no exclusive relationships such as we find in marriage (see Luke 20:27–38), but relationships there will be. In principle, therefore, the concept of being reunited with loved ones is perfectly defensible, provided we realize that we shall be together with many others too.

The resurrection of the body is a wonderful hope and is something to be looked forward to. Something of the spirit of the resurrection is expressed by this epitaph on an old tombstone: 'The body of B. Franklin, printer, like the cover of an old book, its contents turned out and stripped of its lettering and gilding, lies here, food for worms. But the work shall not be lost; for it will, as he believed, appear once more in a new and more elegant edition, corrected and improved by the Author.'

e. Life in the world here and now

In the first place, the resurrection provides a pattern for living. Much is made of the way in which the disciples became changed men as a result of encountering the risen Lord. At one moment they were frightened and meeting behind locked doors, the next moment standing up in public and witnessing to the resurrection of Jesus from the dead. But it is not just the disciples of old who became changed people – we too are called to live changed lives. It is not simply our beliefs that change as a result of the resurrection, but also our lifestyle. Our living and not just our dying is encompassed by the little word *Therefore* (v. 58).

We see something of Paul's changed lifestyle in the way in which he addresses the Christians at Corinth: he calls them *my dear brothers* (v. 58), and no doubt 'sisters' too. If the truth be told, these Corinthians scarcely deserved such an epithet. Many of them belonged to the awkward squad. Some had been rooting for Paul – but many others rooting for Peter and for Apollos (1:10–12). As becomes particularly clear in 2 Corinthians, there was an anti-Paul lobby at Corinth, who questioned his integrity, who called him names, and who refused to accept his leadership. Theologically the Corinthians were not very sophisticated – in fact the very reverse. For all their charismatic pretensions, they were more akin to a group of spiritual pygmies (3:1). As far as their lifestyle was concerned, there was still a lot to be desired. In other words, many of the Corinthian Christians were the last people one might ever have expected to be bosom pals of the great apostle. Yet, for all their failings and faults, he addresses them as *my dear brothers* (and sisters). In spite of everything, Paul was prepared to accept them as brothers and sisters in Christ. That acceptance – that love – was a sign of the difference that the risen Christ made to Paul. The resurrection affects the way we live. It affects the way in which we relate to one another.

The resurrection also gives us a new purpose for our working: *your labour in the Lord is not in vain* (v. 58), or as J. B. Phillips put it, 'Nothing you do for him is ever lost or wasted.' In the first instance Paul is probably speaking of the work of the gospel (see, e.g., 16:16). The time and energy God's people devote to the cause of Christ are never wasted. Yes, there are times when we wonder whether the effort has been worthwhile – for we do not always see the fruit of our labours. We have worked hard and long, and now wonder whether it has all been worthwhile. But as Jesus himself reminds us in the parable of the sower, where the seed is sown, there is always a harvest (Mark 4:8, 20). Maybe we shall not see the harvest in our lifetime, but a harvest there will be. As another parable of Jesus reminds us, however, there are times when we are called not simply to sow the seed of the word, but to give our very lives as seed in the service of God: 'unless a grain of wheat falls into the earth and dies, it remains just a single grain; but if it dies, it bears much fruit' (John 12:24, NRSV). In the first instance Jesus was speaking of himself. But the words that follow indicate that he also had his disciples in mind (John 12:25–26a). We are never losers in the service of God – the principle of resurrection applies to us, as well as to Jesus.

The resurrection also gives us a new purpose in the more general world of work. Sometimes Christian people wonder whether it really is worth trying to apply their faith to their life in the world beyond the church: the world of work, that cut-throat world, where dog eats dog, where so many people seem to be out for themselves, where standards of honesty, integrity and industry seem to be in question. Particularly when we see ruthless ambition and unfair practices winning the day, we wonder what practical difference living a Christian lifestyle at work really makes. Are there any rewards for those who are considerate of others, who refuse to compromise, who don't cheat, who don't tell untruths? If this life is the be-all and end-all, then maybe not. But this existence is not all there is. There is a new world coming – where right, and not just might, will triumph, where justice and fairness will prevail, where God will take account of the way in which we have lived, at work, as well as at home (see 2 Cor. 5:10). Nothing we do for God is ever 'in vain'.

4. Resurrection – present and future (2 Cor. 4:7 – 5:10)

But we have this treasure in jars of clay to show that this all-surpassing power is from God and not from us. [8]*We are hard pressed on every side, but not crushed; perplexed, but not in despair;* [9]*persecuted, but not abandoned; struck down, but not destroyed.* [10]*We always carry around in our body the death of Jesus, so that the life of Jesus may also be revealed in our body.* [11]*For we who are alive are always being given over to death for Jesus' sake, so that his life may be revealed in our mortal body.* [12]*So then, death is at work in us, but life is at work in you.*

[13]*It is written: 'I believed; therefore I have spoken.' With that same spirit of faith we also believe and therefore speak,* [14]*because we know that the one who raised the Lord Jesus from the dead will also raise us with Jesus and present us with you in his presence.* [15]*All this is for your benefit, so that the grace that is reaching more and more people may cause thanksgiving to overflow to the glory of God.*

[16]*Therefore we do not lose heart. Though outwardly we are wasting away, yet inwardly we are being renewed day by day.* [17]*For our light and momentary troubles are achieving for us an eternal glory that far outweighs them all.* [18]*So we fix our eyes not on what is seen, but on what is unseen. For what is seen is temporary, but what is unseen is eternal.*

[5:1]*Now we know that if the earthly tent we live in is destroyed, we have a building from God, an eternal house in heaven, not built by human hands.* [2]*Meanwhile we groan, longing to be clothed with our heavenly dwelling,* [3]*because when we are clothed, we will not be found naked.* [4]*For while we are in this tent, we groan and are burdened, because we do not wish to be unclothed but to be clothed with our heavenly dwelling, so that what is mortal may be swallowed up by life.* [5]*Now it is God who has made us for this very purpose and has given us the Spirit as a deposit, guaranteeing what is to come.*

[6]*Therefore we are always confident and know that as long as*

we are at home in the body we are away from the Lord. ⁷We live by faith, not by sight. ⁸We are confident, I say, and would prefer to be away from the body and at home with the Lord. ⁹So we make it our goal to please him, whether we are at home in the body or away from it. ¹⁰For we must all appear before the judgment seat of Christ, that each one may receive what is due to him for the things done while in the body, whether good or bad.

The key to this passage is found in Paul's statement, that God *raised the Lord Jesus from the dead* (2 Cor. 4:14). This is the heart of Christian believing and preaching (4:13; see also Rom. 10:9 and 1 Cor. 15:1–2, 11). This too is the ground of Christian hope. The resurrection of Jesus is the basis of our resurrection: *the one who raised Jesus from the dead will also raise us with him* (4:14; see also Rom. 8:11; 1 Cor. 6:14). The resurrection of Jesus affects not only our future, however, but also our present. In this excerpt from 2 Corinthians the difference Jesus makes to life and to death comes particularly to the fore. For Paul the resurrection of Christ was not simply a doctrine to be believed – it was a power to be experienced, and a hope to inspire.

This passage from 2 Corinthians falls into two sections. The first highlights the difference that the resurrection of Christ makes to the present (4:7–18); the second highlights the difference that the resurrection of Christ makes to the future (5:1–10). Needless to say, the present and the future impinge on each other.

a. Present implications of the resurrection (4:7–18)

In the context of defending himself and the ministry he has received from God, in these next few verses Paul introduces the themes of death and resurrection, of weakness and of power. He writes: *But we have this treasure in jars of clay to show that this all-surpassing power is from God and not from us* (v. 7). The *jars of clay* Paul has in mind are in fact the small pottery oil lamps to be found in any home; while the *treasure* is the light of Jesus shining in the hearts of his people (v. 6). The metaphor is doubly applicable. On the one hand, the cheapness of the clay lamps represents the very ordinariness of those who, in their lives as also in their words, preach the gospel of Jesus Christ; and in turn the ordinariness of the human bearers of the gospel makes a striking contrast with the infinitely precious treasure of the gospel. On the other hand, the fragility of the clay lamps represents the frailty and weakness of those who preach the gospel of Jesus Christ; and in turn their frailty and weakness make a striking contrast with *the all-surpassing power* of

God. It is this latter contrasting parallel that Paul develops. The ministry God has given him reflects both human weakness and divine power; but more than that, his ministry reflects both the weakness of the crucified Christ and the power of the risen Christ. Parallels and contrasts abound!

Paul begins by acknowledging that he, as a bearer of the gospel of light, is in one sense nothing more than a common clay pot. Paul, by contrast with the message he had to proclaim, acknowledges his ordinariness and his weakness. In using this picture, was Paul reflecting the contrast the Jews sometimes made between the Torah and those who taught it? According to a Jewish commentary on Deuteronomy 11:12, 'as it is not possible for wine to be stored in golden or silver vessels, but only in one which is least among the vessels, an earthenware one, so also the words of Torah can be kept only with one who is humble in his own eyes'.[10] Similarly the teaching of a certain Rabbi Jehoshua ben Hanaiah, whose outward appearance was unattractive, was likened to 'glorious wisdom in a repulsive earthen vessel'.[11] Perhaps Paul was also conscious that his opponents criticized him for being an unimpressive figure (see 2 Cor. 10:1, 10).

By contrast, God's power is *all-surpassing* (v. 7), it is 'extraordinary'. No other power can compare with it. God's power has no rivals. This is the power he displayed in the resurrection of Jesus. In the later words of Paul to the Ephesians, God's 'incomparably great power . . . is like the working of his mighty strength, which he exerted in Christ when he raised him from the dead' (Eph. 1:19–20). Yet paradoxically it is also the power displayed in the cross of Christ. As Paul wrote in an earlier letter to the Corinthians, 'we preach Christ crucified . . . the power of God' (1 Cor. 1:23–24). This power, however, was not limited to Christ, but is available to his followers.

The clear implication of verse 7 is that Paul had experienced God's all-surpassing power in his ministry. Contrary to Paul's charismatic opponents at Corinth, however, this power had been displayed not in 'signs, wonders and miracles', but rather in trouble, adversity and difficulty. Paul will express the same thought in 2 Corinthians 12. It is precisely in 'weakness' that Christ's resurrection 'power' is 'made perfect' (12:9–10). Christ's power does not drive out weakness. On the contrary, it comes to full strength only in weakness.

The same thought is probably found in Philippians 3:10, where to 'know Christ' is to experience 'the power of his resurrection and the fellowship of sharing in his sufferings'. The fact that Paul's mention

[10] *Sifre* Deut. 48. [11] *b. Ta'anit* 7a.

of resurrection precedes suffering is a pointer to the fact that this power is experienced in the midst of suffering. In this life, death and resurrection, resurrection and death, are experienced not successively, but simultaneously.

In a series of four contrasts, Paul goes on to show how he not only preached the resurrection but also lived out the resurrection. *We are hard pressed on every side, but not crushed; perplexed, but not in despair; persecuted, but not abandoned; struck down, but not destroyed* (vv. 8–9). In fulfilling his God-given calling as a minister of the gospel, Paul had known all kinds of difficulties (see 2 Cor. 11:23–28). Yet as he reflects on these difficulties, he does not act as a Stoic. For him, ministry is not a matter of 'grinning and bearing it'. Christian ministry is about experiencing the power of Christ in the midst of human weakness. The fact that Paul was not out for the count, but still on his feet, was due to the working of God's resurrection power in his life and ministry.

It is important that we note that the experience of God's resurrection power did not give Paul a trouble-free life; rather, it gave him the inner resources to cope with life's troubles. Earlier in this letter to the Corinthians, Paul had written in similar vein: '*We were under great pressure, far beyond our ability to endure, so that we despaired even of life . . . But this happened that we might not rely on ourselves but on God, who raises the dead. He has delivered us . . . and he will deliver us*' (2 Cor. 1:8–10). God did not deliver Paul by removing all the difficulties, but rather enabled him to live through the difficulties.

Here in 2 Corinthians 4 Paul continues to develop his theme of power in weakness, of resurrection in the midst of death. *We always carry around in our body the death* (more accurately, the 'killing', *nekrōsis*) *of Jesus, so that the life of Jesus may also be revealed in our body* (v. 10). Paul chooses his words carefully here. When he means to speak of death, he uses (on at least forty-five occasions) the common Greek word *thanatos* (e.g. v. 11); but here (and elsewhere only in Rom. 4:19) he uses a different word, *nekrōsis*. *Nekrōsis* describes the process of being put to death. Paul felt that his sufferings were almost 'killing' him. Life for Paul was a constant (*always*) experience of crucifixion. Yet in the midst of the dying, he also experienced the resurrection *life of Jesus*. Paul is not referring here to the resurrection life of Jesus that he would experience in the future (1 Cor. 15:35–49), but rather to the resurrection life of Jesus mediated through his Spirit in this present time (see 1:22; 5:5). Already in the here and now the Spirit's renewing power may be experienced (4:17).

This resurrection *life* of Jesus is 'revealed' (*phanerōthē*) in Paul's *body* (v. 10). It is perhaps significant that the same word is used of the appearance of the risen Christ in John 21:14. This suggests that the power Paul experienced was not a subjective experience known only to him. Others too noticed the difference. For those with eyes to see, the risen Christ was present in the sufferings of the apostle, so that precisely in those moments of weakness Paul was given the strength to cope (2 Cor. 12:9). Whereas others might have become bitter and resentful toward God, Paul for his part was able to be content with his lot (2 Cor. 12:10).

Paul more or less repeats himself in verse 11. There are differences, however. For instance, this time he speaks of *death* (*thanatos*) rather than of 'killing' (*nekrōsis*). He also speaks of the *life* of Jesus being revealed in *our mortal body*. The NIV translation is not quite accurate here, for Paul does not actually speak of the 'body', but rather of the 'flesh'. In Paul's writings the 'flesh' is an expression denoting our human-centred form of existence, our this-worldly, mortal existence. Yet even here the transforming power of Jesus is visible.

For the third time, Paul speaks of *death* being *at work in us* (v. 12), but suddenly a new thought is developed. 'Life' is at work not simply in him and those working with him, but also *in you* (v. 12). Paul's sufferings, which are so intimately related to his work as a minister and preacher of the gospel, are the means of bringing *life* to the Corinthians; they bring benefit to the church at Corinth (v. 15), not least by sparing the church some of the suffering God's people were expected to endure before the final establishment of his kingdom (the so-called messianic woes: see Col. 1:24 and possibly 2 Cor. 1:5).

It is with his work as a preacher of the gospel in mind that Paul quotes from Psalm 116:10: '*I believed; therefore I have spoken*', and adds, *With that same spirit of faith we also believe and therefore speak* (v. 14). Paul's faith in the Lord Jesus impelled him to speak of his Lord (1 Cor. 9:16). Like the psalmist, he finds that speaking is the natural outcome of believing. There is more to the quotation, however, than initially meets the eye. Paul was undoubtedly aware of the context of his quotation. Psalm 116 was written by one who had known great distress. Indeed, the psalmist declared in the very next sentence, 'I am greatly afflicted' (116:10b). In the midst of his distress, however, he had also experienced the Lord's deliverance:

For you, O LORD, have delivered my soul from death,
    my eyes from tears,
    my feet from stumbling.

(Ps. 116:8)

Paul, like the psalmist, had also experienced deliverance from trouble.

It is with that deliverance in mind that Paul continues: *we know that the one who raised the Lord Jesus from the dead will also raise us with Jesus and present us with you in his presence* (v. 14). Here is a difference from the preceding verses. There Paul had written of experiencing the power of the risen Christ in the present. Now he looks forward to the resurrection to come. The resurrection in question is not Christ's, but Paul's and that of other Christians too. Christ has already been raised from the dead. To be raised *with Jesus* is therefore to be raised up as Jesus was raised up. In the resurrection to come, Christians will be made to stand *in his presence*. The resurrection offers hope for the future, as well as power for the present.

In the meantime, Paul's sufferings are *for your benefit*, for as a result God's *grace* reaches *more and more people* (v. 15). The Greek here is difficult. The NIV translation refers to *more and more people* coming to faith. Alternatively, Paul may be speaking not so much of numerical growth as of spiritual growth taking place among the majority of people in the church. Whether more people join the church or grow in grace, however, the result is the same – an increase in *thanksgiving* to God which in turn redounds to his *glory*.

In the light of all this, *we do not lose heart* (v. 16; see 4:1). In the midst of so much trouble and difficulty, it would be understandable for Paul to despair. But this is where the resurrection of Christ again makes such a difference. There is so much to look forward to. This world is not the be-all and end-all. There is a life to come! As Paul looks to the future, he sees three contrasting sets of circumstances.

First, Paul notes the contrast between the 'outward' and 'inner' forms of existence (v. 16). He may here be picking up terms used by his opponents at Corinth. What Paul has in mind is the 'natural' body over against the 'spiritual' or 'supernatural' body of 1 Corinthians 15:44. The former is 'wasting away', not simply physically, but because it belongs to 'this world' which 'in its present form is passing away' (1 Cor. 7:31). The latter, however, is *being renewed* on a daily basis (see Rom. 12:2). There is a new world coming!

Secondly, there is the contrast between the *momentary troubles* and the *eternal glory* to come (v. 17). These *momentary troubles* Paul describes as *light*, but they are only *light* in comparison with the glory that *outweighs them all*. By themselves Paul's troubles were overwhelmingly heavy, so much so that at one stage Paul felt that he was under 'sentence of death' (2 Cor. 1:9). But this is where faith makes all the difference. Christian faith gives a new perspective to this life.

Thirdly, there is a contrast between the *seen* and the *unseen* (v. 18). What is visible is but *temporary* and limited to this world. The things that are *unseen*, however, are eternal. It is this *eternal* dimension that Paul now turns to explore.

b. Future implications of the resurrection (5:1–10)

The resurrection of Jesus not only impacts the present, but also affects the future. The resurrection leads to eternal life. Paul, the tentmaker, likens this present life to one vast transit camp. We live, as it were, in tents. They represent the insecurity and impermanence of the present life. A tent by definition is a temporary structure. However, *we know that if the earthly tent we live in is destroyed, we have a building from God, an eternal house in heaven, not built by human hands* (5:1). Paul is not indulging here in speculative theology; he is expressing something 'known', something certain and common to the Christian tradition. The only thing Paul did not know was whether or not he would be around at the coming of the Lord. If his tent were to be 'dismantled', however, he knew that the Lord had some permanent accommodation for him. Indeed, so certain is Paul of this life to come that he uses the present rather than the future tense: *we have (echomen) a building from God*. Although Paul does not make this explicit, the thought must be that by comparison with what God has to offer, even the most luxurious of living conditions in this world will seem but a slum.

The precise nature of the *house in heaven* which awaits believers is not defined. The most natural interpretation is to see the house as representing the new resurrection body. Another possibility, albeit less likely, would be to view the house in question not as an individual dwelling, but rather as a home – a heavenly temple? – where there is room for many. This would certainly harmonize admirably with the teaching of Jesus in John 14:1–3 (as also with Mark 14:58 and John 2:19), and would perhaps more easily account for Paul's use of the present tense (*we have a building from God*).

In the meantime *we groan* (v. 2). Indeed, two verses later Paul repeats himself and adds a phrase: *we groan and are burdened* (v. 4). The fact is that, as Paul has just demonstrated in the previous chapter, this life is full of trouble (4:8–12). Thank God there is a world to come where we can put behind us the trials and tribulations of this life! The only other occasion when Paul speaks of groaning is in Romans 8, where, in the context of the 'present sufferings' (Rom. 8:18), he writes that not only 'the whole creation' has been 'groaning as in the pains of childbirth' (Rom. 8:22), but also 'we ourselves, who have the firstfruits of the Spirit, groan inwardly as we wait eagerly for our adoption as sons, the redemption of our bodies' (Rom. 8:23). Indeed, in this time of weakness even the Spirit's prayers are characterized by 'groans that words cannot express' (Rom. 8:26).

At this point the metaphor begins to change. From housing, Paul turns to clothing – but not completely, with the result that we end up with a somewhat strange and mixed metaphor. We long *to be clothed with our heavenly dwelling* (v. 2). The building is now something to be worn! Paul here (and in v. 4) uses an unusual doubly compounded verb (*ependysasthai*) to express his hope of putting this new construction 'over and on' his present *tent*. Like any good Jew, he has a horror of being *found naked* (v. 3).

Unfortunately, Paul's use of this metaphor has brought about major differences of interpretation. These can be summarized in two principal points of view. The traditional view is that Paul wishes to avoid having to experience some kind of 'disembodied' intermediate state between his death and the coming of the Lord. Paul would much prefer to be still alive when the Lord returns. The thought of being *naked* (like the bare or 'naked' seed of 1 Cor. 15:37) in this disembodied state is abhorrent. He longs to be able to put on God's new *heavenly dwelling* (v. 4) over his present dwelling. But is this really what Paul had in mind? If so, it seems strange that he makes no reference to such a possibility in 1 Corinthians 15, or indeed anywhere else. An alternative, and indeed preferable, view is that Paul has no thought of any 'intermediate state'; rather, he simply expresses his longing to be clothed with a new 'spiritual' body (see 1 Cor. 15:44). As he does so, however, Paul attacks those 'enthusiastic' Corinthians who denied any future resurrection; as far as he was concerned, a hypothetical 'bodiless' or 'naked' existence held no attractions. That Paul was repudiating a Corinthian desire for 'disembodiment' is indicated by his sentence construction (*not . . . but*), which he often uses to express disagreement with a viewpoint not his own (e.g. 1 Cor. 4:9; 6:13; 2 Cor. 10:4).

For Paul, therefore, there is no gap between death and the resurrection. In terms reminiscent of 1 Corinthians 15:54, he writes that at death *what is mortal* will be *swallowed up by life* (v. 4). The term *life* is a pointer to the fact that the unseen reality that lies beyond death is not some shadowy existence, but life in a new dimension – life that makes our present state appear to be mere existence by comparison. In terms of this imagery, it is not just the seriously ill who may lack quality of life – it is all of us. One day those who are Christ's will really live.

A sign of the new life that *God . . . has made us for* is the presence of the Holy Spirit in our hearts, *guaranteeing what is to come* (v. 5).

Here, as in 2 Corinthians 1:22 and Ephesians 1:14 (see also Rom. 8:23), the Holy Spirit is likened to a down payment or 'deposit' (*arrabōn*). In modern Greek the same word is used of an engagement ring, the promise of so much more to come. Similarly the Spirit, who belongs to the era of resurrection and new creation, is a promise of God's salvation, which will be fully experienced only in the kingdom of God.

Because of the gift of the Holy Spirit, Paul can write, *Therefore we are always confident* (v. 6; see also 5:8; 7:16; 10:1–2). Paul is able to face up to the prospect of death with boldness. He does not fear the dissolution of this present body, because he knows that he will not be *naked*; God will instead supply a replacement that will be greatly superior.

Paul turns to use another metaphor, that of going home. We *know that as long as we are at home in the body we are away from the Lord* (v. 6). In one sense Paul has never been separated from the Lord. His life as a Christian is lived 'in Christ'. Yet full fellowship with the Lord will be achieved only when we see him 'face to face' (1 Cor. 13:12). In the meantime, we *live by faith, not by sight* (v. 7). The underlying metaphor is that of an ongoing pilgrimage. Literally, Paul writes, 'we are walking by faith'. The life of faith is a way of faith (see Acts 9:2; etc.)

Once more Paul expresses his 'confidence' in the God of resurrection. We *... would prefer to be away from the body and at home with the Lord* (v. 8). Significantly there is no reference to any intermediate state, because that possibility does not cross Paul's mind. Certainly, from Paul's point of view, there would have been nothing to have been gained from a 'sleep of the soul'. Paul's desire rather is to be *at home with the Lord*. As he writes later to the Philippians, to 'be with Christ . . . is better by far' (Phil. 1:23). The implication in both 2 Corinthians 5:8 and Philippians 1:23 is that Paul expects to be consciously 'with Christ' at the moment of death. Death for Paul means heaven now. This equation of the moment of death with entry into heaven may appear to contradict Paul's teaching on the resurrection on the last day (see, e.g., 1 Cor. 15:51–54). There is no necessary contradiction however. For although we mortals live within a world bounded by time, life within heaven is beyond time. From the perspective of eternity, therefore, our individual deaths and the resurrection on the last day may well be collapsed into a single 'moment'.

Paul's goal – both in this life and the life to come – is *to please* his Lord (v. 9), not least because there will be a day when *we must all appear before the judgment seat of Christ* (v. 10; see also Rom. 2:16; 14:10, 12). The thought that his future was secure did not lull

Paul into any false sense of security. Because he knew that death was not the end, he was determined to be all the more obedient. Although our eternal destiny depends on our response to God's love in Christ, that does not save even Christians from the day when all will be exposed to God's searching light. In his earlier letter to the Corinthians, for instance, Paul had talked about the 'fire' of judgment testing 'the quality of each man's work'; on that day our apparent achievements may prove worthless, although even those of us who have built poorly on Christ will be saved, albeit with the smell of fire upon us (1 Cor. 3:10–15).

c. Resurrection power

The greatest demonstration of power is neither the Niagara Falls nor the nuclear bomb, but rather the resurrection of Jesus from the dead. The resurrection of Jesus puts every other achievement in the shade – God's power is *all-surpassing* (4:7). The fact is that in spite of all the efforts of medical science, we have not been able to defeat death. We may be able to develop life in a test tube, but we can only extend life by a few years, and even then the quality is all too lacking. The fact is that death is inevitable. In the words of Benjamin Franklin, 'in this world nothing can be said to be certain, except death and taxes'. But in raising Jesus from the dead, God has done what we could never do – he has defeated death. What makes this 'feat' even more powerful is that even at a distance of almost two millennia we too can experience that power in our lives. For the God *who raised the Lord Jesus from the dead will also raise us with Jesus* (4:14).

Even more 'extra-ordinary' is that we don't have to wait until we die before we can experience God's resurrection power in our lives. Already in the here and now God is waiting to break into our lives. We don't have to be special people to experience God's power. God specializes in working in the lives of weak and ordinary people, who feel that not only do they have feet of clay, but clay characterizes all they do and are. We don't have to be supermen or superwomen for God to use us. Where faith expresses itself in a desire and willingness to serve, God takes what we offer and by his all-surpassing power transforms it for his glory (4:15).

The fact is that God is in the business of resurrection – and resurrection involves transformation. Because God is in the business of resurrection and transformation, he is happy to deal with the weak and the ordinary. Indeed, God works in the lives only of weak and ordinary people. The strong and the powerful rule themselves out from God's attention (see 2 Cor. 12:9–10). The details of our lives may differ from those of Paul's. Yet many of us know what it is to feel *hard pressed, perplexed* and *struck down*; there may even be times when, because we have had the courage to live by our convictions, we have felt *persecuted*. Life – at home or at work or indeed in the church – can be tough. The good news, however, is that when we feel most 'dead', God can bring life. For the resurrection is not just a doctrine to be believed, but a power to be experienced. The risen Lord Jesus can be relied upon as an ongoing resource in the here and now. God doesn't promise to deliver us once and for all from the troubles of life – for that, we may have to wait until death itself. He does, however, promise that when we feel as if we are *given over to death*, the *life of Jesus* will break through (4:10), even in all-too-human, 'flesh'-centred people like us (4:11). There are no limits to what God, in his resurrection power, can do.

d. Facing death

However much we watch our cholesterol level, however hard we may try to powder over the wrinkles, we must ultimately face death. Death always turns up trumps! In the words of the psalmist,

> The length of our days is seventy years –
> or eighty, if we have the strength.
>
> (Ps. 90:10)

But that is it! What then? What happens at death? For men and women without faith, there is no hope of life beyond the grave – death is the end. It is oblivion. It is curtains. As Shakespeare's Claudio says, it is 'to die, and go we know not where; to lie in cold obstruction and to rot'.[12] But for us who believe that on the third day God raised Jesus from the dead, there is hope. Death is but the gateway into the very presence of God. Death issues in life. Death leads to security, to wholeness, and to home. This is the confidence of Paul as outlined in 2 Corinthians 5.

First, death leads to security. *Now we know that if the earthly tent we live in is destroyed, we have a building from God, an eternal house in heaven, not built by human hands* (5:1). Paul did not just hope; he was not just fairly certain; he was sure that at death a permanent home awaits those who have put their trust in the Lord Jesus Christ. His only uncertainty was whether or not the Lord might return before he died. What is certain, however, is that God will rebuild our lives in a totally secure and permanent fashion.

Secondly, death leads to wholeness. One of the things we dread

---

[12] W. Shakespeare, *Measure for Measure*, III.i.

about death is that it seems to diminish us. Even the process that leads to death is often one of shrinkage. We lose weight; we become bent over; our skin and flesh seem to shrivel; our hair begins to drop out, as do our teeth. Virtually every bodily function slackens in its efficiency. In the face of such reduction it is a struggle to cling to full selfhood; our egos wane to the point where they scarcely cast a shadow. We are no longer what we were. As we watch our human tent begin to fray and unravel, and finally to split at the seams, we feel that our personhood is seeping out and running away. 'Nakedness' is what we fear; we worry that we shall be embarrassingly unclothed. That is, we fear being incomplete, not whole, lacking in some essentials of personality. But there is no need to have that fear. Death will lead to wholeness. We shall not be *naked* (5:3), for God will clothe us with a new body.

Thirdly, death leads to home. From housing and clothing Paul now turns to introduce a third image – the image of being *at home with the Lord* (5:8). It has been said that going home means going home not to a place, but to a person. What is true of human families is even more true when we go home to the Lord. Whatever heaven may be like, the centre of it all will be the Lord himself. We shall be at home with the Lord, and with all who love him, for ever. To die is not to go into the great unknown; rather, it is to return home to God. And nothing can better that.

5. The resurrection life (Col. 3:1–4)

Since, then, you have been raised with Christ, set your hearts on things above, where Christ is seated at the right hand of God. ²Set your minds on things above, not on earthly things. ³For you died, and your life is now hidden with Christ in God. ⁴When Christ, who is your life, appears, then you also will appear with him in glory.

For the Christian, life in the here and now is lived in the light and power of the resurrection of Jesus. The resurrection does not simply give hope for the future; it transforms the way in which we live in the present.

In these four verses Paul works out the theological implications of Christian baptism: *you died* (v. 3); *you have been raised with Christ* (v. 1). For Paul Christian baptism involves the identification of the believer with the Lord who died and rose for us. We were 'buried with him in baptism and raised with him through [our] faith in the power of God, who raised him from the dead' (Col. 2:12). The picture here is not of a bath in which sins are ritually washed away, but rather of a watery grave, in which the believer is buried with Christ, only then to rise to a new life with Christ. A similar picture is found in Romans 6:4: 'We were . . . buried with him through baptism into death in order that, just as Christ was raised from the dead through the glory of the Father, we too may live a new life.' For Paul, baptism marks the end of the old life and the beginning of a new life in Christ. This new life inevitably involves a new lifestyle. There is a difference in emphasis, however, between the two letters. For whereas in both Romans 6 and Colossians 2–3, Paul works out the ethical implications of what it means to die with Christ, it is only in Colossians 3 that Paul draws out the ethical implications of what it means to rise with Christ. Colossians 3:1–4 is in fact a call to embrace the implications of the resurrection in daily living.

The use of tenses in this passage is highly significant. When Paul refers to baptism, he uses the simple past (the Greek aorist): *You have been raised with Christ* (v. 1), *you died* (v. 3; see 2:20). The Greek indicates a one-off act in the past. Although conversion may often be a drawn-out process, the public commitment to Christ in the waters of baptism takes place at a particular moment of time. At that moment a death takes place. The links with the old way of living are – in principle at least – severed. In identifying ourselves with the Christ who died and rose for us, we declare our resolve to die to self and to live for Christ alone. . . . *your life is now hidden with Christ in God* (v. 3). Here Paul uses a Greek perfect (*kekryptai*) which describes the ongoing effects of this past event: 'your life has been hidden and remains hidden with Christ'. The origins of this imagery are uncertain. Paul may be alluding, however, to the pagan idea that in death we are 'hidden' in the earth. But whereas, in death, unbelievers are dead and gone for ever, Christians, in dying with Christ, are but entrusting their lives to God's safe keeping. On the day of Christ's appearing, the secret will be out for all to see: *you also will appear with him in glory* (v. 4). But that moment of revelation remains for the future. In the meantime we are called to live out the life of Christ in the here and now.

Paul's use of the present imperative is of particular interest: *set your hearts on things above, where Christ is seated at the right hand of God* (v. 1); *set your minds on things above, not on earthly things* (v. 2). The use of the present tense indicates that this focus on the heavenly life involves no simple one-off act, but rather calls for a lifetime's striving. The present imperative speaks of a continual effort: 'keep on setting your hearts on things above . . . keep on setting your minds on things above'. There is nothing magical or automatic about the effects of baptism. Baptism is a spiritual event that must be constantly affirmed and worked out in our lives. As Paul makes clear elsewhere in his letters, salvation can never be limited to one tense; rather, it involves the past, present and future: we have been saved, we are being saved, and we shall be saved. Our salvation may be a gift of God's grace, but we also have to work out our salvation (see Phil. 2:12–13). Or, to put it another way, we have to work at becoming what by God's grace we already are.

There is little difference between the two verbs Paul uses to urge his readers to live out the resurrection life that is theirs in Christ. The first imperative, translated in the NIV as 'set your hearts on', is derived from a verb (*zēteō*) which has the general meaning of to 'seek' (so NRSV). It is, for example, found in Matthew 6:33: 'But seek first his kingdom and his righteousness' (see also Rom. 2:7; 1 Cor. 10:24), and refers to the orientation of a person's will. Significantly, the phrase *things above* is qualified by the additional clause *where Christ is seated at the right hand of God.* That is, Christ is to reign not only in heaven above, but also in our lives below. He is to be the head of the body (1:18) as well as the head over every power and authority (2:10). To seek the things above is to be focusing supremely on Christ's concerns rather than on our own selfish interests, to allow Jesus to be Lord of our lives, to live out lives 'worthy of the Lord' (1:10). In practical terms, this means that in our life together we are called to live holy lives marked by compassion, kindness, humility, gentleness and patience (3:12). Where forgiveness is exercised (3:13) and love is displayed (3:14), there the peace of Christ rules (3:15) and the word of Christ dwells (3:16).

Set your minds on things above, not on earthly things (v. 2). Here Paul is essentially repeating himself. To set one's mind (*phroneō*) on things above is to adopt the attitude (*phroneite*) of Christ Jesus (Phil. 2:5), which resulted in a lifetime of humble service. In other words, Paul is calling not so much for an act of the intellect as for a movement of the will surrendered to the service of Christ. Indeed, there was a related Greek phrase (*ta tinos phroneō*), which means to 'take someone's side', to 'espouse someone's cause'. To be 'heavenly minded', therefore, has nothing to do with mysticism, but rather everything to do with living.

The opposite of being 'heavenly minded' – setting one's mind *on earthly things* – is spelt out in the verses that immediately follow. It is to live a life characterized by sexual immorality, impurity, lust, evil desires and greed (v. 5). It is to engage in anger, rage, malice, slander and filthy language (v. 6) as also to fail to be honest with one another (v. 9).

Our new life in Christ is to lead to a new lifestyle. But if this is to happen, then an ongoing act of the will must be involved. To live Christlike lives we must actively rid ourselves of the old self and its practices (3:9). At first sight this new lifestyle appears to be very much a matter of human effort and achievement. Yet the truth is that the resurrection life is not a self-improved life; it is a life lived out in the power of the risen Christ. This comes to particular expression in the opening words of this third chapter: *Since, then, you have been raised with Christ* (v. 1). The passive mood is a reminder that God is at work – he it is who has raised us from death to life. Through our faith his power is at work in our lives (2:12). Similarly, a little later, Paul speaks of Christians having put on 'the new self, which is being renewed in knowledge in the image of its Creator' (3:10). Here again a divine passive is used, to indicate that this is God's doing. The changes in our lives are not self-contrived, but rather enabled and brought about by God himself. True, we have to play our part. We have to set our hearts and minds on the things above. But this aligning of our wills with the things of the risen Christ is consequent upon the work of God in our lives. By God's grace we have been made capable of doing his will.

The fact is that in Christian baptism we do not just resolve to die to self and live for Christ. There in the waters of baptism we become one with Christ. We have become 'united with him in his resurrection' (Rom. 6:5). This is not just a future promise. Already in the here and now we share in the life of Christ. Indeed, here in Colossians Paul goes so far as to describe the risen Christ as *your life* (v. 4). As Paul tells the Philippians, for him 'to live is Christ' (Phil. 1:21; see also Rom. 8:2, 10; 2 Cor. 4:10; Gal. 2:19–20). Life in its deepest sense is to be found not in us, but in Christ. However, this present experience of Christ has yet to be fully consummated – our resurrection has not already taken place (see 2 Tim. 2:18). The future has yet to break into our lives fully. For now, we have only a foretaste of the things to come. It is only on the day of Christ's appearing that we shall truly be 'with him' (see Phil. 1:23: also 1 Thess. 4:17; 2 Cor. 4:14; 13:4).

Furthermore, on that day we *will appear with him in glory* (3:4). The NIV translation here is not helpful. In the first place, it does not bring out the contrast with the previous verse. Our life, *now hidden with Christ*, 'will be revealed' (*phanerōthēsesthe*). On that day not only will Christ be revealed to be the Son of God; we too will be revealed as the children of God (see Rom. 8:19). This day of revelation will therefore be a day of vindication. Then the rightness of our decision to follow Jesus will be seen by all; then our baptismal confession of Jesus as Lord will be vindicated. Secondly, the NIV translation fails to do justice to the passive mood, 'When Christ is revealed . . . we shall be revealed.' This day of revelation will be God's doing. The God who raised Jesus from the dead, and whose power has already been at work in our lives (see Col. 2:12), will on that day complete his work of resurrection: then the 'hope of glory' (1:27) will be fully realized.

a. Baptism and the resurrection

For Paul Christian baptism is the gateway into the resurrection life. Baptism opens up the three tenses of resurrection life.

First, the past tense: the funeral is over! The river, pool or baptistery in which a believer is baptized is likened to an aquatic graveyard (2:12; see Rom. 6:4), in which believers are buried with Christ, only then to rise to a new life with him. This 'death and resurrection' experience has ethical implications too. For there in the waters of baptism we say a final goodbye to the world's way of living and adopt a new way of living – Christ's. All this is in mind when Paul writes, *you died* (3:3); *you have been raised with Christ* (3:1). In New Testament terms baptism marks the end of the conversion process and the entrance into a new life lived in the light and power of the resurrection: 'the old has gone, the new has come!' (2 Cor. 5:17). Resurrection from this perspective is a past experience.

Secondly, the present tense: become what you are! The resurrection is not simply a past experience; it is also a present experience. For as we share in the resurrection of Jesus, we discover that it transforms the way in which we live in the here and now. Our new life in Christ leads to a new lifestyle. Yet if the resurrection is to be a present experience, we must continually work out its implications in our lives. We must constantly maintain our focus *on things above, not on earthly things* (v. 2). Negatively, this means we have to turn our back on our old way of living (v. 8). In the words of the old Church of England catechism, we have to renounce 'the devil and all his works, the pomps and vanity of this wicked world, and all the sinful lusts of the flesh', and to do so not just once, at the time of our baptism, but daily as we seek to walk with Christ. Positively, this means we have to strive to make Jesus Lord of our lives. Indeed, our lives will be shaped by the risen Christ only as, on a daily basis, we work out our baptismal vows of love and loyalty to our Lord.

Thirdly, the future tense: glory has yet to come! We have yet to share in the resurrection life of Christ in all its fullness. Our lives, for the moment still *hidden with Christ in God* (v. 3), appear to be out of step with the world. But, *When Christ . . . appears* (v. 4) then the truth will out and we shall be seen to be marching to the one tune that counts, namely God's tune. On that day the future will fully break into our lives. On that day our hope in Christ will be fully realized and we shall be *with him in glory* (v. 4). What a wonderful day that will be!

6. The resurrection hope (1 Thess. 4:13–18)

Brothers, we do not want you to be ignorant about those who fall asleep, or to grieve like the rest of men, who have no hope. [14]*We believe that Jesus died and rose again and so we believe that God will bring with Jesus those who have fallen asleep in him.* [15]*According to the Lord's own word, we tell you that we who are still alive, who are left till the coming of the Lord, will certainly not precede those who have fallen asleep.* [16]*For the Lord himself will come down from heaven, with a loud command, with the voice of the archangel and with the trumpet call of God, and the dead in Christ will rise first.* [17]*After that, we who are still alive and are left will be caught up together with them in the clouds to meet the Lord in the air. And so we will be with the Lord for ever.* [18]*Therefore encourage each other with these words.*

It would appear that in his brief stay at Thessalonica Paul had led the new church there to believe that Jesus would be returning very soon to usher in God's final kingdom and to welcome his people into his presence. In the few months that had elapsed since Paul's visit, however, not only had Jesus not returned, but also some of the new Christians at Thessalonica had died. These deaths had come as a great shock to many in the church, and had caused them to wonder what the future held for their loved ones. In response to their doubts and concerns, Paul wrote to reassure his new converts. In particular, here in 1 Thessalonians 4:13–18 he sought to point out to them the tremendous future that awaits those who have put their faith in Christ.

Paul tackles the issue head-on: *we do not want you to be ignorant about those who fall asleep* (v. 13). In talking about death here, he uses a euphemism found elsewhere in the New Testament (see John 11:11–13; Acts 7:60; 13:36; 1 Cor. 7:39; 11:30; 15:20). It is tempting to assume that the very euphemism is a pointer to resurrection hope. Certainly, from a Christian perspective, death is as natural as sleeping. Just as sleep holds no terror for anyone, neither need death hold any terror for those who believe – for one day we shall wake up to a new life lived in God's nearer presence. It is unlikely, however, that Paul was wanting to make such a theological point. The fact is that this euphemism is not peculiar to the Christian faith, and is found both in the Old Testament (e.g. Gen. 47:30; Deut.

31:16; 1 Kgs. 2:10; 22:40) and in the ancient world as a whole. Far from having a positive connotation, it could in fact have a negative thrust. In contemporary paganism, death was viewed as a sleep from which there would be no awaking. The Greek playwright Aeschylus, for instance, refers to death as 'one unending night of sleep'.[13] Similarly the Roman poet Catullus wrote, 'The sun can set and rise again, but once our brief light sets, there is one unending night to be slept through.'[14] Here in 1 Thessalonians 4, however, there appears to be no such negative connotations. Paul is using the euphemism in a neutral fashion.

Although some Greek philosophers, such as Plato, taught a belief in the afterlife (a belief also found in some of the mystery religions of Paul's day), these beliefs were lacking in substance and amounted to little more than viewing the life to come as a poor reflection of the present. Furthermore, these beliefs were not widespread. For unbelievers in general (the rest), the future held no hope (v. 13; see Eph. 2:12). According to Theocritus, 'hopes are for the living; the dead are without hope'.[15]

The hopelessness experienced by the pagan world in the face of death is well expressed in a letter of condolence dating from the second century AD, written by an Egyptian lady named Irene to a couple whose son had just died. She had suffered a similar bereavement. 'I sorrowed and wept over your dear departed one as I wept over Didymas [her husband? her son?] . . . but really, there is nothing one can do in the face of such things. So, please comfort each other.'[16] For Irene, as indeed for non-Christians in general, death held within it no silver lining, for all hope of an afterlife was missing. This sense of hopelessness also comes to expression in a letter of Plutarch to a friend whose son has died: there he urges reason as the best cure of grief, in recognition of the fact that all people are mortal.[17] Seneca, in one of his letters, similarly appeals to reason, and scolds a friend for his unseemly display of excessive grief: 'You are like a woman in the way you take your son's death.'[18] In the ancient world there was little more that could be done in the face of death than maintaining, as it were, a stiff upper lip.

Attitudes have not changed much. John Diamond, for instance, an agnostic Jewish journalist, has written an honest but witty account of his encounter with terminal cancer, underneath which is

---

[13] Aeschylus, *Eumenides* 651.
[14] Catullus 5.4–6.
[15] Theocritus, *Idyll* 4.42.
[16] *Oxyrhynchus Papyri* 115.
[17] Plutarch, *Letter to Apollonius* 103F–104A.
[18] Seneca, *Epistle* 99.2.

a deep sense of sadness. The final sentence of his account is about the purchase of a dog: 'A dog is a happy thing, and it will be happy for me for whatever time I've got left and as happy as things can be for the family when I am gone.'[19]

Against this sense of hopelessness Paul exhorts his readers not *to grieve like the rest of men, who have no hope* (v. 13). When Paul's pagan contemporaries grieved, they grieved at the fact that death was the end – their loved ones had been cut off from the land of the living and from all the delights that life holds. Christians, who are inspired 'by hope in our Lord Jesus Christ' (1:3; see 2:19), may mourn for themselves and their own sense of personal loss (see Rom. 12:15; 1 Cor. 12:26), but they do not need to mourn over those who have died in Christ. When Roy Castle, the British entertainer, died on 2 September 1994, his widow, Fiona was able to say to her friends, 'No flowers, no fuss, no mourning, just lots of joy!'

The basis of Christian hope is, of course, the resurrection of Jesus. Using a form of words probably derived from an earlier Christian creed, Paul states, *We believe that Jesus died and rose again* (v. 14). Significantly, Paul never speaks of Jesus as 'sleeping' in death: *Jesus died* (see also 5:10). The stark truth of that statement underlines the dreadful reality of the death of Jesus, who, when he died, endured the full horror of the wages of sin (Rom. 6:23); it also underlines the mighty miracle of the resurrection.

The corollary of the death and resurrection of Jesus is *that God will bring with Jesus those who have fallen asleep in him* (v. 14). The NIV does not perhaps do justice to one particular nuance of the Greek text. Literally, Paul writes of those who have fallen asleep 'through' (*dia*) Jesus. The unusual use of this preposition suggests that for those who have died trusting in Jesus, Jesus becomes the bridge between their death and eventual resurrection. The resurrection of those who have died in Christ, however, is implicit rather than explicit here, for Paul's focus is on the return of Christ rather than just on the resurrection. Nevertheless, the bringing of the dead with Jesus presupposes the resurrection of the dead.

At this point the apostle launches into the fullest description of Christ's return in the New Testament, a description *According to the Lord's own word* (v. 15). This statement, however, creates difficulties, for there is no known word of Jesus that corresponds exactly to what we have here in 1 Thessalonians 4. The nearest parallel is found in Matthew 24:31: 'And he will send his angels with a loud trumpet call, and they will gather his elect from the four winds, from one end of the heavens to the other.' Because there is no closer parallel, some

---

[19] J. Diamond, *C: Because Cowards Get Cancer Too* (Vermillion, 1998), p. 256.

have wondered whether Paul is citing a saying of Jesus not preserved in the four canonical Gospels. Others have suggested that Paul is citing a Christian 'prophecy' uttered in the name of the risen Lord (see, e.g., Rev. 16:15). Alternatively, rather than alluding to a particular text, Paul may simply be summing up the teaching of Jesus found in the Gospels relating to the return of Christ (see especially Matt. 24:29–31, 40–41) and applying it to the present situation.

As Paul looks ahead to the Lord's return, he distinguishes between two groups: *those who have fallen asleep* and those *who are left* (v. 15). The clear impression is that at this stage Paul anticipates belonging to the latter group, for twice he writes of *we who are still alive* (vv. 15, 17), whereas in his later writings he reckons with the possibility, if not the likelihood, of his own death (1 Cor. 6:14; 2 Cor. 4:14; Phil. 1:20). We should not make too much, however, of this apparent change of emphasis. For, like Jesus himself, Paul refused to speculate about the timing of the end (5:1). Paul's concern was with the fact of Christ's coming, and not 'whether we are awake or asleep' (5:10).

When the Lord returns, *we who are still alive . . . will certainly not* (an emphatic double negative is used – *ou mē) precede those who have fallen asleep* (v. 15). It would appear that some at Thessalonica feared that their loved ones who had died in Christ would be at a disadvantage. A similar idea current in Judaism was that those who were alive at the end of the world would do better than those who were dead (see, e.g., Dan. 12:12: also *Psalms of Solomon.* 17:50; 2 Esdras 13:24). By contrast, Paul stresses that the dead in Christ will not miss out on anything.

On the great day of resurrection *the Lord himself will come down from heaven, with a loud command, with the voice of the archangel, and with the trumpet call of God* (v. 16). Although there is no direct quotation from the Gospels, there are a number of echoes of the words of Jesus. For instance, the descent of the Lord recalls Jesus' description of the appearing of the Son of Man: 'They will see the Son of Man coming on the clouds of the sky, with power and great glory' (see Matt. 24:30; Mark 13:26; Luke 17:24). Similarly in Matthew 24:31; and Mark 13:27 (see also Mark 8:38; Luke 9:26), 'angels' – as distinct from an 'archangel' (to which Jude 9 is the only reference in the Bible) – are associated with the coming of the Son of Man. There may well be a parallel to the 'loud command' of John 5:25, where Jesus declares that 'the dead will hear the voice of the son of God and those who hear will live'. 'The trumpet call of God', a frequent feature of Old Testament theophanies (e.g. Exod. 19:16; Is. 27:13; Joel 2:1; Zech. 9:14), is found in Matthew 24:31: 'And he will send his angels with a loud trumpet call' (see also 1 Cor. 15:52; Rev. 11:15).

It is a moot point whether or not we should distinguish the loud command from the voice of the archangel and the trumpet call. Probably they are just three different ways of expressing the same thought. The loud command is likened to the voice of an archangel (the lack of the definite article in the original Greek indicates that no particular archangel is in mind) and to the sound of a trumpet. Needless to say, the details of these events are not to be pressed. Ultimately these events defy description. What we have here is not so much a detailed programme as an artist's impression. Yet underlying the pictures is an essential truth. Christ is coming again in triumph. With an irresistible authority the Lord will rouse those who are sleeping, *and the dead in Christ will rise first* (v. 16). Far from missing out, those who have died *in Christ* will be the first to experience his glory.

Then *we who are still alive and are left will be caught up together with them in the clouds to meet the Lord in the air* (v. 17). The coming of the Lord is reminiscent of the words of Jesus regarding the coming of the Son of Man, who comes 'on the clouds' (see Matt. 24:30; Mark 13:16; also Dan. 7:13). Clouds are a regular feature of biblical theophanies, and are always a symbol of the divine glory (see Exod. 19:16; 24:15–18; 40:34; 1 Kgs. 8:10–11). The Lord comes in glory.

This coming of the Lord is marked by a 'reunion': when the dead and the living are reunited in Christ. *We . . . will be . . . together* (v. 17). What a wonderful thought this must have been for the Thessalonians! Heaven is a place of togetherness. Death may separate us from our loved ones, but in Christ we are brought together.

This coming of the Lord in glory is also marked by an event traditionally known as the 'rapture'. The word 'rapture' is derived from the Latin equivalent (*rapere*) of the Greek verb (*harpazō*), which often implies violent action (see Acts 8:39; 23:10; Rev. 12:5). In certain evangelical circles this word came to be used of a secret 'rapture' of the saints, which was supposed to precede Christ's one-thousand-year reign. The basis for this belief was found in combining 1 Thessalonians 4:17 with Matthew 24:40: 'Two men will be in the field; one will be taken and the other left.' However, here in 1 Thessalonians 4 there is nothing secret about the rapture – nor is there any hint of an intervening millennium. Rather, the living are described as *caught up . . . in the clouds*, that is, they are 'seized' or 'snatched away' by the irresistible power of God, *to meet the Lord in the air*. They too share in the Lord's victory. For no longer is *the air* the place where the powers of evil hold sway (see Eph. 2:2) – it is now the place where Jesus is acknowledged as Lord of all.

Traditionally this verse has been interpreted as speaking of the saints marching heavenwards. The opposite, however, may be the case. Paul may be thinking of the Christians going out to meet King Jesus and then accompanying him back to earth. For the Greek phrase (*eis apantēsin tou kyriou*) was used in Hellenistic times to describe the action of the leading citizens of a town who would go out to meet a visiting dignitary with a view to then escorting him back to their city. Indeed, the same phrase is found in Acts 28:15, where Luke describes how Paul was met by the Roman Christians some miles from the city. It is also found in Matthew 25:6, where the bridal party goes out to meet the bridegroom in order to escort him back to the wedding banquet. Although it is true that this interpretation is not demanded by the text, it accords with Paul's expectation of a 'creation . . . liberated from its bondage to decay' (Rom. 8:21). The fact is that Paul and the early church in general (see 2 Pet. 3:13; Rev. 21:1, 10) looked forward to a new order of life in a new world of God's making.

And so we will be with the Lord for ever (v. 17). This is the climax of Paul's vision of the future, and it contains the heart of the Christian hope. For what matters ultimately is not the place of meeting, but rather the being *with the Lord for ever* (see Phil. 1:23). As Paul makes clear toward the end of his letter, to be with the Lord is to experience salvation from the wrath of God (5:9–10). There, in the presence of the Lord, we are beyond the reach of evil, pain and suffering. It is this new quality of life – life with God – that makes the thought of its being *for ever* so desirable.

Therefore encourage each other with these words (v. 18; see also 5:13). Literally, 'keep on encouraging' one another, for a present imperative is used. Significantly these words are not addressed to the leaders of the church, but to the church in general. Pastoral care is a task in which all Christians are involved (see 1 Cor. 12:25). Furthermore, as Paul makes clear, pastoral care is not just a matter of listening to others, important as listening may be. Pastoral care also involves the application of Christian truth to living. This truth centres around the resurrection of Jesus and its implications for those who believe.

a. Encouragement for All Saints' Day

There is nothing harder than losing a loved one. To lose a loved one is to lose part of oneself. 'Death', wrote the Swiss psychiatrist Carl Jung in his *Memoirs*, 'is indeed a piece of brutality. There is no sense in pretending otherwise. It is brutal not only as a physical event, but far more so psychically: a human being is torn away from us, and what remains is the icy stillness of death.' As those who have experienced bereavement know to their cost, the loss of a loved one calls for radical and painful adjustments, which are often still difficult to accept even after many years'. Even a widow of twenty or more years' standing may still miss her husband. Bereavement is something we never truly get over, for when we have loved deeply, we also hurt deeply.

The result is that for people of no Christian faith, death is the bleakest of experiences. The grieving of those *who have no hope* (v. 13) is a bitter experience. 'Death', said the ancient Greek philosopher Aristotle, 'is the most terrifying of all ills, for it is the end.' Tom Stoppard's play *Rosencrantz and Guildenstern are Dead* is equally pessimistic when Guildenstern comments grimly on Hamlet's deliberations about suicide: 'No, no. It's not like that. Death isn't romantic . . . death is not anything . . . death is . . . not. It's the absence of presence, nothing more . . . the endless time of never coming back . . . A gap you can't see, and where the wind blows through it, it makes no sound.'[20]

Thank God, there is more to say than that death (and life, for that matter) is bleak. For Paul makes it clear that with Jesus there is hope. Yet at the time of death there is sadness – there would be something wrong with our relationships if we did not shed copious tears when a loved one died. Even Jesus wept at the tomb of his friend Lazarus (John 11:35). As counsellors know all too well, all kinds of complications arise if people do not 'work out' their grief. But Christians do not have *to grieve like the rest of men, who have no hope* (v. 13). For *we believe that God will bring with Jesus those who have fallen asleep in him* (v. 14). The result is that when we mourn, as mourn we do, we mourn not so much for our loved ones as for ourselves. The grief we experience and the tears we shed are over the loss that is ours. Our hope is in Jesus, who *died and rose again* (v. 14). Because of what God has done in the past, we know that we can be certain of the future, both for ourselves and for our loved ones. Christian hope is not a whistling in the dark – it is rooted in the reality of a past event.

Because of our hope in Jesus, death is not to be feared, although we may fear the process of dying. While dying can be a painful and degrading affair, it is amazing what the hospice movement has achieved in this respect. For the Christian, however, death itself need not be feared, for *God will bring with Jesus those who have fallen asleep in him* (v. 14). To develop the metaphor, one day we shall wake up and live *with the Lord for ever* (v. 17). Martin Luther put

[20] *Rosencrantz and Guildenstern are Dead*, ed. T. Bareham (Macmillan, 1990).

it this way: 'I shall go to sleep, and I shall know nothing more until an angel knocks on my tombstone and says, "Time to get up, Dr Luther! Judgment Day!"' What a difference Jesus makes – both to death and to life. In him we may find great comfort (v. 18).

b. The five R's of Christian hope

Although most people can cope with death when it happens in a detective thriller, many find it difficult to cope with death when it happens to themselves or to their loved ones. This was true at Thessalonica, where the unexpected deaths of loved ones had given cause for deep concern. Even today, to people without any Christian faith, there is little we can say of any real comfort. They *have no hope* (v. 13) Those who have put their trust in Jesus, however, can face the future with confidence. Here in 1 Thessalonians 4 the Christian hope can be summed up in five 'R's'.

Resurrection. The resurrection of Jesus is not to be likened to a single rabbit God pulls out of the hat to demonstrate that Jesus is his Son. Rather, it is the basis for all Christian hope. The consequence of believing that *Jesus died and rose again* is that *God will bring with Jesus those who have fallen asleep in him* (v. 14).

Return. On the great day of resurrection, *the Lord himself will come down from heaven* (v. 16). The words of Paul here echo the words of Jesus regarding the coming of the Son of Man. Both Jesus and Paul were taking up traditional Jewish symbols relating to the end times (e.g. *the voice of the archangel, the trumpet call*, v. 16) and then applying them to the distinctive Christian concept that at the end of time Jesus will return to wind up the historical process. If the truth be told, some Christians are embarrassed by this concept and would prefer to believe in a more sophisticated form of the Christian faith. This facet of Christian believing, however, is not an optional extra. In this respect C. S. Lewis was right when he wrote: 'It seems to me impossible to retain in any recognisable form our belief in the divinity of Christ and the truth of the Christian revelation while abandoning, or even persistently neglecting, the promised and threatened return.'[21]

Rapture. The coming of the Lord in glory will be marked by an event known as the 'rapture', when the living will be 'seized' by the irresistible power of God *to meet the Lord in the air* (v. 17) with a view to then accompanying the Lord as he comes to take up his kingdom here on earth. While Christians have indulged in a good

---

[21] C. S. Lewis, *The World's Last Night and Other Essays* (Harcourt Brace Jovanovich, 1960), p. 93.

deal of speculation about the rapture, it is important to grasp that what we have here is not so much prose as poetry, not so much a programme as an artist's impression. Yet underlying the picture is an essential truth: Christ is coming again in triumph.

Reunion. This coming of the Lord will be marked by a reunion, when the dead and the living are reunited in Christ: *we . . . will be . . . together with them* (v. 17). One day we shall be together again with our loved ones who have died in Christ, but earthly relationships will no longer have the same significance they once had. The marriage bond, for instance, has significance in this world only (see Luke 20:34–35). There is no reason, however, to believe that we shall not recognize our loved ones and delight in their company. Nevertheless, we need to be aware that heaven will be far more than a private family reunion. It will be the greatest reunion of all time, with people 'from every tribe and language and people and nation' (Rev. 5:9).

Rejoicing. The new life will be a life of unending joy, for *we will be with the Lord for ever* (v. 17). If all that God had to offer was more of the same, then few of us would want to live for ever. For many people, life as it is now is far from being a constant source of joy – there is much pain around (sadly sometimes in the church and not just in the world). But the new life will be lived in the presence of God, where God will be 'all in all' (1 Cor. 15:28). Nothing more wonderful could be imagined.

We can therefore *encourage each other* (v. 18). 'Without Jesus death is horrible,' wrote Blaise Pascal, 'but with Jesus it is holy, kind and the joy of the true believer.'

6. The witness of Peter and his friends to the resurrection

The book of Acts has with good reason been called 'the Gospel of the Resurrection'. The apostles preached the good news of Jesus risen from the dead (see, e.g., 2:24, 31–32; 3:15; 4:2, 10, 33; 5:30–31; 10:40; 12:30; 13:30, 32, 34, 37; 23:6; 24:15, 21; 26:8, 23. In all the speeches of Acts the resurrection occupies the central place. Jesus is Lord, because God has raised him from the dead.

The preaching of the apostles has its roots in the 'commission' of the risen Lord in Acts 1:8: 'you will be my witnesses in Jerusalem, and in all Judea and Samaria, and to the ends of the earth'. Although the witness of the disciples is not limited to the resurrection, their witness centres on it. So, when the disciples came to appoint a successor to Judas, the key qualification is that the new apostle 'must become a witness with us of his resurrection' (1:22).

The themes of witness and resurrection are so closely intertwined that, with the sole exception of Acts 1:8, the witness of the apostles is always coupled with resurrection. The first half of the book of Acts is concerned with the witness of Peter. On the day of Pentecost, for instance, Peter states: 'God has raised this Jesus to life, and we are all witnesses of the fact' (2:32). To the crowd in Solomon's Colonnade he declares: 'God raised him from the dead. We are witnesses of this' (3:15). In one of his summary statements, Luke writes: 'the apostles continued to testify [literally, 'give witness', *apedidoun to martyrion*] to the resurrection of the Lord Jesus' (4:33). To the Sanhedrin Peter and the other apostles declare: 'The God of our ancestors raised Jesus from the dead . . . We are witnesses of these things' (5:30, 32). When invited to preach to Cornelius and his friends, Peter says, 'We are witnesses . . . God raised him from the dead on the third day' (10:39–40) and mentions the fact that the risen Lord was 'seen . . . by witnesses whom God had already chosen' (10:41).

In the second half of the book of Acts, Paul takes centre stage. He too is portrayed by Luke as a witness to the resurrection. His conversion on the Damascus road, for instance, is an encounter with the risen Lord, as a result of which he is commissioned to be 'his witness to all men of what [he has] seen and heard' (22:5). The same theme is present in his retelling of his conversion story to Agrippa. He tells Agrippa how he was appointed to be 'a witness, of what he has seen of Christ' (26:16), and then moves on to speak of 'the Christ . . . as the first to rise from the dead' (26:23). Similarly at Pisidian Antioch Paul and his friends preach the resurrection (13:30, 33–34, 37) and in so doing 'are now his witnesses' (13:31).

With this introduction we now turn to two speeches in which first Peter and then Paul preach the resurrection. For the purposes of this book, we shall not look at the speeches as a whole, but rather limit ourselves to the sections where the primary focus is on the resurrection.

1. Preaching the resurrection in Jerusalem (Acts 2:22–32)

'Men of Israel, listen to this: Jesus of Nazareth was a man accredited by God to you by miracles, wonders and signs, which God did among you through him, as you yourselves know. ²³This man was handed over to you by God's set purpose and foreknowledge; and you, with the help of wicked men, put him to death by nailing him to the cross. ²⁴But God raised him from the dead, freeing him from the agony of death, because it was impossible for death to keep its hold on him. ²⁵David said about him:

"I saw the Lord always before me.
Because he is at my right hand,
I will not be shaken.
²⁶Therefore my heart is glad and my tongue rejoices;
my body also will live in hope,
²⁷because you will not abandon me to the grave,
nor will you let your Holy One see decay.
²⁸You have made known to me the paths of life;
you will fill me with joy in your presence."

²⁹'Brothers, I can tell you confidently that the patriarch David died and was buried, and his tomb is here to this day. ³⁰But he was a prophet and knew that God had promised him on oath that he would place one of his descendants on his throne. ³¹Seeing what was ahead, he spoke of the resurrection of the Christ, that he was not abandoned to the grave, nor did his body see decay. [32]*God has raised this Jesus to life, and we are all witnesses of the fact.'*

After the initial explanation of the speaking in tongues (2:14–21), Peter moves on to the heart of his sermon, *Jesus* (2:22). It is at this point that Peter's specifically Christian preaching begins. Indeed, true Christian preaching always begins with Jesus.

After a brief summary of the life and ministry of Jesus (2:22), Peter moves on to speak of the death of Jesus on the cross. Peter has no hesitation in attributing direct responsibility to the Jews of his day: *'you, with the help of wicked men, put him to death by nailing him to the cross'* (v. 23). The Romans may actually have carried out the crucifixion, but they were only the agents of the Jews. The NIV somewhat unfairly describes the Romans as *wicked*: the Romans, like any other Gentiles, were in fact 'without the law' (*anomos*) in the sense that they were not 'under the law'. Wickedness lay with the Jews, and in particular with the chief priests, who handed Jesus over to the Romans.

Such an ending to the life of one *accredited by God* (2:22) must have seemed strange. Peter, however, makes clear that what appeared to be a free action on the part of human beings was in fact fully in line with the will of God: *'This man was handed over to you by God's set purpose and foreknowledge'* (v. 23). God had already 'decided beforehand' what should happen (4:27). The cross of Jesus was no unfortunate accident – it was part of the divine plan. At this stage Peter has no developed theology of the cross. The one thing he knew was that even in this most terrible of events God was at work. Indeed, as Luke is at pains to show in his writings, there was a divine necessity in the death of Jesus, for only in this way could Scripture be fulfilled (Luke 24:26–27, 44–46; Acts 3:18; 13:27; 26:23).

But God raised him from the dead (2:24; see 3:15). The resurrection is an act of God. Jesus did not just rise from the dead; rather, it was God who raised Jesus (see also 2:24, 32; 13:34; 17:31). In the act of resurrection God reversed the sentence of death passed on Jesus. The resurrection is God's seal of approval on the crucified Saviour – it is God's 'yes' over against the human 'no'.

Peter goes on to define a little more closely what was involved in the resurrection: in raising Jesus God was *freeing him from the agony of death* (2:24). Peter borrows an expression from Psalms 18:5 and 116:3, which in the original Hebrew speak of the 'cords' of death, but which in the Greek version quoted by Peter speak of the 'pangs' or 'pains' (*ōdines*) of death. The latter word normally refers to 'birth pains' (see 1 Thess. 5:3), and was often used of the messianic woes expected at the end of time (see Matt. 24:8; Mark 13:8). We appear therefore to have a complex combination of metaphors present. The resurrection marked freedom from the bondage of death; the end of 'labour pains' as new life came to birth; and a transition point between the sufferings of the old order and the joys of the new messianic age.

Peter continues: '*it was impossible for death to keep its hold on him*' (2:24). If Peter was thinking of 'labour pains', then maybe he was saying that death could no more hold Jesus down than a pregnant woman could hold her unborn child in her body. It may be that his mind was on Psalm 16, however, which he was about to quote: if so, the inevitability of the resurrection lay in the fact that it was foretold by David.

Peter then launches into an extended quotation from the Greek version of Psalm 16:8–11. His argument is that David, whose tomb could still be seen (2:29), could not have been speaking of himself, for the psalm speaks of one who is alive. In its original setting Psalm 16 is a hymn of praise to God, who has saved the psalmist by protecting him from death. By interpreting it in the light of the resurrection, therefore, Peter is in fact dramatically reinterpreting the message of the psalm. Interestingly, Paul draws upon the same psalm when preaching at Pisidian Antioch (13:35–37). The key to this form of biblical exegesis is found in the figure of David, who, as God's anointed king, was seen as the prototype of the Messiah. As a result, such psalms as Psalms 2; 110; and 16 were all seen by the early church as finding their fulfilment in Jesus.

'*I saw the Lord always before me*' (v. 25). The inference is that at all times, and perhaps not least as he faced death on the cross, Jesus was conscious of living in the presence of God. This sense of God's constant presence with him in turn gave him the confidence that God would always be there to protect him:

> '*Because he is at my right hand,*
> *I will not be shaken*' (v. 25).

Even in death '*my body also will live in hope*' (v. 26): it is possible that Peter had in mind the interval between Good Friday and Easter Day. The hope lay in the belief that '*you will not abandon me to the grave*' (v. 27); that is, God will not allow his body to experience the *decay* of decomposition (see v. 31). Instead, '*You have made known to me the paths of life*' (v. 28): the 'path' (singular), which for the psalmist was the way that is well-pleasing to God, and so leading to life, is now the way leading out of death and back to life. So the psalm concludes, '*you will fill me with joy in your presence*' (v. 28), the joy that comes from being made alive to live again in the presence of God.

'*Seeing what was ahead, he spoke of the resurrection of the Christ*' (v. 31). David did not consciously speak of the resurrection of Jesus. His words were fulfilled in a way he could never have dreamt of. Yet in one respect Peter's reinterpretation is true to David's original intention: God, and not death, has the final word.

Peter's sermon now reaches a climax: '*God has raised this Jesus to life, and we are all witnesses of the fact*' (v. 32). In spite of the Christianized exposition of Psalm 16, the truth of the resurrection does not rest on a rereading of Scripture, but rather on the witness of Peter and the other apostles. Peter and the early church would never have interpreted Psalm 16 as speaking of the resurrection if they had not themselves encountered the risen Christ. The truth of the resurrection rests on the apostles' experience of the risen Lord.

At this point Peter returns to his theme of the gift of the Spirit: it is this risen and exalted Lord Jesus who '*has poured out what you now see and hear*' (v. 33).

a. Witnessing together to the truth of the resurrection

A witness by definition is a person who is able to give evidence to the truth of a particular incident. Only a person who has first-hand knowledge of an event can be a witness. In a court of law, hearsay evidence is disallowed: the court is interested only in what the witness has heard and seen. Truth is of the essence in witnessing. So when the risen Lord Jesus, as he was about to ascend to his Father, commissioned his disciples to be his witnesses (Acts 1:8), he was in effect telling those who had shared his life for the past three eventful years to give evidence on his behalf regarding all that they had seen and heard. The disciples did not forget his words. When they came to replace Judas Iscariot and bring the apostolic team up to strength, nominations were restricted to those who 'have been with us the whole time the Lord Jesus went in and out among us, beginning from John's baptism to the time when Jesus was taken up' (1:21–22). Right from the start the first Christians were concerned for truth. This concern for truth therefore gives us great confidence when we approach the New Testament documents. For instance, in his Gospel and in his history of the early church, Luke was clearly not writing as an impartial observer; nevertheless, he did not seek to pervert the truth. Rather, in the prologue to his Gospel he states that he sought to base his work on a careful investigation of eye-witness evidence (Luke 1:1–4).

From the Acts of the Apostles we discover that the disciples witnessed in particular to the truth of the resurrection of Jesus. The key qualification for Judas's successor was that he had to be 'a witness with us of his resurrection' (1:22). On the day of Pentecost Peter was concerned above all to witness to the fact that God had raised Jesus to life (2:32). What was true then must be true of our witness today. When we speak to non-Christians about Jesus, we must be sure to speak about his resurrection. For the resurrection is the great miracle of the Christian faith; it is the heart of the Christian gospel. Without the resurrection of Jesus his life and death have no meaning (see 1 Cor. 15:17). The message of the resurrection is the message the world needs to hear. In this respect some advice from the evangelist Michael Green may be pertinent:

> Major on Jesus and the resurrection . . . the person of Jesus is the most attractive in the world. And the evidence for his being more than just a man is overwhelming. I love to face enquirers with that. And then I encourage them to go away and read the five accounts of the resurrection, to see how it reverberates from practically every page in Acts, and then to attempt to argue against it. It is a formidable case to dismantle, and they do not succeed. God has not given us the answer to all manner of questions we would love to have unravelled. But he has seen fit to provide very strong supporting evidence for the divinity of Jesus Christ and the fact of his resurrection from the dead.[1]

In a court of law, although it is possible for the evidence of one individual witness to swing a trial, a case is much more likely to be made if a series of witnesses can be called to give evidence. Indeed, in the Old Testament, charges could not be brought against anybody on the basis of the evidence of only one witness. 'A matter must be established by the testimony of two or three witnesses' (Deut. 19:15). It is sometimes suggested that the reason Jesus sent his disciples out two by two was that in this way their preaching would be strengthened as they corroborated one another's testimony. Although, on the day of Pentecost, Peter did the preaching, he was conscious that he was speaking on behalf of a group of witnesses: 'We are all witnesses of the fact' (v. 32), he said. The same is true of preaching today: the preaching of a minister is a witness to the corporate faith of the church in the risen Lord Jesus. Although there is a very necessary place for individual witnessing, the witness of a church as a whole has normally a vital role to play.

The corporate witness of the church is evident not only in what is said from the pulpit, but also in how life is lived in the pew. If

---

[1] M. Green, *Evangelism through the Local Church* (Hodder & Stoughton, 1990), p. 138.

others are to believe, then the gospel of the resurrection has to be evident in the way in which a church lives its life together. This was certainly true of the early church. Luke, for instance, describes how the believers shared their possessions, and then adds, 'With great power the apostles continued to testify to the resurrection of the Lord Jesus' (4:33). The implication is that it was this demonstration of the life of the church that gave great power to the preaching. Mahatma Gandhi once said to a group of missionaries in India, 'You work so hard at it. Just remember that the rose never invites anyone to smell it. If it is fragrant, people will walk across the garden and endure the thorns to smell it.' If our lives are full of the fragrance of the risen Lord Jesus, people will be drawn to the message we preach. The fact is that we witness through how we live as much as through what we say.

2. Preaching the resurrection in Athens (Acts 17:16–21, 30–32)

While Paul was waiting for them in Athens, he was greatly distressed to see that the city was full of idols. [17]*So he reasoned in the synagogue with the Jews and the God-fearing Greeks, as well as in the market-place day by day with those who happened to be there.* [18]*A group of Epicurean and Stoic philosophers began to dispute with him. Some of them asked, 'What is this babbler trying to say?' Others remarked, 'He seems to be advocating foreign gods.' They said this because Paul was preaching the good news about Jesus and the resurrection.* [19]*Then they took him and brought him to a meeting of the Areopagus, where they said to him, 'May we know what this new teaching is that you are presenting?* [20]*You are bringing some strange ideas to our ears, and we want to know what they mean.'* [21]*(All the Athenians and the foreigners who lived there spent their time doing nothing but talking about and listening to the latest ideas.)*

[30]*'In the past God overlooked such ignorance, but now he commands all people everywhere to repent.* [31]*For he has set a day when he will judge the world with justice by the man he has appointed. He has given proof of this to all men by raising him from the dead.'*
[32]*When they heard about the resurrection of the dead, some of them sneered, but others said, 'We want to hear you again on this subject.'*

Athens, with its Parthenon and many temples, was one of the most impressive and glorious cities of the ancient world. When Paul visited the city, however, he was not overwhelmed by its beauty, but was deeply pained to see the extent to which the Athenians worshipped other gods. Luke was not exaggerating when he said that *the city was full of idols* (v. 16). The city was well-nigh covered with them. The Greek historian and travel writer Xenophon described Athens as 'one great altar, one great sacrifice'. There were said to be more statues of pagan gods in Athens than in all the rest of Greece put together. One Roman satirist remarked that it was easier to meet a statue in Athens than to meet a man! So Paul was not just being diplomatic when he described the Athenians as 'very religious' (v. 22). They were by common assent reckoned to be the most religious of human beings in the ancient world. Pausanias, for instance, wrote that 'the Athenians venerate the gods more than others'.[2]

Paul *was greatly distressed* (v. 16) at this sight. The Greek word (*parōxyneto*) expresses more than mere upset; it suggests anger too. The only other occurrence is found in 1 Corinthians 13:5: 'love is not easily angered'. It is the verb the Greek version of the Old Testament regularly uses to describe God's reaction to idolatry (e.g. Deut. 9:7, 18, 22; Ps. 106:28–29; Is. 65:2–3; Hos. 8:5). Paul was 'provoked' (RSV) to anger, as well as no doubt to grief. For what he saw was a contravention of the first two commandments of the law. In the first place, God had said, 'You shall have no other gods before me' (Exod. 20:3), yet the Parthenon, by its very title, claimed to embrace every god going. Indeed, just to be on the safe side, the Athenians had even erected an altar to an unknown god (v. 23)! Secondly, God had said, 'You shall not make for yourself an idol in the form of anything in heaven above or on the earth beneath or in the waters below' (Exod. 20:4), yet the city abounded in every kind of distorted representation of divine beings.

Faced with such a rank display of paganism, Paul found himself 'compelled to preach' (1 Cor. 9:16). Luke gives the impression that the prime reason for his going to Athens was not so much to preach the gospel as to find a safe haven where he could wait for Silas and Timothy to follow him with news of the church at Thessalonica (17:14–15). Nevertheless, while he waited for them, Paul could not remain silent. Like Jeremiah, he knew what it was like to experience the 'burning fire' of God's word in his heart, and he could not hold it in (Jer. 20:9).

So he reasoned (v. 17) with the Athenians. The Greek verb (*dialegomai*) gives us our English word 'dialogue'. It is regularly

---

[2] Pausanias, *Description of Athens* 1.17.1: similarly Sophocles, *Oedipus at Colonus* 260; and Josephus, *Against Apion* 2.130.

used by Luke to describe Paul's communication of the good news of Jesus (Acts 17:2; 18:4, 19; 19:8–9; 20:7, 9; 24:12, 25). Paul did not so much 'preach' as conduct a 'discussion' or 'argument' with his listeners, in which no doubt a good deal of debate took place.

In the first place, *he reasoned in the synagogue with the Jews and the God-fearing Greeks* (v. 17). The *God-fearing Greeks* were 'devout' (NRSV) Gentiles who, dissatisfied with the gods of Olympus and hungering for the living God, had converted to Judaism. Presumably these discussions took place on the Sabbath. The synagogues did not have ministers or other fixed people to speak. Instead, the synagogue officials tended to invite any distinguished person to speak. Paul, almost certainly still dressed as a Pharisee (see 1 Cor. 9:20), would have been a natural person to invite to speak.

During the rest of the week Paul *reasoned . . . in the market-place day by day with those who happened to be there* (v. 17). The market-place or Agora was not just a market; it was the great city square of Athens, as much a centre of social and intellectual life as of commercial activity. In a later aside, Luke tells us that *All the Athenians and the foreigners who lived there spent their time doing nothing but talking about and listening to the latest ideas* (v. 21). The Greeks, born with curiosity in their souls, loved nothing better than splitting philosophical hairs with one another.

It was presumably there in the Agora that Paul met a group of *Epicurean and Stoic philosophers* (v. 18). Two more different philosophical schools of thought could scarcely be found. In essence, the Stoics tended to be serious, earnest people, possessed of a great sense of moral duty; the Epicureans by contrast tended to be fun-lovers who lived for pleasure and little else.

It may well have been the Epicureans who dismissed Paul as a *babbler* (v. 18). The underlying Greek word (*spermologos*) meant literally a 'seed-picker', and was originally used of birds pecking for food. The term came to be used to describe people who snapped up the ideas of others and then spread them about, without having any understanding of what those ideas actually meant.

The Stoics, possibly, took Paul a little more seriously: *'He seems to be advocating foreign gods'* (v. 18). The word for 'gods' (*daimonia*) could be used of lesser gods as well as of demons. By word of explanation Luke adds, *They said this because Paul was preaching the good news about Jesus and the resurrection* (v. 18). In their ignorance, some of Paul's hearers thought that he was talking about two gods, a male god called 'Jesus' and his female companion 'Anastasis' (the Greek word for resurrection). It may even be that some mistook the name of Jesus (*Iēsous*) for the Greek word for healing (*Iasis*), and then concluded Paul was speaking about two gods of health, namely 'Iasis' (healing) and 'Anastasis' (which could mean 'restoration', viz. to full health). Here we discover how central the resurrection was to Paul's preaching. For Paul, to preach Jesus was indeed to preach the resurrection.

At this point they took him off to the court of *the Areopagus* (v. 19), which took its name from the place where its meetings were held on the Hill of Ares, otherwise known as Mars Hill. Originally a criminal court capable of handing down the death sentence, it had become a kind of debating club for the leading people of the city. Paul's speech to the Areopagus was largely an exercise in 'natural theology', and as such is not of relevance to our purposes. What is of interest, however, is that from speaking of the way in which God had made himself known in the world of nature, Paul moved on to speak of the way in which God had made himself known in Jesus. 'Natural theology' in itself never converts anybody, but rather is a 'preparation' for the gospel.

Paul had taken as the starting point for his sermon the Athenians' worship of an unknown God (v. 23). He now draws his sermon to an end by reverting to the topic of his hearers' ignorance: *'In the past God overlooked such ignorance'* (v. 30). Such ignorance had always been culpable. For as Paul had pointed out to the people of Lystra, 'the living God . . . has not left himself without testimony' (14:15, 17). Now Paul makes a similar point to the Athenians. As the creator of the universe (v. 24), the sustainer of life (v. 25) and the ruler of the nations (v. 26), God is knowable, as 'he is not far from each one of us' (v. 27). The Greek poets Epimenides and Aratus were right: 'For in him we live and move and have our being' . . . 'we are his offspring' (v. 28).

With the coming of Jesus, ignorance of God is no longer excusable: *but now he commands all people everywhere to repent* (v. 30). People need to repent, because this is God's world. It is a moral world, where God's standards count. The Athenians needed to copy the Thessalonians, who 'turned to God from idols to serve the living and true God' (1 Thess. 1:9).

Furthermore, *'he has set a day when he will judge the world with justice by a man he has appointed. He has given proof of this to all men by raising him from the dead'* (v. 31). Nobody will be able to escape that judgment. As Paul later wrote to the church at Corinth, 'we must all appear before the judgment seat of Christ' (2 Cor. 5:10; see Rom. 14:10). If proof is wanted, then one need look no further than the resurrection of Jesus. The inference is that in being raised from the dead, Jesus was vindicated in his claim to be the Son of God, who will share in the judgment of God (see John 5:27).

The Athenians' response was mixed. *When they heard about the resurrection of the dead, some of them sneered* (v. 32). Had Paul spoken of the immortality of the soul, most would have listened with respect, but to speak of resurrection appeared crass. So some 'began to mock' (*echleuazon* – Luke uses the imperfect tense); talk of resurrection seemed laughable. For to them it was an article of faith that dead men do not rise from the dead. In the words attributed to Apollo, expressed on the occasion when that very court of the Areopagus was founded, 'Once a man dies and the earth drinks up his blood, there is no resurrection.'[3] There are many today who like to think that the Christian gospel with its message of resurrection is one big hoax. Certainly, if Jesus did not rise from the dead, it is the cruellest of jokes. But supposing he did? Others responded, *'We want to hear you again on this subject'* (v. 32). These hearers were more polite. There is a real danger, however, in deferring a decision about Jesus. It has been said that 'tomorrow' is the most dangerous word in the English language – for it may well be that 'tomorrow' will never come. 'A few', however, 'believed' (v. 34). They believed in *Jesus and the resurrection* (v. 18).

a. A model in evangelism

Paul was conscious that he was a man with a mission. He believed that right from the moment of his birth he had been set apart by God to tell others the good news of Jesus (see Gal. 1:1, 15). On the Damascus road the risen Lord Jesus had not only appeared to him, but had also commissioned him to take the gospel to the Gentiles (Acts 9:15). When Paul arrived in Athens, therefore, he could not behave like any other tourist. Distressed at the sight of so many idols and in turn so much spiritual hunger, he had to tell others *the good news about Jesus and the resurrection* (v. 18). Like Paul, we too have been entrusted with a mission. We too are called to share the good news of Jesus and his resurrection. Furthermore, like Paul at Athens, we too find ourselves living in a society cluttered with idols. Our own idols may not be statues of stone – instead, the gods of sex and success, power and security, money and materialism, work and the family, leisure and sport, are expressed in different forms. Unlike Paul, however, we tend to forget our mission and look upon our society not with distress, but with apparent equanimity.

When it came to method, Paul began with the synagogues, partly for theological reasons (see Rom. 1:16), but also partly for practical reasons. The synagogues provided a natural, ready-made audience of people interested in God. Paul did not, however, limit himself to the

---

[3] Aeschylus, *Eumenides* 647–648.

'God-fearing' fringe. He also went to the market-place, to the café society of his day, and talked to people where they were. Furthermore, in going to the court of the Areopagus, he took the opportunity to meet with the opinion-makers of the city on their own turf. In all these meetings with people, Paul did not preach 'six feet above contradiction'. Paul was happy to enter into discussion with people about God, and in particular about Jesus and the resurrection. Paul did not simply preach Jesus; he also sought to persuade men and women of the truth as it is in Jesus. Although in the final analysis we can never argue people into the kingdom of God, we can remove a number of blockages.

Paul's message was always centred on the living God, who has made himself known in Jesus. Unfortunately, we have no full transcript of what Paul said to the court of the Areopagus. Luke's nine verses, which take only two minutes to read, are a bare summary. If Acts 17:18 is anything to go by, Paul will have majored on *Jesus and the resurrection*. With an audience that included Stoic philosophers, he would have pointed to the cross of Jesus as a sign of God's love (see Rom. 5:8). This message of God's love would have made the Stoics sit up and listen, for one of their central tenets was that God has no feelings. With an audience that included Epicurean philosophers, Paul would have spoken of the resurrection of Jesus as a sign of God's offer of life. This would have made the Epicureans too sit up and listen, for they regarded death as the greatest enemy of happiness. This twin message of Jesus and his resurrection is a message our world still needs to hear.

3. A resurrection benediction (Heb. 13:20–21)

In what is in effect a heavy theological treatise, it may well seem strange that it is only in the closing benediction that the unknown author of the letter to the Hebrews refers explicitly to the resurrection of Jesus. In a context where Jewish Christian converts were wavering in their faith, however, it proved necessary for the author to demonstrate the superiority of the Christ by emphasizing the exaltation of Jesus to the 'right hand of the Majesty in heaven' (1:3; see also 8:1; 10:12; 12:2) and the eternal high-priesthood of Jesus (5:6; 7:7, 25; 8:25). Yet inevitably the exaltation of Jesus, as also his eternal high-priesthood, implies the resurrection. Indeed, it is no exaggeration to say that the resurrection of Jesus is presupposed throughout the letter. For instance, the resurrection of Jesus surely underlies the description of Christ as having destroyed the one holding the power of death, and who then freed those held in slavery by their fear of death (2:14–15). Likewise the resurrection of Jesus must surely be presupposed by the attribution to Jesus of an 'indestructible life' (7:16; see also 7:25; 13:8). 'The resurrection of the dead', together with the associated doctrine of 'eternal judgment', is included among the 'elementary teachings' (6:1–3) derived from Judaism, which gained a new significance in the light of the Christian faith, and not least through the resurrection of Jesus from the dead. None of this, however, takes away the fact that it is not until almost the very end of the letter that we have an explicit reference to the resurrection of Jesus. As we shall see from the exposition of the benediction, this reference was no mere throwaway, but was included for a particular purpose.

May the God of peace, who through the blood of the eternal covenant brought back from the dead our Lord Jesus, that great Shepherd of the sheep, [21]equip you with everything good for doing his will, and may he work in us what is pleasing to him, through Jesus Christ, to whom be glory for ever and ever. Amen.

The benediction begins with an invocation to God as *the God of peace*. In the context of the final chapter of the letter, it would appear that this description of God as the source and giver of peace was particularly appropriate in view of certain leadership tensions present in the church (see 13:7, 17).

A doxology apart, the benediction concludes with a twofold prayer that God will first *equip* the recipients of the letter *with everything good for doing his will* and then that God may *work in us what is pleasing to him*. The main thrust of the prayer is found in the first petition. The Greek verb (*katartizō*), translated by the NIV as *equip*, has an interesting range of meanings, but refers in particular to restoring things or to putting them in order. It could be used of the mending of nets (see Matt. 4:21). In the context of surgery it could be used of setting a bone in a leg that had been broken. It often has the sense of completing something lacking (e.g. 1 Thess. 3:10). In the light of this range of meanings, the NIV translation, with its prayer that God may 'equip you with everything good', is perhaps a little misleading. The same criticism may be made of the GNB, which renders the prayer: 'May the God of peace . . . provide you with every good thing.' Both the NIV and the GNB give the impression that what is lacking in the lives of the recipients of the letter is the tools for the job. The actual issue, however, is that people need an inner transformation if God's will ('what is pleasing to him') is to be done. The NRSV gets close to this meaning with its translation, 'Now may the God of peace . . . make you complete in everything good'. The REB gets perhaps even closer when it adopts the language of the old Authorized Version: 'May the God of peace . . . make you perfect in all goodness.' As I have already noted, not everything had been sweetness and light ('perfect'!) in the church's life. Perhaps their church meetings had not been as harmonious as they might have been. Not everybody was keen to accept the leadership being offered. This is the context in which the prayer for 'completeness' or 'perfection' is made.

It is in this context too, where the need for 'completeness' or 'perfection' is uppermost, that the author refers to the death and resurrection of Jesus. The prayer of the benediction gains added strength because the *God of peace* is the God *who through the blood of the eternal covenant brought back from the dead our Lord Jesus, that great Shepherd of the sheep.*

Significantly, Jesus is described as *that great Shepherd of the sheep.* The attribution of this title to Jesus is often thought to be due to the fact that the author is at this point drawing upon the Greek translation of Isaiah 63:11, where Moses is described as 'the shepherd of the sheep'. At this particular junction, however, such a comparison (Moses was a 'shepherd', but Jesus is the *great Shepherd*) does not appear to be particularly relevant. The comparison with Moses has already been dealt with at an earlier stage in the letter (see 3:1–6). Although it is possible that there is a reference back, it is perhaps more probable that the author drew upon Isaiah 63:11, not because he was seeking to emphasize again the superiority of Jesus to Moses, but rather because in this closing section of the letter he has been dealing with the issue of 'shepherding', or church leadership. Certainly this allusion to Jesus as *that great Shepherd of the sheep* is particularly apposite for two reasons. First, the author's chief concern throughout the letter has been to encourage church members, tempted 'like sheep' to go astray, to 'return' to Jesus, 'the Shepherd' (see 1 Pet. 2:25); and secondly, as the author has just emphasized, church leaders too must give an account of their leadership to Jesus, the Chief Shepherd (see 1 Pet. 5:1–4). Furthermore, the author may have been conscious that this 'great Shepherd', whom *God brought back from the dead* just as he led Moses out of the land of Egypt, is also the 'good shepherd' who laid down his life for the sheep (John 10:11). The imagery lends itself both to death and to resurrection.

In terms of resurrection, the choice of the verb (*anagō*) may be due to the fact that it is used in the Greek of Isaiah 63:11. Interestingly, it is also used in the Psalms of God's 'leading out' the psalmist from the realm of the dead (Pss. 29 English Bibles [30]:4, LXX; 70[71]:20, LXX; 85[86]:13, LXX). By implication, there is also a reference to Jesus, in turn, leading his sheep from the realm of the dead, as Moses led the people of Israel out of Egypt. The presence of such a reference is strengthened by the verbal allusion in the following phrase to Zechariah 9:11, where God promises Zion that 'because of the blood of my covenant with you' he will release her prisoners from the 'waterless pit'. The 'waterless pit' is an image often used in the Psalms for the realm of the dead (e.g. Pss. 27[28]:1, LXX; 29[30]:3, LXX; 87[88]:46, LXX; 142[143]:7, LXX). Jesus is the *great Shepherd of the sheep* not least because he leads his sheep from the land of the dead into the land of the living.

In terms of the death of Jesus, the author declares that God raised the great Shepherd *through* or 'by virtue of' *the blood of the eternal covenant*. The emphasis here is very much on the resurrection. The resurrection of Jesus is a public demonstration and confirmation of the fact that his sacrifice has been accepted and that a new *eternal covenant* has been established (see chs. 8 – 9).

This focus on Jesus as the great Shepherd, crucified and risen from the dead, now becomes relevant in the light of the prayer that God will transform his people by making them 'complete' or 'perfect'. Such a transformation is possible only on the basis of the death and resurrection of Jesus. In his death, Jesus has established a new covenant, one that by offering forgiveness leads to 'perfection' (see 10:14). Above all, in his resurrection from the dead, Jesus, as the forerunner (6:20), has carved out a way that leads from death to life. Although 'completeness' or 'perfection' is found only at death, it is perhaps not too much to infer that the power that raised Jesus from death to life is available in the here and now to lead his followers from a 'dead' way of living to one that is *pleasing* to God.

a. A benediction of perfection

God wants us to be perfect. He wants us to become 'perfect in all goodness': as the REB puts it, God wants us not to become reasonably good but to strive for 'perfection'. But how can this be? In one sense, we can never attain perfection in this world – even the best we offer God is always tainted (see 1 John 1:8). We can, however, begin the journey toward such a goal. The benediction gives some pointers.

In the first place, it is God who makes us perfect. It is God who achieves perfection in us. True, we need to cooperate with him; perfection does not come without effort on our part, but neither does it come without help on God's part. Just as James and John had to do a repair job on their fishing tackle (Matt. 4:21), so God needs to do a repair job on our lives. Just as, when we have broken a leg, we may need a doctor to set the limb straight, so we need God to straighten our individual lives, as well as, sometimes, our life together in his church.

In the second place, God makes us perfect through the power of the cross of Jesus. It is 'by the blood of the eternal covenant' made through the self-giving death of Jesus on the cross that God is able to put things right. As the letter to the Hebrews makes clear, Jesus is 'the mediator of a new covenant' (9:15); it is by his 'shedding of blood' that there is 'forgiveness' of sins (9:22). God puts things right in our lives by the death of his Son, and sets us back on the road toward 'perfection'.

In the third place, God makes us perfect through the power of the resurrection of Jesus. God doesn't want just to forgive us; he also wants to change us. He changes us by the power of the resurrection. The basis for the prayer in the benediction is that the same divine creative energy that raised Jesus from the dead can be available to us; the power that shattered the bonds of death for Jesus can shatter the bonds of sins and failure which all too often hold us in their grip. How do we receive this power? Jesus showed that the road to Easter Day lay through Good Friday. He experienced God's power in his life as he surrendered himself to the cross. The way to power is always the way of self-surrender. What is true in the life of individuals is also true in the life of the church. If a church is to experience God's power in its life together, then there are times when individuals may need to surrender their own whims and preferences and accept the direction that God gives through those whom he has called to lead.

This process of 'perfection' or transformation will not be complete in this lifetime, but it needs to begin. Furthermore, this process is not easy – it requires determination on our part. But it is possible. C. S. Lewis once put it this way:

> He said (in the Bible) that we were 'gods' and He is going to make good His words. If we let Him – for we can prevent Him, if we choose – He will make the feeblest and filthiest of us into a god or goddess, a dazzling, radiant, immortal creature, pulsating all through with such energy and joy and wisdom and love as we cannot now imagine, a bright stainless mirror which reflects back to God perfectly (though of course, on a smaller scale) His own boundless power and delight and goodness. The process will be long and in parts very painful, but that is what we are in for. Nothing less. He meant what he said.[4]

[4] C. S. Lewis, *Mere Christianity*, in *Selected Books of C. S. Lewis* (HarperCollins, 1999), pp. 452–453.

4. Resurrection joy (1 Pet. 1:3–9)

Peter wrote his first letter to encourage a group of Turkish (v. 1) churches. This theme of encouragement is made explicit at the end of the letter, but is in fact implicit throughout: 'I have written to you briefly, encouraging you and testifying that this is the true grace of God. Stand fast in it' (5:12). Peter's readers needed encouragement, for Nero was on the throne. The letter was probably written around the end of AD 63, or perhaps the beginning of AD 64: that is, shortly before Nero's persecution of the church, during which Peter probably lost his life. The theme of suffering is constantly to the fore (e.g. 1:6; 3:13–17). In this context Peter begins his letter by encouraging his readers to face up to death. In spite of the threatening storm clouds of imminent persecution, they had no cause to fear. As a direct consequence of the resurrection of Jesus they had been given *a living hope* (v. 3).

The context in which most Christians find themselves today is very different. Certainly in the West we are surrounded by apathy rather than persecution. In spite of all the advances in medical science, however, death still has a sting. Rousseau's maxim that 'he who pretends to face death without fear is a liar' is as true today as ever it was. In other words, Christians today also need to be encouraged to think through what it means to be filled with a living hope.

> *Praise be to the God and Father of our Lord Jesus Christ! In his great mercy he has given us new birth into a living hope through the resurrection of Jesus Christ from the dead,* *and into an inheritance that can never perish, spoil or fade – kept in heaven for you,* [5]*who through faith are shielded by God's power until the coming of the salvation that is ready to be revealed in the last time.* [6]*In this you greatly rejoice, though now for a little while you may have had to suffer grief in all kinds of trials.* [7]*These have come so that your faith – of greater worth than gold, which perishes even though refined by fire – may be proved genuine and may result in praise, glory and honour when Jesus Christ is revealed.* [8]*Though you have not seen him, you love him; and even though you do not see him now, you believe in him and are filled with an inexpressible and glorious joy,* [9]*for you are receiving the goal of your faith, the salvation of your souls.*

Praise be to the God and Father of our Lord Jesus Christ! (v. 3). Peter begins his first letter on a wonderful note of 'benediction', that is, of praise. He declares that God is to be blessed (praised) because of what he has done for us in Jesus. This paean of praise is often compared to a similar benediction in Ephesians 1:3–12, but there is a signal difference – for whereas the focus of the benediction in Ephesians 1 is the grace of God in Jesus Christ, here the focus of the benediction is the resurrection hope that is ours as the result of the resurrection of Jesus from the dead. God is worthy of praise because *he has given us new birth into a living hope through the resurrection of Jesus Christ from the dead* (v. 3). If comparisons are to be made with other parts of Scripture, it is not so much Paul's benediction in Ephesians 1, but rather his outburst in 1 Corinthians 15:55, that forms the closest parallel:

> Where, O death, is your victory?
> Where, O death, is your sting?

Little wonder that both passages find their way into most funeral services. God is indeed to be praised – for he has raised Jesus from the dead, and in so doing brought hope to us all.

If the apostle Peter is indeed the author of this letter – and certainly the first verse would indicate this – it is not surprising that these opening verses are dominated by the theme of resurrection. For according to Luke, Peter's early preaching was dominated by the resurrection of Jesus (e.g. Acts 2:24, 31–32, 36; 3:15, 26; 4:2, 10; etc.). Although Peter has many other things to say in his first letter, it does seem appropriate that he should begin by praising God for the resurrection hope that is ours in Jesus.

It is significant that in this opening hymn of praise God is defined as *the God and Father of our Lord Jesus Christ* (v. 3). Jesus is not declared to be the Son of God, but rather God is described as the *Father of our Lord Jesus Christ*. It is not that the Son has usurped the place of the Father, but rather it is the Son who makes the Father known. In that sense all truly Christian preaching has to begin with Jesus. If preaching should be focused on what God has done in Christ, so too should all Christian worship. Christian worship is not in the first place the worship of God; rather, it is the worship of God as the *God and Father of our Lord Jesus Christ*. The mighty acts of incarnation, redemption and resurrection must always be to the fore.

But to return to 1 Peter 1:3. Jesus is described as *our Lord Jesus Christ*. Is Peter already anticipating the theme of resurrection here? For, as he declared on the day of Pentecost, it was through raising Jesus to life that God 'made this Jesus . . . both Lord and Christ' (Acts 2:36). Jesus is Lord because God raised him from the dead (see Rom. 10:6). Of interest is the possessive pronoun *our*. Peter underlines the special bond not only between him and his Lord, but also between the Lord and all those who *love him* (1:8). The

Christian religion is a personal religion. Christians do not believe primarily in a set of doctrines. They believe in the Lord who 'loved' them and 'gave himself' for them (see Gal. 2:20).

Perhaps as a result of his own personal experience of having let down the Lord Jesus, Peter was mindful of God's *great mercy* extended to him (see also 2:10). The fact, however, is that none of us deserves the new beginning that God has given us in Christ. Here in itself is cause for praise.

God *has given us new birth into a living hope through the resurrection of Jesus Christ from the dead.* In raising Jesus from the dead, God brought new life not only to his Son, but also to all those who have *faith* (v. 5). Although the 'hope' of life beyond the grave remains only a 'hope' in this life, God has already transformed the lives of those who believe. Peter uses a simple past (aorist) participle to indicate that God 'has caused us to be born again' (*anagennēsas*). Within the New Testament this particular Greek verb (*anagennaō*), found only here and in verse 23, is closely related to the Greek expression in John 3:3, 7 (*gennaō anōthen*), where Jesus talks to Nicodemus of the necessity of being 'born again' if he is to 'see the kingdom of God'. The language is slightly different, but the underlying concept is the same (see also 1 Cor. 15:50).

Here in 1 Peter 1:3 the means God uses to bring about the new birth is *the resurrection of Jesus Christ from the dead*; in 1 Peter 1:23 the means is 'the living and enduring word of God'. In reality, however, there is little difference between the two, for 'the living and enduring word of God' is in fact the gospel message of resurrection. When the preaching of the message of the resurrection encounters faith in the heart of the hearers, there the radical process of new birth takes place.

In the life of the early church, faith in the Lord of resurrection was expressed through baptism (see Acts 2:38), with the result that the concepts of faith, baptism, resurrection and new birth all became interrelated. Something of this interrelationship is seen a little later in 1 Peter, where Peter writes: 'Baptism . . . the pledge of a good conscience towards God . . . saves you by the resurrection of Jesus Christ' (3:21). Baptism of itself does not save anybody; rather, baptism as an expression of faith's 'pledge' (or commitment) towards God is what saves. To put it another way, baptism is faith's response to the love of God in Christ. Because the focus of faith expressed in baptism was the risen Christ, Peter could speak of the resurrection bringing about salvation, that is, effecting new birth. Some have suggested that Peter has baptism in mind also here in 1 Peter 1:3.

It is important to note that faith primarily centres on the risen Lord Jesus and on the life he had to offer. Faith looks back to Easter

Day, but faith also looks forward to the coming of the kingdom of God, when death will be swallowed up in victory and the perishable will inherit the imperishable (see 1 Cor. 15:50–55). Faith, we might say, looks forward in *hope*. This theme of *hope* finds repeated expression in 1 Peter. At the beginning of his letter Peter writes of the *living hope* into which we have been born again through the resurrection from the dead (1:3). This hope is *living* in the sense that it has been engendered by the resurrection of Jesus and remains focused on the resurrection life in Jesus. In 1:13 Peter urges his readers to set their 'hope fully on the grace to be given . . . when Jesus Christ is revealed' and when in turn the kingdom of God is to come in its resurrection fullness. A few sentences later Peter specifically links together the twin concepts of faith and hope with the resurrection as he declares: 'God . . . raised him [Jesus] from the dead . . . and so your faith and hope are in God' (1:21). The theme of resurrection is absent when a little later Peter mentions 'the holy women of the past' who 'put their hope in God' (3:5). Undoubtedly, however, the message of the resurrection is in his mind when he goes on to identify the Christian faith with hope: 'Always be prepared to give an answer to everyone who asks you to give the reason for the hope that you have' (3:15). The hope in question was surely the hope anchored in the resurrection of Jesus.

This hope in the resurrection separated the Christians from their non-Christian neighbours. The non-Christian world at that time was a world 'without hope and without God' (Eph. 2:12). In the ancient world death in particular was a force to be dreaded. According to Aristotle, 'Death is the most terrifying of things, for it is the end.' Sophocles expressed a similar dread: 'Not to be born at all – that is by far the best fortune; the second best is as soon as one is born with all speed to return thither one has come.' Into this darkness the light of the gospel of life shone.

This theme of hope in the resurrection permeates the whole of the benediction in 1 Peter 1. It is, for instance, clearly present when Peter writes of *an inheritance that can never perish, spoil or fade – kept in heaven for you* (v. 4). Peter is here referring to the kingdom of God which those who are born again will inherit (see John 3:3; 1 Cor. 15:50). This inheritance is described by three negative adjectives, each of which seeks to describe that which is beyond description. First, this inheritance is imperishable, that is, it cannot decay with age. The life God has for us in Christ will never come to an end. Secondly, it is undefiled, that is, it cannot be spoilt by sin. The life God has for us in Christ is perfection itself. Thirdly, it is unfading, that is, it cannot be debased with the passing of time. The life God offers in Christ will never lose its value. In addition, Peter writes that this inheritance is *kept in heaven for you.* Peter employs a Greek perfect passive participle (*tetērēmenēn*) to indicate a past activity with results that continue into the present. The participle can have the sense that this life has been indefinitely reserved for the people of faith. Alternatively, it can have the sense that this life in heaven will remain immune from disaster (see Matt. 6:19–20; Luke 12:33).

Furthermore, this resurrection hope belongs to men and women of faith who *are shielded by God's power until the coming of the salvation that is ready to be revealed in the last time* (v. 5; see also 1:20; 4:7). Peter employs a military term to describe the security of Christian believers. Furthermore, he expresses this term by means of a present participle (*phrouroumenous*). The implication is that God's power remains in constant guard over those who put their trust in the God of resurrection. Indeed, it is the power that raised Jesus Christ from the dead that ensures the safety of those who have been born again.

The experience of God's resurrection power at work in the lives of those who have faith, as also the hope of resurrection to come, is the cause for great rejoicing, in spite of present *trials* and tribulations (v. 6). Future joy outweighs present *grief*. Joy was the mood of Easter (see John 20:20; etc.). Joy too was the hallmark of the early church, itself a community of resurrection (see Acts 2:46; also 4:16; 5:41; 16:34). Peter is giving expression to intense joy here. The verb (*agalliaomai*) used here (and in v. 8) is found in the opening lines of the *Magnificat* (Luke 1:46–47), where Mary cries out:

'My soul glorifies the Lord
and my spirit rejoices in God my Saviour.'

The NIV translates the term here as *greatly rejoice;* 'exult' would be a good alternative translation. Although the Greek (*agalliasthe*) could be an imperative ('Rejoice!'), almost certainly we have here the indicative. Those to whom Peter is writing do not have to be told to be joyful – they *already greatly rejoice.*

Peter was able to take a positive view even of their present *trials. These have come so that your faith . . . may be proved genuine* (v. 7). For Peter, even the darkest of clouds can have a silver – or rather a golden – lining. The picture here is of God refining faith as a goldsmith might refine gold – the end product is so much better, as it is now free of impurity (see Ps. 66:10; Prov. 17:3; 27:21; Zech. 13:9; Mal. 3:3). Faith is *of greater worth than gold* because one day even gold will perish (see also 1:18). This thought brings joy in the present, and in the future will *result in praise, glory and honour when Jesus Christ is revealed* (v. 7).

Peter elaborates on this joy, a joy rooted in love for the risen Lord Jesus, unseen and yet present by his Spirit: *Though you have not seen him, you love him; and even though you do not see him now, you believe in him and are filled with an inexpressible and glorious joy* (v. 8). Unlike Peter (see 2 Pet. 1:6), the Christians to whom he wrote had never had the privilege of physically seeing the Lord Jesus. Yet they had come to *love him*. Here again is a reminder that the Christian faith is primarily a relationship and not a philosophy or a moral code. Until the day when they will indeed see him 'face to face' (1 Cor. 13:12), they *now* are called to *believe* in him. It is difficult to think that Peter is not alluding to the words of the risen Lord Jesus recorded after Thomas's encounter with him: 'Because you have seen me, you have believed; blessed are those who have not seen and yet have believed' (John 20:29). As a result of their relationship with the risen Lord Jesus and the hope that is theirs in him, they exult with a joy which is beyond description and which is 'shot through with that glory which belongs to God himself'.[5]

This joy is all the more deepened, because, as a result of their faith in the risen Lord Jesus, they are *receiving . . . the salvation* of their *souls* (v. 9). Peter employs a present participle (*komizomenoi*): their future salvation is already in the process of being worked out in the present. Already they have been born again – however, their *hope* of sharing in the resurrection of Jesus has yet to be realized. The *salvation of your souls* is the nearest Peter comes to the Pauline doctrine of the resurrection of the body. The soul, for Peter, undoubtedly has the Semitic sense of the essential self, and refers to humans as living beings (see Gen. 2:7). In other words, the salvation Peter has in mind is not some shadowy disembodied spirit familiar to the spiritualist seance, but rather a new and fuller life lived together in the kingdom of God, a life described by Eugene Peterson in *The Message* as 'total' salvation.

a. The Easter hope

The Easter hope means there is *a life beyond the grave*. There is a fascinating tombstone in Bolsover, Derbyshire, which reads:

> Here lies in a horizontal position the outside case of
> Thomas Hinde, Clock and Watchmaker,
> Who departed this life wound up
> in the hope of being taken in hand by his Maker
> and being thoroughly cleaned, repaired and set a-going
> in the world to come.

[5] J. N. D. Kelly, *The Epistles of Peter and of Jude* (A. & C. Black, 1969), p. 57.

No such hope, however, was to be found among the tombstones of the great and mighty of classical times. In the graveyard on the Appian Way, just outside the city of Rome, not one of the epitaphs expresses any hope for the future. Instead, one reads: 'The sun will rise and set, but it is eternal darkness for me.' By and large the epitaphs are sarcastic in tone; for example, 'A cocktail for you and a cocktail for me . . . and that is life'; or 'Life is constituted of lust. But lust is not good for the constitution.' Similarly, in many circles today, there is also little hope. Most people would dearly love to believe in life after death. Because they are uncertain about what lies ahead, however, they do their best to minimize or forget death. Death becomes the last thing they talk about – even at the moment of dying. But the good news is that with the resurrection of Jesus, 'hope' has been brought into the world.

Easter hope means that there is *a life to be certain of*. Christian hope has nothing in common with that false hope many of us experience when we go on a diet. We can be certain of the future. because of what has happened in the past. Our *hope* is based on the resurrection of Jesus (v. 3). This hope is all the more certain in so far as the blessings of this new life are *kept* for us by God in heaven (v. 5), and because God keeps them we know they can never be taken away. People can tie us to the stake, throw us to the lions, gas us in a concentration camp, exterminate us with a bomb, or gun us down, but they cannot take away the life God has for us. What a hope! Here amid all life's uncertainties is something certain – something truly secure.

Easter hope is about *a life to experience now*. Faith in Jesus not only affects the future. It also affects the present. Christianity is not simply about 'pie in the sky when you die'. Already in the here and now God *has given us new birth* (v. 3). Here of course we are dealing with a metaphor, as nobody is literally born again. And yet the underlying truth is that in this life the Christian undergoes a radical change. Life becomes a joyful experience (v. 8). It is not that life suddenly becomes any easier. Indeed, for Peter's readers the reverse was the case – the sheer fact of being Christians invited persecution. No, the joy comes from knowing that our sins are forgiven and so the past can never return to haunt us; that God is our Father and is present with us through his Spirit; that Jesus is our Saviour and with him our future is for ever secure.

Easter hope is about *a life to receive today*. The good news is that this resurrection life is not the preserve of the few, but is open to all who believe in the Lord Jesus (v. 8) and so receive God's *salvation* (v. 9).

The story is told of a medieval king who gave his new court jester the fool's sceptre and told him to keep it until he met a bigger fool than himself. Years later the king lay dying and sent for the jester. 'I'm going on a long journey,' he said.

'Where are you going, and how will you travel?' asked the jester.

'I don't know,' replied the king.

'Have you made any provision for the journey, Your Majesty?'

'No,' replied the king.

The jester handed the king his fool's sceptre. 'Then this belongs to you.'

5. A vision of the risen Lord (Rev. 1:9–18)

I, John, your brother and companion in the suffering and kingdom and patient endurance that are ours in Jesus, was on the island of Patmos because of the word of God and the testimony of Jesus.
¹⁰On the Lord's Day I was in the Spirit, and I heard behind me a loud voice like a trumpet, ¹¹which said: 'Write on a scroll what you see and send it to the seven churches: to Ephesus, Smyrna, Pergamum, Thyatira, Sardis, Philadelphia and Laodicea.
¹²I turned round to see the voice that was speaking to me. And when I turned I saw seven golden lampstands, ¹³and among the lampstands was someone 'like a son of man', dressed in a robe reaching down to his feet and with a golden sash round his chest.
¹⁴His head and hair were white like wool, as white as snow, and his eyes were like blazing fire. ¹⁵His feet were like bronze glowing in a furnace, and his voice was like the sound of rushing waters.
¹⁶In his right hand he held seven stars, and out of his mouth came a sharp double-edged sword. His face was like the sun shining in all its brilliance.
¹⁷When I saw him, I fell at his feet as though dead. Then he placed his right hand on me and said: 'Do not be afraid. I am the First and the Last. ¹⁸I am the Living One; I was dead, and behold I am alive for ever and ever! And I hold the keys of death and Hades.'

When John had his vision of the risen Lord he was languishing in exile on the island of Patmos (v. 9). Patmos (present-day Patino) is one of the Sporades Islands off the west coast of Asia Minor. Some thirty miles in circumference, it is relatively small. We have no idea of the conditions John had to endure. Some have speculated that he may have been forced to work in the saltmines that were found there. It may well be, however, that his punishment was not so much hard labour as separation from his family and friends. Ephesus was some fifty miles away – with the sea in between. Fortunately, as the past tense *was* indicates, the exile proved temporary. According to Eusebius, following the death of the Roman emperor Domitian (AD 96), John was allowed to return to Ephesus thanks to an edict of the Roman senate recalling all those who had been banished.

The cause of John's banishment was his preaching the word of God and his testimony (*martyria*) of Jesus (v. 9). As the leader of the church in Ephesus, John had apparently been considered a threat to the community. His preaching, far from sending people to sleep, appears to have stirred up trouble. So he had been taken into 'protective custody'.

John described his period of exile as being a time when he shared in the *suffering and kingdom and patient endurance that are ours in Jesus* (v. 9). Like his readers, John knew what it was like to be 'under pressure' – the Greek noun (*thlipsis*) is derived from a verb meaning to 'press' or to 'squash', which was often used metaphorically to describe a variety of mental and emotional ordeals and is variously translated as 'agony', 'distress', 'tribulation', 'oppression' or, as here, *suffering*. John's experience of exile no doubt included ostracism, slander, poverty and even violence. It was not a happy time. Emperor Domitian (AD 51–96) and his servants were beginning to cause trouble for the church. Indeed, at Pergamum, Antipas had actually died for his faith (2:13).

But this was not the whole picture. As a result of the death and resurrection of Jesus, John and his readers, even in the moment of their suffering, were also sharing in the life of the kingdom (see v. 6). For John, this experience of sharing in both the suffering and the kingdom that are ours in Jesus formed the two aspects of present Christian existence. Contrary to some modern 'prosperity' teaching, membership of Christ's kingdom does not shield us from suffering – rather, for John and his readers, membership of the kingdom was the cause of their suffering. To be in Jesus is to take up our cross and follow the crucified (see Mark 8:34).

Not surprisingly John therefore includes *patient endurance* as the third mark of Christian living (v. 9; see also 2:2–3, 19; 3:10). In these 'in-between' times, when Christ's kingdom is hidden and is yet to be revealed, 'steadfast perseverance' is called for if we are to 'overcome' (see 2:7, 11, 17, 26; etc.) all that the world can throw at us.

It was *on the Lord's Day* (1:10), when John received his vision of the risen Christ. The expression *the Lord's Day* is found only here in the New Testament, and is closely related to the expression 'the Lord's Supper' (1 Cor. 11:20). In both phrases an adjective is used (*kyriakos*) which means 'belonging to the Lord (*kyrios*)'. The Lord in question, of course, is Jesus – not Caesar! Significantly there was a day in the month dedicated to Caesar, on which his accession to the throne was celebrated. It may be that the Christian use of the term 'the Lord's Day' as also their celebration of the resurrection on the 'first day of every week' (see 1 Cor. 16:2; Acts 20:7) contained an implicit protest against 'Caesar's day'. Jesus alone is Lord, for he is not seated on Caesar's throne, but shares the very throne of God himself (5:13).

Although John may have been the only Christian on Patmos, he may have been observing the Lord's Day by focusing on the Lord in worship. As he did so he found himself *in the Spirit* (v. 10; see 4:2; 17:3; 21:10). The Spirit 'took control' (GNB) of him and enabled him to see into heaven itself. The setting of the vision is significant: John and his readers were very conscious of the rising hostility against them; humanly speaking their prospects were far from good. A sense of fear, if not of hopelessness, must have been experienced by many. In such a setting John sees the risen Christ, and in seeing him everything else begins to shrink back into proportion.

The vision-like nature of the experience is emphasized by the use of the word *like* (v. 10). The use of this particle, which occurs some fifty-six times in Revelation, brings out the fact that John was dealing with heavenly realities for which earthly speech was inadequate.

The *loud voice* (see 5:2, 12; 6:10; 7:2; etc.) John heard was *like a trumpet* (v. 10). Every feature of the vision of the risen Christ is overwhelming. A little later his voice is described like the sound of rushing waters (1.15). This voice is not to be likened to the 'gentle whisper' Elijah heard (see 1 Kgs. 19:12), nor to some gently babbling brook, but rather to the mighty Niagara or Victoria Falls. The sound of this trumpet-like voice drowns out all other sounds – the voice of the risen Lord alone prevails.

Significantly the voice of the figure before him comes from among *the seven golden lampstands* (v. 12). There among the lampstands was someone *'like a son of man'* (v. 13). *The seven golden lampstands* symbolize *the seven churches* of Asia Minor to which John is commanded to write (v. 20). This imagery goes back to Zechariah 4:1–14, but whereas there the people of God are represented by a single seven-branched lampstand, here each of the seven churches are represented by a lampstand of their own – the change in symbolism is no doubt accounted for by the fact that in the New Testament each local church is representative of the universal church as a whole. Important as this understanding of the local church is, however, the key point John wishes to make is that the risen Lord is among his people (see Matt. 18:20). The risen Lord may share the throne of God, but this does not mean to say he is an absentee Lord, who will return only at the end of time. He is already with his people.

The description of the risen Lord is full of Old Testament allusions, but in particular draws upon the description of the Ancient of Days in Daniel 7:9–14 and of the angel in Daniel 10:5–6. For example, the risen Lord is likened to *a son of man*. The omission of the definite article is significant. In the Gospels the term 'the Son of Man' frequently conveys the idea of humility (e.g. Matt. 8:20) – but here the anarthrous phrase refers back to Daniel 7:13–14 and emphasizes his glory; for in Daniel 7 'one like a son of man . . . was given authority, glory and sovereign power; all peoples, nations and men of every language worshipped him. His dominion is an everlasting dominion that will not pass away, and his kingdom is one that will never be destroyed.'

This *son of man* figure was *dressed in a robe reaching down to his feet and with a golden sash around his chest* (v. 13). Although many commentators think that John is describing the risen Lord in priestly garments (see Exod. 28:4; 39:29; Ezek. 9:2; 44:18), the fact is that a robe and sash were basic articles of clothing common to both men and women in the ancient world. Certainly nowhere else in the book of Revelation is Jesus presented as a priest. The allusion is rather to Daniel 10:5, where the angel is described as 'dressed in linen, with a belt of the finest gold round his waist'. This allusion is confirmed by the later reference to *his eyes* being *like blazing fire. His feet were like bronze glowing in a furnace, and his voice was like the sound of rushing waters . . . His face was like the sun shining in all its brilliance* (1:14–16). The angel in Daniel 10:6 is similarly described as having 'eyes like flaming torches', 'arms and legs like the gleam of burnished bronze, a 'voice like the sound of a multitude' and a 'face like lightning'. The emphasis here is upon the exalted glory of the Lord. Whether or not the detail is significant is perhaps open to question. The *eyes like blazing fire* may symbolize the omniscience of the risen Lord, from whom no secret is hidden; the feet *like bronze glowing in a furnace* may signify the omnipotence of the Lord, who will brook no opposition to his rule (see 2:18, 23).

The risen Lord is also described as having *head and hair . . . white like wool, as white as snow* (v. 14). The allusion is to Daniel 7:9, where God is depicted as 'the Ancient of Days', whose clothing was 'as white as snow', and whose hair was 'white like wool'. At first sight the image here in Revelation 1 is somewhat strange, for it seems that the risen Lord is depicted as an old man. That is not the point, however. John's concern is to associate Jesus closely with God, who in Daniel 7 is depicted as the judge of the nations.

Further, writes John, *In his right hand he held seven stars* (v. 16). What does John have in mind? Some have drawn attention to the fact that in antiquity the 'seven stars' were often used to represent the seven 'planets' (Sun, Moon, Jupiter, Mercury, Mars, Venus and Saturn), and have suggested that here we have a picture of the cosmic Lord. Jesus – and not the stars – has the destiny of the world in his hands. This is an attractive suggestion, strengthened by the fact that the Roman emperors took the symbol of the seven stars and used it on their coins to underline their claim to be the world rulers. The stars here, however, as John makes clear later, represent 'the angels of the seven churches' (1:20). John is saying here that the Lord has the churches in his hands – he has his hold on them: they are in his care (see John 10:28).

But there is no room for complacency. For John also writes: *out of his mouth came a sharp double-edged sword* (v. 16). The risen Lord comes with the sword of judgment (see 2:16; 19:15, 21). Furthermore, this sword of judgment threatens not only the nations of the world (19:15), but also the church (2:16). As the churches are reminded in the seven letters, the Lord is concerned to root out sin within the church as much as within the world.

Not surprisingly, at the sight of this exalted figure, John, like the angel in Daniel 10:7–9, was overwhelmed and fell to the ground (v. 17). Indeed, fear and falling to the ground are typical reactions to the appearance of a supernatural figure (see Is. 6:5; Ezek. 1:28; 3:23; Luke 5:8). Unique to the book of Revelation, however, is the phrase *as though dead*. John is revived only by the touch of the risen Lord, a detail possibly symbolic of the difference the risen Christ can make to us all.

At this point the vision reaches its climax. Undoubtedly the words of the risen Lord are intended to reassure not just John, but also his readers as they faced an increasingly hostile future: *'Do not be afraid. I am the First and the Last. I am the Living One; I was dead, and behold I am alive for ever and ever! And I hold the keys of death and Hades'* (1:17–18).

The first ground for confidence is that the risen Lord is *the First and the Last* (v. 17; see 2:8; 22:13), reminiscent of the description of God as 'the Alpha and the Omega' (1:8; 21:6). This phrase is also reminiscent of a Jewish expression that spoke of keeping the law from 'aleph to tau' (the first and last letters of the Hebrew alphabet), and meant keeping the law in its entirety – the first commandment and the last commandment and everything in between. Therefore, the implication of the fact that the Lord is the First and the Last, the Alpha and the Omega, is that he is the beginning of history and the end of history and Lord of all the time that lies between. Indeed, as the beginning and the end and Lord of all the time in between, he is Lord of history and sovereign of all. This sovereignty is reinforced by the way in which the phrase is prefaced by an allusion to the divine name, *I am* (*egō eimi*; see Exod. 3:14, 'I AM WHO I AM'). The risen Lord, as 'the One who is', is the ever-present Lord in the sense that he is ever present to act on behalf of his people. He is the Lord who is always able to meet the needs of the hour.

As the ever-present Lord he is *the Living One* (v. 18). John uses a favourite rabbinic title for God. But there is a double meaning, for the phrase refers not just to the traditional Jewish designation for God but also to the triumph of the risen Lord Jesus over death. This latter reference is confirmed by the startling words '*I was dead.*' Incomprehensibly, the Eternal One experienced death. But the Lord immediately goes on: '*and behold I am alive for ever and ever!*'

The second ground for confidence is contained in the final affirmation: '*And I hold the keys of death and Hades*' (v. 18). 'Hades' is the normal Greek word for 'underworld' (the Hebrew term was Sheol) and does not refer to 'hell' as such, but rather to the place of the dead. Jesus holds *the keys*. Some commentators maintain that this image of Jesus as the key-bearer is derived from the popular Hellenistic conception of the goddess Hekate as the key-bearer to the world of the dead. The phrase could also have Jewish roots, however. For instance, the Jerusalem Targum on Deuteronomy 28:12 has the comment: 'Four keys are delivered into the hand of the Lord of the world which he has given to no ruler: the key of life, the key of the graves, the key of food, the key of rain.' Whatever the source of the imagery, the implication is clear: Jesus has 'authority over death and the world of the dead' (GNB). He is able to lead his followers out from death into life. For those facing the prospect of martyrdom (2:13), it must have been a great comfort to know that death was not the end. Because of this they could give themselves to his service, whatever the risks, knowing that their ultimate future was secure. Indeed, there is great comfort here for us all. Death need not be feared, for Jesus has conquered death and offers life to all who will accept the 'water of life' (see 21:6–7).

a. Jesus is Lord!

Jesus is Lord – of the world! It was not without significance that the Spirit took control of John *on the Lord's Day*, the day of resurrection, when Christians celebrated the truth that Jesus shares the very throne of God himself (see 5:13). The risen Lord, who appeared to him in all his glory, is likened to 'the Ancient of Days', to whom was given all authority and all power. From first to last John's Revelation is dominated by this idea of divine sovereignty. He is saying to those who lived under the shadow of Caesar's throne, and found that shadow made darker by the shadow of Satan's throne, 'Do not be afraid – the one truth that matters above all is that there is a greater throne above! Jesus is Lord!' John's contemporaries needed to hear that message, and so too do we. In a world where so many things seem to go wrong, it is tempting to believe that this world is out of control. John's message is that, ultimately, right will out and evil will have its come-uppance, for Jesus is Lord.

Jesus is Lord – of the church! In his vision, John sees the risen Lord *among the lampstands*, that is, the Lord who reigns on high is with his people. Indeed, in the vision the Lord holds the churches' representatives (*the seven stars*) in his hand. What a wonderfully comforting picture for churches that are struggling and that seem overwhelmed by the 'competition' the world appears to provide. The Lord who has the 'whole wide world in his hands' is also the Lord who has each of his churches in his hands. But there is no room for complacency. For this same Lord, who protects his people, also comes with *a sharp double-edged sword* to judge not only the world, but also the church. With the risen Lord in the midst there is no room for lovelessness in any shape or form. Jesus is Lord of his church!

But there is a more personal application of the vision. The risen Lord holds *the keys of death and Hades*. As a result of his death and resurrection, death need no longer have the last word; death need no longer be 'the king of terrors' (Job 18:14; see also Ps. 55:4). To those who have made him their Lord, Jesus says, *'Do not be afraid.'* For we too may share with him that life which is *for ever and ever.*

b. The Lord's Day

John's use of the term *the Lord's Day* suggests a number of different approaches to the Christian use of Sunday. First, Sunday is a day for *celebration*. As the first day of the week, it is the day when we celebrate the resurrection of Jesus. It is the day when we celebrate Jesus' triumph over sin and death. Jesus, not Caesar, is on the throne of the world! Indeed, it is not simply the *day* that belongs to him – we too belong to him.

Secondly, Sunday is a day for *commemoration*. The Lord's Day is the day when the Lord's Supper is served. It is the day when we break bread and remember that Jesus died for us. Because the Lord's Supper takes place on the Lord's Day, however, we remember not simply one who died, but one who is *alive for ever and ever.* Commemoration becomes celebration.

Thirdly, Sunday is a day for receiving the *collection*. Although this thought is not present in Revelation 1, the theological rationale implied by the lordship of Jesus over all aspects of life is present in the description of Jesus as the exalted Son of Man. It is *on the Lord's Day* that we acknowledge that all that we have belongs to him and is therefore held in trust (see 1 Chr. 29:14). Or, as Paul writes to the church at Corinth, it is 'on the first day of every week' that each one of us is to 'set aside a sum of money in keeping with his income' (1 Cor. 16:2).

Fourthly, Sunday is a day for *comprehension* – for gaining a deeper understanding of God's purposes for our lives and for the life of this world. For John and his readers, such comprehension was gained through a series of visions. For us, such comprehension comes as we encounter the risen Lord in worship and in the exposition of the Word of God. Sunday is a day when we see life in its true perspective – when we see life in the light of the risen Lord.

6. A vision of life around the throne (Rev. 7:9–17)

After this I looked and there before me was a great multitude that no-one could count, from every nation, tribe, people and language, standing before the throne and in front of the Lamb. They were wearing white robes and were holding palm branches in their hands. [10]*And they cried out in a loud voice:*

> *'Salvation belongs to our God,*
> *who sits on the throne,*
> *and to the Lamb.'*

[11]*All the angels were standing round the throne and around the elders and the four living creatures. They fell down on their faces before the throne and worshipped God,* [12]*saying:*

> *'Amen!*
> *Praise and glory*
> *and wisdom and thanks and honour*
> *and power and strength*
> *be to our God for ever and ever.*
> *Amen!'*

[13]*Then one of the elders asked me, 'These in white robes – who are they, and where did they come from?'*
[14]*I answered, 'Sir, you know.'*
And he said, 'These are they who have come out of the great tribulation; they have washed their robes and made them white in the blood of the Lamb. [15]*Therefore,*

> *'they are before the throne of God and serve him day and night*
> *in his temple; and he who sits on the throne will spread his tent*
> *over them.*
> *16Never again will they hunger; never again will they thirst.*
> *The sun will not beat upon them, nor any scorching heat.*
> *17For the Lamb at the centre of the throne will be their shepherd;*
> *he will lead them to springs of living water.*
> *And God will wipe away every tear from their eyes.'*

From John's vision of the risen Lord in Revelation 1 we turn to his vision of life beyond resurrection promised to those who remain faithful to their Lord. As we have already seen, John is writing at a time when widespread persecution appeared to be imminent. 'The hour of trial' (3:10), otherwise known as 'the great tribulation' (7:14), was about to come upon the world. Martyrdom appeared to be the certain lot of those who remained faithful to their Lord (6:9). But to those who 'overcome' (2:7, 11, 17, 26; 3:5, 12, 21), death will not have the final word. For 'the Lion of the tribe of Judah . . . has triumphed' (5:5). The risen Lord is 'the Living One' and holds 'the keys of death and Hades' (1:18). This is the context in which Revelation 7:9–17 and 21:1–5 are to be placed.

From first to last John's 'revelation' is dominated by *the throne* of God (v. 9). Caesar's throne is as nothing compared to God's throne. As John delights to repeat, the Lord God is the 'Almighty' Lord, who is sovereign over all (Rev. 1:8; 4:8; 11:17; 15:3; 16:7, 14; 19:6, 15; 21:22). John's message is that the God who is enthroned in heaven is the God who is working out his purposes here below. In the words of the heavenly chorus,

> 'Hallelujah!
> For our Lord God Almighty reigns.'
>
> (19.6)

God, however, does not sit on his throne alone. Sharing the throne of God is *the Lamb* (7:9, 10; see also 5:6). The Lamb (*arnion*) is John's principal and distinctive title for Jesus, and, apart from John 21:15, is found only in the book of Revelation, where it occurs no fewer than twenty-nine times (5:6, 8, 12, 13; 6:1, 16; 7:9, 10, 14, 17; etc.). With the exception of 13:11, where it is used of the Antichrist, who is the antitype of Jesus, it always refers to the exalted Jesus.

As the Lamb of God, Jesus is in the first instance the Redeemer Lamb, God's Passover Lamb. In this respect he is the Lamb who 'was slain' (5:6, 12; 13:8) and who ever bears the marks of his suffering. It is significant that John never uses a simple past participle to describe Jesus as the one who was slain, but rather a perfect participle (*esphagmenon*, 5:6), which represents the continuing effects of a once-for-all past act. But Jesus is not just the crucified Saviour; he is also the risen Lord. As the risen Lord he is God's Warrior Lamb. In this respect he is the Lamb who has seven 'horns' (5:6), symbols of power (see Deut. 33:17; also Rev. 17:3, 12). The Warrior Lamb overcomes the forces of evil, because he is 'Lord of lords and King of kings' (17:14). This image of the Messiah as a Warrior Lamb was familiar in Jewish apocalyptic writing[6] and may account for John's use of the Greek word *arnion* for 'lamb', as distinct from the more usual term *amnos*, used elsewhere in the New Testament to describe Jesus as God's Lamb (see John 1:29, 36; Acts 8:32; 1 Pet. 1:19).

Here in Revelation 7, however, the initial focus of John's vision is not so much the throne as the vast crowd standing before the throne. In his vision, John centres on the church 'triumphant', which he describes as *a great multitude that no-one could count* (v. 9). Literally, 'no-one could do the arithmetic'! God's promise to Abraham that his people would be as the stars of the heavens in number (Gen. 15:5), and as the sand of the sea (Gen. 32:12), had been well and truly fulfilled. What an encouragement this vision must have been to the small struggling churches to which John was writing!

Furthermore, this huge crowd came *from every nation, tribe, people and language* (v. 9; see also 5:9; 11:9; 13:7 and 14:6 for the same fourfold division). The people of God have transcended their Jewish roots. This massive, international gathering can be likened to a heavenly United Nations.

As an aside, we may note that there is no need to see any distinction from, or contradiction with, John's earlier description of the redeemed as '144,000 from all the tribes of Israel' (Rev. 7:4). The 144,000 is not meant to be an exact figure, but rather the product of $12 \times 12 \times 1,000$, and is just another way of expressing the complete number of the redeemed. Nor is John seeking to distinguish between Jewish believers and Gentile Christians; rather, the twelve tribes are a symbol of the church as the new Israel.

The people making up the enormous crowd *were wearing white robes* (v. 9): that is, they had received what was promised to those who overcame at Sardis (3:5). The significance of these white robes

---

[6] See, for example, *Testament of Joseph* 19:8–9: 'And all the beasts rushed against him [the lamb], and the lamb overcame them, and destroyed them and trod them underfoot . . . His kingdom is an everlasting kingdom, which shall not pass away.'

is unpacked a little later in the vision. There, one of the elders declares, that *'they have washed their robes and made them white in the blood of the Lamb'* (v. 14). To our way of thinking this is nonsense – blood stains rather than cleans! We are dealing here with symbolism, however. The symbolism of dirty clothes for an unclean life occurs frequently in the Old Testament (e.g. Is. 64:6; Zech. 3:3), as also the corresponding idea of clean clothes for a pure life (see Zech. 3:4). Here the blood of the Lamb, which washes clean, is a symbol of the sacrificial death of Jesus on the cross, which cleanses us from sin (see Heb. 9:24; 1 John 1:7). It was through the outpouring of his life at Calvary that Jesus, the Lamb of God, took away the sin of the world (see John 1:29; 19:34). There may also be an allusion to Isaiah 1:18 (see also Gen. 49:11):

'Though your sins are like scarlet,
    they shall be as white as snow;
though they are red as crimson,
    they shall be like wool.'

Here we have a reminder that God's people owe their place in heaven first to Jesus, the Lamb of God, and only secondly to their faith expressed in courage and endurance. Nevertheless, if the blood of Jesus is to cleanse, a response of faith is needed. This faith, subsequently lived out in lives of ongoing faithfulness, is publicly expressed in baptism. Certainly the simple past tense (*washed*, *eplynan*) suggests that there was a particular moment when they washed their robes and made them white: baptism (see Acts 22:16), rather than martyrdom, would seem to have been that moment, not least because their robes were washed in the Lamb's blood rather than their own.

The crowd were also *holding palm branches in their hands* (v. 9). These palms are surely symbols of joy and victory (see John 12:13; also 1 Macc. 13:51; 2 Macc. 10:7). The waving of palms may be likened to the modern custom of waving scarves and banners at a football match. The crowd raise their voices to praise God and the Lamb. *'Salvation belongs to our God, who sits on the throne, and to the Lamb'* (v. 10). This is no mere liturgical response. This is a shout of praise (*they cried out in a loud voice*). Indeed, John actually uses the present tense (*krazousin*) here, with the implicit suggestion that the crowd keep on shouting out. It is almost as if they cannot contain themselves with pride and delight at what God has done in Christ. Just as a crowd of jubilant football fans might go wild celebrating their team's success, so God's people continually celebrate his salvation with understandable excitement.

But what precisely are they celebrating? The word *salvation* can be understood in several ways. With reference to the cleansing power of the blood of Christ, salvation may be understood as salvation from sin and from the dire consequences of sin. The use of the term 'salvation' in Revelation 12:10 and 19:1 may suggest, however, that the primary reference is to the Hebrew concept of salvation as deliverance from enemies, that is, 'victory' over them (see, e.g., 1 Sam. 14:6, 45; Ps. 118: 14–15, 21) – God in Christ has saved his people by gaining the victory over the powers of evil. Alternatively, with reference to the political ideology of the time, which claimed Caesar to be the source of total well-being, salvation may be understood in terms of the true well-being to be found only in God and the Lamb. Clearly all three concepts are closely interrelated. We have much reason to celebrate.

At this point the angels also join their voices in praise to God. They echo the praise of the redeemed (*'Amen!'*) and in turn ascribe their own worship to God:

> *'Praise and glory*
> *and wisdom and thanks and honour*
> *and power and strength*
> *be to our God for ever and ever.'*
>
> (v. 12)

Six of the seven attributes occur in their earlier doxology (5:12), but in an entirely different order, with *thanks* replacing 'wealth'. At first sight it appears that John has heaped together a random collection of words of praise, with the intention of making an effect through their sheer quantity. Yet there is significance in each of the terms, for each of them expresses a different response to the divine. *Praise* (or 'blessing', *eulogia*), for instance, represents the loving adoration for his grace beyond measure (see Eph. 1:3–10). *Glory* (*doxa* – from which is derived our English word 'doxology') represents the awesome acknowledgment of God's inestimable worth (Luke 2:24). *Wisdom* (*sophia*) is the joyful boast that God's wisdom is wiser than any human wisdom (1 Cor. 1:18–31). Whether or not there are any 'eucharistic' allusions, *thanks* (*eucharistia*) surely includes thanksgiving for the broken body and poured-out blood of Jesus (1 Cor. 11:23–25). *Honour* (*timē*) is the reverential respect due to the King of the universe (the *Pantocrator*). *Power* (*dynamis* – from which is derived our English word 'dynamite') is the insightful confession that God is able to do 'immeasurably more than all we ask or imagine' (Eph. 3:20). *Strength* (*ischys*) is the celebration of the might of God, who raised Jesus from the dead and 'appointed him to be head over everything for the church' (Eph. 1:22). Although this outpouring of praise is attributed to the angels, this 'hymn' is also a fitting medium of praise for humans. We too can add our *Amen!*

The focus of the vision now switches back to the crowd dressed in white: *'These are they who have come out of the great tribulation'* (v. 14). The use of the definite article probably indicates that the reference is primarily to the final series of 'trials' that will immediately precede the end (3:10; see also Dan. 12:1; Mark 13:19). With the hindsight of the years, however, it is perhaps not without significance that John uses a present participle (*erchomenoi*) – people not only *have come*, but also continue to come, out of tribulation. Down through the centuries trials and tribulations have been an ongoing experience of God's people (see John 16:33; Acts 14:22). Interestingly, the noun *tribulation* (*thlipsis*) can refer to the process of 'grinding' or 'milling', a process in which corn is ground between two heavy 'pressurizing' stones. Time and again the people of God have found themselves 'between a rock and a hard place', crushed between the demands of their faith and the 'pressures' of this world. But John reminds his readers that to those who keep the faith a wonderful future is in store. Drawing upon a number of Old Testament passages, he develops a picture of life beyond the resurrection.

First, in this life beyond the resurrection, *'they are before the throne of God'* (v. 15). As they live their life in the presence of God, *'they serve (latreuousin) him day and night in his temple'* (see 22:3). The 'service' John has in mind is the worship of their hearts and minds (see, e.g., Matt. 4:10 and Luke 4:8, where *latreuō* is a synonym for *proskyneō*, to 'worship'). As 'priests', they *serve* through the offering of their adoration and praise (see 1:6). Together with the heavenly host they now share in the constant round of the worship of God.

Secondly, in this life beyond the resurrection they are enveloped by the presence of God and by his accompanying glory. For *'he who sits on the throne will spread his tent over them'* (v. 15). This expression anticipates John's description of the holy city in Revelation 21:3: 'Now the dwelling [literally, 'tent', *skēnē*] of God is with men and he will live [literally, 'pitch his tent', *skēnōsei*] with them.' In the Old Testament (see, e.g., Exod. 40:34–38) the 'tent of God's presence' was where God revealed his glory (*kābôd*). John, no doubt, was also recalling the prophecy of Isaiah 4:5–6: 'Then the Lord will create over all of Mount Zion and over those who assemble there a cloud of smoke by day and a glow of flaming fire by night; over all the glory will be a canopy. It will be a shelter and shade from the heat of the day, and a refuge and hiding-place from the storm and rain.'

Thirdly, in this life beyond resurrection God's presence will both protect his people from all harm and also meet their deepest needs:

> *'Never again will they hunger;*
>   *never again will they thirst.*
> *The sun will not beat upon them,*
>   *nor any scorching heat.*
> *For the Lamb at the centre of the throne will be their*
>   *shepherd;*
> *he will lead them to springs of living water'.*
>
> (vv. 16–17)

Here John not only anticipates Revelation 21 – 22, but also draws upon Isaiah 49:10 with its description of the exiles returning home from Babylon:

> They will neither hunger nor thirst,
>   nor will the desert heat or the sun beat upon them.
> He who has compassion on them will guide them
>   and lead them beside springs of water.

There is also an undoubted reference to Psalm 23:1–2, where the Lord, 'my shepherd . . . leads me beside quiet waters' (see also Ezek. 34:23). Through these images John conveys a picture of safety and security. He also points to the ultimate satisfaction of our deepest longing for spiritual wholeness: our thirst for God will be quenched (see Ps. 42:1–2; also Matt. 5:6; John 4:14; 6:35; 7:37), for we shall live in his very presence.

Fourthly, in the life beyond resurrection all past hurts, and indeed causes of hurts, will disappear. For *'God will wipe away every tear from their eyes'* (v. 17) John here anticipates Revelation 21:4 and alludes to Isaiah's vision of the day when God 'will swallow up death for ever' and 'will wipe away the tears from all faces' (Is. 25:8). The tears of grief and pain will belong to the past. Sorrow will be replaced by delight. What a wonderful future indeed! John sought to encourage and strengthen his readers through this vision. The trials and tribulations of this life are passing. There is a life beyond resurrection, a life of joy and of ultimate well-being.

a. The wonderful reality that is heaven

'Mummy,' asked a little girl, 'do men ever go to heaven?'

'Why, yes, of course, my dear,' answered her mother. 'Why do you ask?'

THE MESSAGE OF THE RESURRECTION

'Because,' said the little girl, 'I've never seen angels with whiskers.'

'Well,' replied the mother, 'some men do go to heaven, but they only get there by a close shave!'

Heaven is the butt of many jokes. Yet the fact is that heaven is a wonderful reality, the hope of which has sustained Christians down through the centuries when life has been tough. However dark life may be, when we look to heaven we shall always have cause to praise and thank God.

Heaven is home to the greatest family in the world. John describes the church triumphant as *a great multitude that no-one could count* (v. 9). If that was true in John's day, how much more true today! The number of God's people must be vast. Various estimates of the population of heaven have been made. According to one recent estimate, there have been over 5,500 million Christian deaths between the resurrection of Jesus and the present day. Needless to say, this kind of calculation needs to be taken with a pinch of salt. The wideness of God's mercy is such that there is little doubt that at the end of time we are going to be in for all kinds of surprises. The one known fact is that the company of heaven will be so large that it will be beyond computation. At a time when church congregations in the West are generally declining and Christians are increasingly a marginalized minority, it is easy for Christians to become depressed. But John encourages us to lift up our eyes beyond ourselves and realize that we are part of the greatest family of all time. One consequence is that even when numbers attending worship are few, the fact is that the congregation is vast, for in worship we join our voices 'with angels and archangels and with all the company of heaven' to proclaim God's 'great and glorious name'.

Heaven is also a place where God is on *the throne* (v. 9). As a child I used to sing the chorus:

God is still on the throne, and he will remember his own;
Though trials may press us and burdens distress us
He never will leave us alone.
God is still on the throne, and he will remember his own.
His promise is true, he will not forget you,
God is still on the throne.

There must have been times when John and his fellow church members were tempted to doubt whether God was still on his throne. Everything about their circumstances pointed to the fact that Caesar was very much on the throne. But in his vision of heaven John came to see that above the throne of Caesar was the throne of the Lord God Almighty. To him belongs *salvation*, to him belongs the victory (v. 10). To him too belong

> *Praise and glory*
> *and wisdom and thanks and honour*
> *and power and strength.*
>
> (v. 12)

We too need to take heart from John's vision. For there are times when we also are tempted to doubt whether God is still on his throne. Indeed, when the storm of life is threatening our frail bark and we feel as if we are going under, we perhaps begin to wonder whether God is indeed wise or powerful. In those times we need to look up and see that there in heaven God is on the throne and is working his purposes out. Indeed, the sight of *the Lamb* sharing his throne (v. 9) will remind us that tragic 'Fridays' may be followed by Easter Day!

Heaven is the place where the tribulations of life are over. When John wrote of those *who have come out of the great tribulation* (v. 14), he had in mind men and women who had come through the fires of persecution: who had been put to death by the sword, been thrown to the lions in the Colloseum, or who had perished in deep dungeons. However, there are other forms of tribulation too. Life can be bruising, for instance, for Christians who refuse to compromise their values with the values of the world of business, entertainment or politics. Life can be tough in other ways too, for Christians are not exempt from the general pain and suffering of the world. Cancer will strike, loved ones will die, hopes will be disappointed, redundancy will take place. But the day is coming when the trials and tribulations of life will be over, and when *God will wipe away every tear from* our *eyes* (v. 17).

This day, however, is reserved for those who *have washed their robes and made them white in the blood of the Lamb* (v. 14). Here we have a 'theological' rather than a 'visual' picture. John is speaking of the blood of Jesus that 'purifies us from all sin', however deeply stained our lives may be. In other words, the hope of heaven is for those who have put their trust in the Lord Jesus and in what he did for us on the cross. We can look forward with confidence because we are able to look back in thanksgiving. Here is cause for further *Praise and glory* (v. 12).

7. A vision of life in the new city (Rev. 21:1–5)

Then I saw a new heaven and a new earth, for the first heaven and the first earth had passed away, and there was no longer any

> sea. ²*I saw the Holy City, the new Jerusalem, coming down out*
> *of heaven from God, prepared as a bride beautifully dressed for*
> *her husband.* ³*And I heard a loud voice from the throne saying,*
> *'Now the dwelling of God is with men, and he will live with*
> *them. They will be his people, and God himself will be with them*
> *and be their God.* ⁴*He will wipe every tear from their eyes. There*
> *will be no more death or mourning or crying or pain, for the old*
> *order of things has passed away.'*
>
> ⁵*He who was seated on the throne said, 'I am making*
> *everything new!' Then he said, 'Write this down, for these words*
> *are trustworthy and true.'*

John's vision of the new Jerusalem forms the climax of the book of
Revelation, and indeed of the Bible as a whole. The story that began
in the Garden of Eden now comes to an end in the city of gold. In
dealing with those heavenly realities, which are beyond our
experience, language inevitably has to be stretched. Metaphor
becomes the order of the day as John seeks to describe the
indescribable. John paints a wonderfully vivid picture in broad
brush-strokes – the details are unimportant compared to the overall
impression.

Although John's vision contains no specific reference to the
resurrection of Jesus, the resurrection is everywhere presupposed.
Death has passed away (v. 4) because Jesus now holds the keys of
death and Hades (1:18). As the 'new' song of heaven suggests (5:9),
everything is being made *new* (v. 5) as a direct consequence of the
triumph of the Lion of Judah on Easter Day (5:5). The 'life' (v. 6)
the Lord God offers is life in Christ (see John 4:14; 7:37–39). Those
who overcome (21:7) are those who have shared in Christ's victory
over sin and death (3:21).

First and foremost John is concerned to show that in the life
beyond resurrection 'everything' will be radically *new* (v. 5). There
will be *a new heaven and a new earth* (v. 1), and a *new Jerusalem*
(v. 2). The 'newness' of the coming new world is in part indicated
by the word John employs. For the underlying Greek adjective
(*kainos*) denotes something quite unknown, strange, remarkable –
even marvellous. The *new* order (like the new covenant, *kainē diathē
kē*) is by definition superior and renders the old obsolete. Life in the
kingdom of God will not just be radically different; it will also be
radically better. So when the *old order of things* will have *passed
away* (v. 4), so too will the accompanying seven elements of *sea,
death, mourning, crying, pain*, all that is under God's 'curse', and
'night' (21:1, 4; 22:3, 5).

The starting point for John's description of *a new heaven and a new earth* (v. 1) is found in Isaiah 65:17-23, where the prophet looks to the day in Jerusalem's history when children do not die, when old people live in dignity, when those who build houses live in them, and when those who plant vineyards eat their fruit. The vision begins with these words of the Lord:

> Behold, I will create
> > new heavens and a new earth.
> The former things will not be remembered,
> > nor will they come to mind.
> But be glad and rejoice for ever
> > in what I will create,
> for I will create Jerusalem to be a delight
> > and its people a joy.
>
> (Is. 65:17, 18)

Whereas Isaiah 65 has in view a transformation of the present order, however, John appears to envisage the creation of a completely new world, in which the distinction between heaven and earth is abolished – for heaven comes down to earth – and in which such a key distinctive geographical feature as the sea disappears. Yet the difference must not be pressed. As we have already recognized, we are dealing with a vision, where the overall impression rather than the detail is what counts.

In this new earth *there was no longer any sea* (v. 1). To those of us accustomed to an island home, the lack of a seaside might appear to be a positive disadvantage. But not for John. For John in exile on the island of Patmos, the sea symbolized separation from his friends and loved ones. The sea kept John prisoner. The disappearance of the sea therefore represented the coming of freedom and the end of oppression. Freedom is also the hallmark of the future glory depicted by Paul: 'the creation itself will be liberated ... and brought into the glorious freedom of the children of God' (Rom. 8:21). In this world we all suffer limitations of one kind or another, but with the coming of the new heaven and new earth we shall be free at last.

There is another and more important thought present, however. For John and his readers, the sea represented the power of evil. The roots of this metaphor are found in the ancient Near Eastern mythologies. In Babylonian mythology, for instance, the sea represented the element of chaos which God had to overcome before he created the earth. God's triumph over Tiamat (Leviathan), the sea monster, was represented as a triumph over the sea (see Ps. 74:13–14; Is. 51:10). The sea in Jewish thought therefore became the symbol of all that was evil. Indeed, according to one famous Jewish rabbi, Rashi, hell could be likened to the sea (*Shabbat* 104a). Here in the book of Revelation the sea is the place where the dragon goes when he is cast down from heaven (12:8); similarly it is from the sea that the Antichrist beast rises (13:1). The absence of the sea in the new world that is coming represents the abolition of evil. The devil has been thrown into the 'lake of burning sulphur' (20:10), as have death and Hades (20:14) and all those guilty of sin in its many, multifaceted forms (21:8). God's new city is *holy* (21:2); 'Nothing impure will ever enter it' (21:27). This is a wonderfully encouraging thought: one day sin and evil will be no more. It is also, however, a challenging thought: only those who *have washed their robes and made them white in the blood of the Lamb* (7:14) will be there.

This holy city is named *the new Jerusalem* (v. 2). Ever since Jerusalem was destroyed by the Babylonians in the sixth century BC, the Jews had dreamed of a rebuilt Jerusalem. These dreams continued even after the physical rebuilding of Jerusalem at the end of the sixth century, and surfaced even more vigorously after the destruction of the temple in AD 70. In the New Testament the idea of a heavenly Jerusalem is found in Galatians 4:26 and Hebrews 12:22 (see also Phil. 3:20; Heb. 11:10; 13:14). In the letter of the risen Christ to Philadelphia those who remain faithful are to be inscribed with 'the name of the city of my God, the new Jerusalem, which is coming down out of heaven' (3:12).

John sees the new Jerusalem *coming down out of heaven from God* (v. 2; also 21:10). What to us might appear as an element out of a science-fiction film is in fact a theological statement. The very descent of the new Jerusalem *out of heaven from God* is a pointer to the fact that this new world is of God's making, and is not the product of human effort (see Pss. 46; 48; Is. 2:1–4). '*I am making everything new!*' declares the one who is seated on the throne (v. 5). The kingdom of God is not something we achieve, but is something God alone brings about. The kingdom of the world becomes 'the kingdom of our Lord and of his Christ' on the day when God takes up his rule and reigns (11:15–18).

The new Jerusalem is pictured *as a bride* (v. 2). The image of the people of God as the bride of God has its roots in the Old Testament (see Is. 54:8; 61:10), and is taken up by Jesus (see John 3:29–30: also Matt. 9:15; 25:1–13) and developed by Paul (2 Cor. 11:2; Eph. 5:29–30). John himself has already described the coming of God's reign as being the moment of the wedding of the Lamb, for which 'his bride has made herself ready' (19:7; see also 21:9; 22:17). The picture of a bride coming to meet her husband conveys the thought of joy and festivity, union and fulfilment.

Like any bride on her wedding day, she is *beautifully dressed for her husband* (v. 2). The beauty of the city is further highlighted in John's listing of the precious stones making up the foundations of the city wall: jasper, sapphire, chalcedony, emerald, sardonyx, carnelian, chrysolite, beryl, topaz, chrysoprase, jacinth and amethyst (21:19–20). With gates of pearl and the great street of gold (21:21), and with the glory of God and the Lamb giving light (21:23), beauty is of the city's essence. The contrast between the new Jerusalem in all its bridal glory and the bride of Christ as she is today is immense: what a transformation will have to take place to rid her of the stains, wrinkles, and other blemishes (see Eph. 5:27) that currently mar her beauty!

The new Jerusalem becomes God's new home. For a voice from the throne declares, *'Now the dwelling of God is with men, and he will live with them. They will be his people, and God himself will be with them and be their God'* (v. 3). John is alluding here to the promise given to the people of God as they wandered in the wilderness: 'I will put my dwelling place among you, and I will not abhor you. I will walk among you and be your God, and you will be my people' (Lev. 26:11–12: see also Jer. 31:33; Ezek. 37:27; Zech. 8:8). The new Jerusalem is characterized by the presence of God. In the words with which Ezekiel closes his great vision of the restored Jerusalem, 'THE LORD IS THERE' (Ezek. 48:35). As 'the Alpha and the Omega, the Beginning and the End' (Rev. 21:6), God does not bring the world to an end; he *is* the End. In the words of the apostle Paul, at the end God will be 'all in all' (1 Cor. 15:28).

John modifies the Old Testament prophecy, however, in one important respect. Unfortunately this is not clear in a number of modern English translations. For whereas the NIV, GNB, NEB and REB speak of *his people* in the singular (v. 3), the best Greek texts read 'peoples' in the plural (so the NRSV). The new Jerusalem will be made up of an exceedingly diverse multiracial population, with representatives 'from every nation, tribe, people and language' (7:9). John speaks of 'the kings of the earth' (21:24) bringing their splendour into it, as also of the city's tree of life having leaves for 'the healing of the nations' (22:2). The new Jerusalem is the focal point for the whole world. In the kingdom of God there is room for all.

The voice from heaven continues, *'He will wipe every tear from their eyes. There will be no more death or mourning or crying or pain'* (v. 4). The Old Testament is not quoted literally, but there is a clear reference to Isaiah 25:8; 35:10; and 65:19. In the new world coming, death and suffering will have no place, for they belong to the old order dominated by sin and evil. Interestingly, the new order of things is depicted primarily in terms of what it replaces. In describing the indescribable it is easier to speak of what will not be, rather than what will be, for

> No eye has seen,
>> no ear has heard,
> no mind has conceived
>> what God has prepared for those who love him.
>>>>> (1 Cor. 2:9; Is. 64:4)

a. The new Jerusalem

To attempt to speak about heaven might well appear as meaningful as deaf people discussing a performance of a symphony or blind people giving a detailed visual description of a sunset. Heaven is beyond our experience and therefore beyond our understanding. The difficulty of speaking about heaven is illustrated by the story of a city child who, on his first trip to the country, saw a bird perched on a branch of a tree. 'Poor little bird!' said the five-year-old. 'Poor little bird! He hasn't got a cage to live in.' His understanding was governed by the life he knew. Similarly our understanding of heaven is governed by the life we know. We can scarcely begin to conceive of that world beyond space and time. We are inevitably limited in our thinking. Fortunately we have a guide: John, in exile on the island of Patmos, had a vision. In the light of this vision we can affirm the following truths.

First, the coming new world is going to be a radical improvement on everything we have ever experienced. The new resurrection order will not be a mere extension of life as we know it, but rather a total transformation. Suffering and death, for instance, sadly an integral part of today's world, will be no more. It is hard to imagine a world more different from ours. And yet for all the radical 'newness' of the future, there will also be a sense of continuity with the past. Paul expressed this sense of continuity in his doctrine of the resurrection of the body (1 Cor. 15). In the book of Revelation, John expresses this sense of continuity in his statement that 'the kings of the earth will bring their splendour into it . . . The glory and honour of the nations will be brought into it' (21:24, 26). There may be no room in the new Jerusalem for all that is bad and evil in this world, but there will be a place for all that is good and pure. Heaven is no world-denying nirvana, but rather a place where human achievement receives divine affirmation. In a way that defies our imagination, we may believe that the best of human life and culture will be found, albeit transformed, in the new Jerusalem.

Secondly, the coming new world is going to be an experience of true community. In his vision, John likened the new resurrection order of things to life in a city. For many people today cities are unattractive places, associated with pollution, overcrowding, and the breakdown of law and order. People who have money and opportunity tend to flee the city. They dream of retiring to the country, if not to the seaside. John, however, dreamt of a city, and a *holy* city at that. John's vision of the life to come was a place of community. His idea of heaven was not a lonely desert island, nor was it some small village tucked away in the hills, but rather a mega-city, bursting with life and vitality. The population of this new Jerusalem is too large for any council official to count. The area it covers is vast – 12,000 stadia (i.e. 1,500 miles) square. Indeed, if the height of the walls are anything to go by (for they measure 12,000 stadia too), the new Jerusalem also consists of high-rise dwellings. John's dream of the new Jerusalem was in some ways similar to that of the rabbis, who used to say that Jerusalem would be enlarged until it reached the gates of Damascus and exalted until it reached the throne of God. John dreamt of a new, inclusive community, a community composed not of a faithful few, but of the nations of the world. The book of Revelation may contain pictures of judgment, but it also contains pictures of salvation open to all. In the words of Jesus, 'In my Father's house are many rooms' (John 14:2).

Thirdly, the coming new world will be of God's making. In his vision of the new resurrection order, John sees the new Jerusalem not as built by human effort, but as coming down out of heaven from God (v. 1). It is God who makes all things new. In the forecourt of a Moscow art gallery stands the statue of a workman beating a broad sword with a hammer. The bottom of the sword is assuming the shape of a ploughshare, and underneath is the inscription, 'We must bend our swords into ploughshares.' The inscription is an echo of words found in Isaiah 2:4 and Micah 4:3, but there is one salient difference between the Marxist hope and the biblical hope: the Old Testament prophets believed that men would beat their swords into ploughshares and their spears into pruning hooks on the day when God establishes his kingdom on earth. If our hope is in ourselves, then we look forward in vain. But the Christian hope is in God, who has already acted decisively in his Son, Jesus Christ. Our hope for the future is certain because of what God has already achieved in the cross and resurrection of Jesus.

Fourthly, whatever else heaven is, it is a place where God lives with his people. When God 'lives' (*skēnōsei*) with his people, he does not simply pitch his 'tent' (*skēnē*, translated by the NIV as *dwelling*, v. 3) alongside our tents, but rather his 'tent', his presence, is all-encompassing (see Rev. 7:15). There is much that we do not know about heaven. Speculations about the furniture of heaven, as indeed about the temperature of hell, are futile. But one thing we do know: heaven is life lived in the presence of God. It is important to recognize that God is not just one 'item' in a list of things to be found in the new Jerusalem, but rather the new Jerusalem is defined by the presence of God. The new Jerusalem is depicted as a perfect cube (21:15–16) and as such the whole city forms a 'Holy of Holies', whose height and depth and breadth were also equal. The whole city is a sanctuary in which God is present everywhere and immediately accessible to all. So John could write, 'I did not see a temple in the city, because the Lord God Almighty and the Lamb are its temple' (21:22). No wonder John therefore describes heaven as a ceaseless round of worship (22:3). One day our evangelizing and baptizing will come to an end, but not our worship. In the words of Martin Luther, 'Heaven is not heaven because joy is there, but because the praise of God is there.' Or in the words of John's earlier vision of heaven, the whole creation will sing the praises of God and the Lamb (5:13).

7. The witness of other voices to the resurrection

Today it is generally agreed that the letters of the New Testament contain fragments of a wide variety of hymns, creeds and confessions of faith that were used in the worship of the early church. Many of these hymns, creeds and confessions not surprisingly bear witness to the resurrection of Jesus. In this chapter we look at only four such examples, namely the confessional formula found in Romans 10:9; the hymns found in Philippians 2:9–11 and Colossians 1:15–20; and the creed found in 1 Timothy 3:16. From the very beginning of the church's life, faith in the risen Christ was central to its believing.

1. The risen Jesus is Lord (Rom. 10:9)

> ... if you confess with your mouth, 'Jesus is Lord,' and believe in your heart that God raised him from the dead, you will be saved.

Jesus is Lord. With these words the first Christians were baptized - and later with these words on their lips many Christians were martyred for their faith. This confession of faith was almost certainly not of Paul's invention, but rather had already been formulated by the early church. From the very beginning the first Christians proclaimed the lordship of the risen Jesus. It is probably no exaggeration to say that here we have the earliest Christian confession of faith.

This confession of faith is also found in 1 Corinthians 12:3. There Paul writes, 'no-one can say, "Jesus is Lord," except by the Holy Spirit.' The mark of a Christian, of one possessing the Spirit of God, is the confession that *Jesus is Lord.*

What makes Paul's use of this confession of faith so interesting here in Romans 10:9 is that he links the lordship of Jesus inextricably with the resurrection of Jesus: *God raised him from the dead.* The resurrection is the basis for the lordship of Jesus (see also Rom. 1:4; 4:24; 14:9; 1 Cor. 6:14; 2 Cor. 4:14). The lordship of Jesus and the resurrection of Jesus are not two separate articles of faith, but rather one. In rising from the dead Jesus triumphed not only over death, but also over every power that can be named. The resurrection of Jesus not only offers hope of life to come, but also changes the course of the world. The risen Jesus is the risen Lord.

It is significant too that the resurrection is mentioned as the distinctive belief of Christians. Christians by definition believe that God raised Jesus from the dead. The resurrection is no optional article of belief – it is *the* article. It is faith in the risen Lord that saves. But what precisely did the early church mean by confessing Jesus as Lord? What practical difference did the resurrection make as far as they were concerned? What did the first Christians understand by the lordship of the risen Jesus?

The truth is that there is no one answer to these questions. Everything depended on one's perspective. The lordship of the risen Jesus may have meant one thing to a Christian living in a predominantly Greek culture, another to a Christian living in a mainly Roman culture, and yet another to a Christian living in a Jewish culture. As the death certificate of Jesus indicated, the Roman Empire was diverse (see John 19:20). To confess the lordship of the risen Jesus in one part of the empire could be very different from confessing the lordship of the risen Jesus in another part. Although the empire was one, the word 'Lord' thus conjured up at least three different images: Greek, Roman and Jewish.

Yet we cannot totally isolate the three cultures from one another; apart from anything else, the Roman Empire was characterized by good communications. Perhaps therefore we should speak of the three strands of thought present in confessing the risen Jesus as Lord. With that proviso, let us look at what this confession of faith may have meant.

a. The risen Jesus saves

To the average Greek the confession *Jesus is Lord* would have meant primarily that Jesus saves. At the time when the Christian faith arrived on the scene, there was a very real religious awakening taking place in the world of Greek culture. For most people the rationalism and accompanying scepticism of the traditional Greek philosophers had been swept away, and in its place the ordinary people, at least, were turning to what were termed 'mystery religions'. These mystery religions, as their name implies, were secret societies – in some ways like today's Freemasons.

In a world that seemed cold and hostile, where many people could no longer believe in the frolics of the gods and goddesses of Mount Olympus, the mystery religions supplied the need for personal religion. In particular, they claimed to offer 'salvation' to people who felt themselves bound by evil spirits, the so-called principalities and powers, and in consequence hemmed in by fate. This salvation, which involved the promise of life in the world to come, was gained by participating in rites not dissimilar to those practised by the early church: they practised, for instance, a kind of 'baptism' and they also engaged in fellowship meals. At the centre of their worship were their saviour gods, whom they called 'lords': for example, Lord Seraphis and Lord Mithras.

Against this background many of the first Christians declared that *Jesus is Lord*. In effect they were saying, 'The one who saves is not Lord Mithras or Lord Seraphis, but the Lord Jesus, and the Lord Jesus alone.' In the words of the apostle Paul to the church at Corinth: 'For even if there are so-called gods, whether in heaven or on earth (as indeed there are many "gods" and many "lords"), yet for us there is but one God, the Father . . . and there is but one Lord, Jesus Christ . . .' (1 Cor. 8:5–6).

In other words, when the first Christians confessed *Jesus is Lord* those from within a Greek culture were proclaiming that Jesus, and he alone, could save men and women from the principalities and powers that were believed to control human destiny. They were proclaiming that Jesus, and he alone, could save humankind from the power of fate and the power of death (see Rom. 8:38–39; 1 Cor. 8:5–6; 15:24–28; Eph. 1:20–23; 4:8–10; Phil. 2:9–11; Col. 1:15–20; 2:10, 15; 1 Tim. 3:16).

The fact was that the 'lords' of the mystery religions were mythological in character, for they were but nature gods who were supposed to die annually and then come to life again annually. The salvation the mystery religions had to offer was therefore in fact as mythical as their gods or lords. By contrast, the *Lord* Jesus was a historical figure who died and rose, and who, as a result of his death and resurrection, had broken the power of every evil and malign force. *Jesus is Lord* meant that 'Jesus saves'.

All this at first sight may seem pretty remote from our experience. The mystery religions have long since ceased to be. And yet our world today is in some respects not so different from the first-century world in which the early Christians lived. For we too live in a day of religious resurgence. Although people are not returning to the churches, there is a fresh interest in 'spirituality'. The teachings and the alternative therapies of the New Age are very much the rage. The fact is that the rationalism of secularism does not satisfy the human heart. People are looking for a 'fulfilment' and 'meaning' (we might say 'salvation') in all kinds of weird and wonderful places. In such a context to declare that the risen Jesus is 'Lord' is to declare that Jesus alone is the way to fulfilment and meaning in this world; he alone is the way to life in the world to come; he alone is the way to salvation.

But there is another aspect to this confession of faith that is relevant to the world today. We have mentioned that many in the first century felt helpless against the spiritual forces – the principalities and powers – supposed to be ruling the world. Many people today feel equally helpless. They may not believe that the stars control their destinies, but they do at times feel that they are no longer in control of their destinies; there are other forces at work. In such a context to declare that *Jesus is Lord* is to declare that Jesus is bigger than all our fears and feelings. He is able to save from every power and every situation; there is nothing that can separate us from the love of God that is in Christ Jesus our Lord (Rom. 8:39). All this is contained in the message of the resurrection: the risen Lord Jesus is the Lord who saves.

b. The risen Jesus comes first

But it was not simply people from within a Greek culture who confessed the risen Jesus as Lord. Those from within a Roman culture also shared in that confession. For them, however, this confession had another meaning.

When Christians in the Roman world confessed that *Jesus is Lord* they meant, 'The risen Lord Jesus comes first – and not Caesar.' We must remember that the time when the Christian faith came on the scene was the time when the religious cult of the emperor was developing. In many parts of the empire Caesar was being increasingly worshipped as 'Lord'. Furthermore, such emperor worship was becoming not just an optional extra for the enthusiasts, but rather an obligation for all.

Inevitably conflict developed between church and state. For although Christians were prepared to follow the teaching of Jesus and 'give to Caesar what is Caesar's' (see Mark 12:17; Matt. 22:21; Luke 20:25), they could not worship Caesar as Lord. For Christians there was only 'one Lord, Jesus Christ' (1 Cor. 8:6). The polytheistic Romans, however, with their belief in many gods, failed to understand the Christian point of view. Indeed, they even called Christians 'atheists', that is, people who do not believe in gods. For the upholders of the imperial cult a refusal to acknowledge Caesar as Lord was tantamount to an act of disloyalty, indeed to an act of treason. Such treason was punishable by death. On that basis many Christians were persecuted, and especially in Rome under Nero thousands of them were martyred for their faith in the risen Lord Jesus. We see this conflict reflected in the book of Revelation, where Caesar is depicted as the Antichrist and where the number of the beast – 666 – is a code denoting 'Nero Caesar', that is, 'another Nero' (see Rev. 13:8).

Probably the most famous example of the conflict between the church and Rome is found not within the pages of the New Testament, but rather in the subsequent martyrdom of Polycarp, bishop of Smyrna. At his trial the Roman consul sought to persuade Polycarp to worship Caesar as 'Lord'. But Polycarp refused. The Roman consul pleaded with Polycarp to change his mind. 'Why,' he said, 'what harm is there in saying Caesar is Lord and sacrificing and the rest of it, and so saving yourself? Swear by the divinity of Caesar. Swear and I release you: curse Christ.' But Polycarp replied, 'Eighty-six years have I served Him and He has done me no wrong: how then can I blaspheme the King who saved me?'[1] For Polycarp, as for all the early Christian martyrs, the risen Jesus was *Lord,* and as such he came first, whatever the cost. Jesus alone was Lord.

Although in the West our circumstances today are different from those of Polycarp and the first Christians, we do have one thing in common with the early church: we too experience a conflict between the demands of Jesus and the demands of the world. True, our political masters do not call for our allegiance in the same way that Caesar called for the allegiance of his subjects. But nevertheless we have other 'lords' and other 'gods' that threaten to come between us and Jesus. For instance, although religious terms may not be used for 'money', 'sex' and 'power', these 'false gods' most certainly command the worship of many. Today, as then, to confess the risen Jesus as *Lord* means to go against the stream and to make him Lord of every department of our lives.

c. The risen Jesus is divine

For Christians living within a Jewish culture, to confess the risen Jesus as *Lord* had yet another connotation. For within the Jewish world the word 'Lord' was a term used regularly of God himself. Indeed, it became a substitute for the divine name (Yahweh), which was felt to be too holy to pronounce. So whenever the name Yahweh turned up in the public reading of the Old Testament Scriptures, instead of reading the divine name out loud, Jews substituted the word 'Lord'.

[1] In J. Stevenson (ed.), *A New Eusebius* (SPCK, 1957), p. 21.

For them it was axiomatic that there was only one 'Lord' – God Almighty himself (see, e.g., the 'Shema' in Deut. 6:4). To call anybody else 'Lord' in this sense was tantamount to blasphemy.

But the first Christians, who were of course Jews, dared to call Jesus *Lord*. For example, when Thomas saw the risen Christ, he worshipped him as 'My Lord and my God' (John 20:28). When Matthew came to write his Gospel he spoke of Jesus in terms of 'Immanuel', 'God with us' (Matt. 1:23). Here in Romans 10 Paul attributes to the Lord Jesus words originally spoken of God himself: 'Everyone who calls on the name of the Lord will be saved' (Rom. 10:13; see Joel 2:32). Peter, at Caesarea Philippi, had cried out: 'You are the Christ, the Son of the living God' (Matt. 16:16). It is no exaggeration to say that it was upon this confession of faith, this faith in the divinity of Jesus, that the church was built.

For the Jews such claims went too far. They were willing to acknowledge Jesus as a great teacher. For example, when the Pharisees sought to trip Jesus up about the paying of taxes, they began by acknowledging: 'you teach the way of God in accordance with the truth' (Matt. 22:16). But in no way could they believe that Jesus shared in the nature of God himself.

Many are in the same boat today. They are willing to acknowledge that Jesus was a special person – that he was a great moral teacher – but they are unwilling to worship Jesus as their Lord and God. There have been many who to all intents and purposes have said the same as Gandhi, who declared: 'I may say that I have never been interested in an historical Jesus. I should not care if it was proved by someone that the man called Jesus never lived, and that what was narrated in the Gospels was a figment of the writer's imagination. For the Sermon on the Mount would still be true for me.'

Jesus is far more, however, than the sum of his teaching; he is far more than the sum of his powerful acts of healing. He is the 'Lord'. We know him to be the Lord, because 'by his resurrection' God through his Spirit has 'declared' him 'with power to be the Son of God' (Rom. 1:4). The resurrection is the moment when Jesus is seen to share the throne of God. Or, to use the language of John, the resurrection is the occasion when the world discovers that it was wrong in its evaluation of Jesus (John 16:9–11). The resurrection therefore confirms that in Jesus our search for God is over. The risen Jesus is divine.

d. The risen Jesus is Lord of all

However we understand the confession *Jesus as Lord*, one thing is sure. The basis for this confession is the resurrection of Jesus. To confess with one's mouth Jesus as Lord is but the outward expression of believing in one's heart that *God raised him from the dead.* Confession is dependent upon belief. Our knowledge that Jesus saves, that Jesus comes first, that Jesus shares the divine nature, is based on the resurrection. The resurrection of Jesus cannot be understood just in terms of God's bringing the body of Jesus back to life. In the resurrection of Jesus God upset the world's order – he made Jesus 'Lord of all' (Rom. 10:12).

The resurrection of Jesus, therefore, has cosmic implications. *Jesus is Lord* may have been a personal confession of faith, but in no way could that confession be limited to the life of the individual believer. In confessing Jesus as Lord the early Christians were not in the first place declaring that 'Jesus is Lord of my life'; they were declaring that Jesus was 'Lord of the world'. As Paul makes clear here in Romans 10, the risen Jesus is Lord not only over all those who call upon him (v. 12), but also over all who do not obey the gospel (v. 16). The rule of the risen Christ cannot be restricted to the church. He who is Lord of the church is also Lord of the world.

We cannot overstress the significance of the resurrection. For the early church, faith in the resurrection of Jesus involved far more than hope of life in the world to come. Rather, faith in the resurrection of Jesus caused them to claim the world for Jesus. The audacity of those first Christians is mind-boggling. For in those opening decades of the church's life, the Christians were an exceedingly small minority group. But in spite of their numbers, they did not suffer from any inferiority complex. Instead, the resurrection of Jesus caused them to believe that the world belonged to Christ. 'Jesus is Lord' was their proud claim.

2. The risen Jesus is Lord of all (Phil. 2:9–11)

If in Romans 10:6 we find an early confession of faith, in Philippians 2:6–11 we find not so much a confession as a carefully structured hymn to the risen and exalted Christ. Almost certainly this hymn was not the creation of Paul. Rather, it would appear that here Paul has quoted an early hymn well known both to himself and to the church at Philippi. The vocabulary used in these verses, for instance, is not typical of Paul. Another indicator of its pre-Pauline character is that the second half of the hymn with its theme of the risen and exalted Lord is irrelevant to the ethical motivation that led Paul to cite the hymn in the first place. (By contrast with Jas. 4:6 and 1 Pet. 5:6, the surrounding context does not speak of humility as the way to exaltation.) For these and indeed other reasons it is generally believed that in Philippians 2:6–11 we have to do with a hymn composed by some unknown theologian of the early church.

It is tempting to expound the whole hymn. The opening verses, for instance, contain great insights into the person of Christ. Since our immediate concern is with the message of the resurrection, however, our primary focus will have to be on the second half of the hymn. For whereas the theme of the first half is the incarnate Jesus, the theme of the second half is the risen and exalted Lord.

> *Therefore God exalted him to the highest place*
> *and gave him the name that is above every name,*
> 10 *that at the name of Jesus every knee should bow,*
> *in heaven and on earth and under the earth,*
> 11 *and every tongue confess that Jesus Christ is Lord,*
> *to the glory of God the Father.*

a. The risen Jesus is the exalted Lord

God exalted Jesus *to the highest place.* To be exact, the original Greek version of the hymn declares that 'God more than exalted Jesus'. The addition of a prepositional prefix (*hyper* – which gives us our English prefix 'hyper') to the verb (*hyperypsoō*) indicates that God did not simply restore Jesus to the place of honour that had always been his: rather, through raising Jesus from the dead he elevated him to a yet higher status than he had ever known before. There is a difference in role between the pre-existent Jesus and the risen and exalted Jesus. Jesus, in rising from the dead and being exalted to the Father's right hand, now occupies a new place of honour.

The key to understanding this statement is found in the first half of the hymn. There in the opening lines we read that although, prior to his coming into our world, Jesus was 'in very nature God', he 'did not consider equality with God something to be grasped' (v. 6). Almost certainly there is an allusion to Adam and the fall. Adam, through eating the fruit of the tree of knowledge in the Garden of Eden, sought to be like God (Gen. 3:5). But Jesus, the second Adam, did not seek to put himself on a level with God. Instead, he 'made himself nothing' (v. 7). Literally, he 'emptied himself', that is, he emptied himself of the glory he shared with his Father, and became one with us. This self-emptying is described in terms of 'taking the very nature of a servant' (v. 7). The Lord of glory, in becoming one with us in our humanity, laid aside all the privileges of divinity that were his, and subjected himself to the limitations of our world. He became a 'servant'. Service summed up the whole purpose of his incarnation. As Jesus himself once said, 'For even the Son of Man did not come to be served, but to serve, and to give his life as a ransom for many' (Mark 10:45). It was in his role as a servant that he 'became obedient to death – even death on a cross!' (v. 8); it was as the Servant of the Lord that he 'poured out his life unto death, and was numbered with the transgressors' (Is. 53:12).

This then is the context in which the hymn declares that God 'more than exalted' Jesus. In response to the Son's obedience, which led him to the cross, God the Father raised him from the dead and seated him at his right hand. That equality with God at which Jesus had refused to grasp is now his. In terms of his 'being' there is no change – Jesus from the very first was 'in very nature God' (v. 6). In terms of his 'function', however, through his resurrection from the dead Jesus is now given a new role.

The hymn elaborates upon this new status when it declares that God *gave him the name that is above every name* (v. 9). As the closing confession in verse 11 indicates, the name in question is the name 'Lord'. This is the *name that is above every name*. Moreover, the conferring of this new name on Jesus involves more than a mere bestowal of a new title; it also involves the raising of Jesus to a new status. This is in line with the basic Semitic idea that a name expresses the nature of the person to whom it is attached: 'He is just like his name' (1 Sam. 25:25). God, by the giving of a new name, could give people a new character or a new capacity. For example, Abram, the 'exalted father', became Abraham, the 'father of many' (see Gen. 17:5, 15). Similarly Simon becomes 'Peter', the rock on which Jesus will build his church (Matt. 16:18). Likewise here, the new name of *Lord* indicates that Jesus has been given a new role, that of Lord. The risen Jesus is the exalted Lord.

b. The risen Jesus is the universal Lord

The hymn proceeds to elaborate upon this new role that now belongs to Jesus. God has exalted Jesus to the highest height so that *at the name of Jesus every knee should bow . . . and every tongue confess that Jesus Christ is Lord* (vv. 10–11). The English translation *at the name of Jesus* gives the impression that when the name of Jesus is in one way or another called out, the whole creation bows the knee and in turn proclaims him Lord. However, this is a misleading impression. The hymn actually declares that 'every knee shall bow *in* (*en*) the name of Jesus' (emphasis mine). In the Septuagint, the Greek version of the Old Testament, to do something 'in the name of the Lord' always means to do something 'by invoking the name of the Lord', that is, calling upon the name of the Lord accompanies the action. For example, in 1 Samuel 20:42 Jonathan says to David, 'Go in peace, for we have sworn friendship with each other in the name of the Lord, saying, "The Lord is witness between you and me . . ."' (see also Jer. 44:26). The whole creation honours Jesus by falling on their knees and calling out the name of Jesus. The proclaiming of the name of Jesus here accompanies the act of submission symbolized by the bending of the knee. A parallel may perhaps be drawn with Ephesians 5:26, where the 'word' of confession ('Jesus is Lord'?) accompanies the act of submission expressed in 'washing with water'.

Of even greater significance, however, is the extent of the submission. Every creature *in heaven and on earth and under the earth* is involved. Traditionally, this threefold division of the universe has been taken to refer either to angels, people alive (on earth), and the dead (in Sheol), or to angels, humankind and demons. More recently, however, not a few theologians have argued that the hymn has only the spirit world in mind; the cosmic principalities and powers alone are in view. But is this latter assertion really true? The hymn is in fact drawing upon the statement in Isaiah 45:23, where the Lord declared:

> Before me every knee will bow;
> by me every tongue will swear.

The Lord was speaking there of men and women. This same anthropological thrust is found in Paul's quotation of Isaiah 45:23 in Romans 14:11. The addition here in the Philippian hymn of the line *in heaven and on earth and under the earth* widens the extent of this universal submission. The principalities and powers are now included. However, there is no reason to believe that men and women are excluded! Rather, just as the first Adam was to have had dominion over the whole creation (Gen. 1:26), so now the second Adam is in turn to have dominion over the whole creation too. To the risen and exalted Lord Jesus universal homage is paid. As in Romans 10:6, so also here in Philippians 2 the resurrection of Jesus has cosmic significance. Jesus is Lord of all!

The nature of the homage offered by the whole creation to the risen Lord is described first in terms of genuflection: *at the name of Jesus every knee should bow*. The bowing of the knee is basically a sign of respectful submission. Although prayer was often accompanied by kneeling, there is nothing specifically 'prayerful' about this act. Secondly, the nature of this homage is described in terms of verbal acknowledgment: *and every tongue confess that Jesus Christ is Lord*. There is nothing specifically 'religious' about this acknowledgment. In ordinary first-century usage the underlying Greek verb (*exomologeō*) normally meant to 'recognize something to be valid'. The homage offered by the whole creation, therefore, is not to be conceived primarily in terms of 'worship' but rather in terms of general submission. The reality of the lordship of the risen Jesus is something that has to be acknowledged by all.

When will this universal homage take place? When will the whole creation acknowledge the lordship of Jesus? The hymn is not clear. Some have suggested that it is celebrating the present lordship of Jesus. But such an assertion is hard to square with reality. In no way, either then nor now, can it realistically be argued that we have to do with a present reality here; we live in a world where evil all too often continues to hold sway. Is the bowing of every knee therefore just a future hope, with no expression in the present? Surely not, for already there are many in the church who gladly acknowledge the lordship of Jesus. If Philippians 3:21 be any guide, then we have a process described here which is yet to be completed. Jesus is in the process of bringing everything under control. Yes, Jesus in rising from the dead has already triumphed over the powers of sin and death. Nevertheless, that victory has yet to be total. To use an illustration derived from the Second World War: D-Day is behind us, but V-Day is yet to come. The decisive battle has already taken place, for God has re-established a bridgehead in our world, not least by raising Jesus from the dead. The outcome is therefore already clear; in a sense victory is already secure. For all that, many battles still lie ahead before full surrender is a reality. The risen Jesus is Lord, yet as the writer of the Hebrews states, 'at present we do not see everything subject to him' (Heb. 2:8). This is not to gainsay the magnificent vision of the hymn. The day is coming when Jesus will be Lord of all. Of that we can be certain, because Jesus is now the risen and exalted Lord. The resurrection, a past event, guarantees the future.

c. The risen Jesus is Lord

Once again we see the intimate connection in the thinking of the early church between the resurrection of Jesus from the dead and the lordship of Jesus over the world. Although the kingdom of God had been brought near through Jesus' ministry of preaching and healing (see Mark 1:14; Matt. 12:28; Luke 11:20), the resurrection marks the true beginning of the kingdom of Christ (see Col. 1:13) – it is the basis for his universal reign. Here in Philippians 2 the meaning of the resurrection of Jesus is spelt out in terms of this world, rather than the next; it concerns not so much the reanimation of our bodies as the lordship of Christ over the world. We who believe can be certain of our destiny because Jesus is Lord of all.

Sadly, by comparison the church of today cuts a poor figure. To a large degree we have lost the boldness of the early church. We have to a large extent privatized the resurrection, in that for the most part·

we see there only what Jesus can do for us personally. Indeed, we have to a large extent imbibed the postmodern philosophy of our day and allowed our faith in the risen Lord to become just one way of looking at the world. In this sense the gospel has been reduced to 'views' rather than 'news'. The early church by contrast was much bolder in its understanding of the faith. When it proclaimed Jesus as the risen Lord, it had the world in view and saw the difference Jesus had made to all. In a multicultural and multifaith world the early church shamelessly celebrated the lordship of Christ over all. No wonder the church grew. No wonder the faith of today's church makes so little impact upon the world in general. With our emphasis on what Jesus can do for 'me', we have to all intents and purposes created a ghetto mentality. We need to recover the faith of the early church and see what difference the risen Jesus has made to the world – and then go out and claim the world for him!

3. The risen Jesus is Lord of the world (Col. 1:15–20)

He is the image of the invisible God, the firstborn over all creation. [16]For by him all things were created: things in heaven and on earth, visible and invisible, whether thrones or powers or rulers or authorities; all things were created by him and for him. [17]He is before all things, and in him all things hold together. [18]And he is the head of the body, the church; he is the beginning and the firstborn from among the dead, so that in everything he might have the supremacy. [19]For God was pleased to have all his fulness dwell in him, [20]and through him to reconcile to himself all things, whether things on earth or things in heaven, by making peace through his blood, shed on the cross.

The well-nigh unanimous verdict of New Testament scholarship today is that, as in Philippians 2, so here in Colossians 1 an unknown theologian of the early church celebrates the lordship of Christ. While Paul does not say that he is drawing upon the composition of somebody else, the parallelism in these verses convinces many people that this is no spontaneous lyrical outburst on the part of the apostle. Rather, this is a carefully constructed early Christian hymn. If this is so, then yet again we come face to face with the fact that Paul was not the only theologian of the early church. There were already other Christians at work reflecting on the person of Christ. And as they reflected, they came to make some incredibly daring statements about their Master who had died on a Roman cross less than thirty years before.

My own view is that in Colossians 1:15–20 we have a hymn composed of two main verses (vv. 15–16 and 18b–20) with a short, three-line intermediary verse (vv. 17–18a) holding them together.[2] In our present exposition of this passage, however, our concern is not with the structure of the hymn or with the message of the whole hymn. Rather, we are concerned with what this hymn reveals of the early church's understanding of the resurrection of Jesus. In this connection verses 18–20 will occupy us. For while in the first part of the hymn the author celebrates the lordship of Jesus displayed in his work of creation, in the last part the author celebrates the lordship of Jesus displayed above all in his resurrection from the dead. Before we turn to the second half, however, we shall deal with what I have termed the 'intermediary verse', which gives a flavour of what has gone before and sums up the theme of the hymn, namely that Jesus is Lord.

a. Jesus is Lord

The first line of this intermediary verse in many ways sums up the first half of the hymn. Jesus is Lord because *He is before all things* (v. 17a). Before the world ever came into being, Jesus was there with the Father. Jesus did not come on to the scene as a result of the Father's creative activity. From all eternity he shared in the Father's glory. However, the hymn is concerned to celebrate not just the temporal priority of Jesus, but rather his lordship. The pre-existence of Jesus is here primarily a symbol of his pre-eminence. As the one who is before all things, he is Lord over all things. This emphasis on the lordship of Jesus explains the use of the present tense, for otherwise the imperfect tense would have been expected: Jesus *is* (not 'was') before all things. Jesus reigns supreme over all.

Therefore the hymn goes on to say, *and in him all things hold together* (v. 17b). The word translated here *hold together* was often used by the Stoics to describe the 'binding together' of the universe. In the words of Hebrews 1:3, Jesus is 'sustaining all things by his powerful word'. It is important to note, however, that the hymn is not propounding a particular cosmological theory but is rather making a theological affirmation: Jesus is the sole and rightful Lord of creation, who not only set the universe in motion at the beginning of time, but who is also responsible for all that appears since then. Indeed, in verse 16 even the powers which elsewhere appear to be

---

[2] See P. Beasley-Murray, 'Colossians 1:15–20: An Early Christian Hymn Celebrating the Lordship of Christ', in D. A. Hagner and M. J. Harris (eds.), *Pauline Studies: Essays Presented to F. F. Bruce* (Paternoster, 1980), pp. 169–183.

hostile to Christ are claimed to have their origin and source of being in him! In other words, Jesus is more than a constitutional monarch, holding simply vestigial powers. As the ongoing sustainer of the universe, he remains supreme. Jesus is Lord!

But even more is involved. The underlying Greek verb can imply not only the 'holding together', but also the 'putting together' of sundered parts. An alternative translation is therefore possible: 'In him all things are brought together.' At this point the hymn looks not only backwards to the role of Jesus in creation, but also forwards to the role of Jesus in the new creation. It may well be that this phrase actually acts as the linchpin of the whole hymn, 'binding together' the work of Jesus in both creation and redemption.

This final line of the 'intermediary verse' looks forward to the second half of the hymn. Jesus is not only Lord of creation, but is also *the head of the body, the church* (v. 18a). According to popular first-century psychology – both Greek and Hebrew – people reasoned and purposed not with their head, but with their heart. In other words, the headship of Jesus over the church cannot be considered in physiological terms – he is not here described as the 'brains' of the church. Rather, the hymn is describing Jesus as the 'boss' or 'leader of the church'. In principle, Jesus is Lord of his church. The fact that all too often the church goes its own sinful and foolish way is not a reflection on Jesus, but rather a reflection on his people. Fortunately, as the hymn implies, ultimately Jesus will have his way with his church.

b. Jesus the risen Lord

The second half of the hymn starts with the statement *He is the beginning* (v. 18b). As the very structure of the hymn shows, the author has the church in view, not the world. Jesus is the 'beginning' not of the creation as a whole, but rather of the new creation. He is the beginning of God's new order of life. Jesus is not just *the head of the body, the church* (v. 18a), he is also 'the source of the body's life' (GNB). Although the actual term 'resurrection' is not found, the idea is presupposed. For it is through his resurrection from the dead that Jesus initiates the redemptive process. The same idea is to be found in such New Testament descriptions of Jesus as the 'firstfruits' (1 Cor. 15:20, 23), the 'author' of life (Acts 3:15), the 'first' to rise from the dead (Acts 26:23). Our hope of life beyond the grave is dependent upon Jesus. By rising from the dead, Jesus has breached death's defences, and through faith we may follow him. Although none of this is made explicit in the hymn, this thinking is certainly implicit.

In this context, however, the hymn is concerned to stress that Jesus is the risen Lord. It is significant that the Greek word translated 'beginning' (*archē*) is often used in the LXX in the sense of 'leader', 'chief' (e.g. Gen. 2:10; 40:13, 20; Exod. 6:25; 12:2; Num. 1:2; 4:22; 26:2; Judg. 7:16, 19–20; etc.). If the author of the hymn had this in mind, then we should perhaps see this phrase as describing the risen Jesus as the one who initiates a process of which he is the Lord. He is the Lord of life.

That resurrection is in mind is borne out by the next statement. There Jesus is described as *the firstborn from among the dead* (v. 18c). Through God's act in raising his Son from the dead, Jesus was literally the first to rise from the dead. What is more, as *the firstborn* his resurrection prepares the way for many others too. In many ways this phrase is parallel to the previous one, *he is the beginning*. In the resurrection of Jesus from the dead is to be found the promise of life for all.

As with the earlier description, *the firstborn over all creation* (v. 15b), here the phrase *the firstborn from among the dead* has less to do with temporal priority than with the idea of sovereignty. For in Jewish thinking the firstborn has authority over others. We see this in the story of Esau and Jacob, where Jacob gains his brother's birthright and in consequence gains Jacob's blessing on the firstborn:

> 'May nations serve you
>   and peoples bow down to you.
> Be lord over your brothers,
>   and may the sons of your mother
>   bow down to you.'
>
> (Gen. 27:29)

We see this also in Psalm 89:27, where the Lord says:

> 'I will also appoint him my firstborn,
>   the most exalted of the kings of the earth.'

Similarly in Hebrews 1:6ff. the angels worship Christ as the firstborn. In the light of these associations new light is thrown upon Colossians 1:18. As the *firstborn from among the dead* Jesus is given authority over all others – he is Lord by virtue of his resurrection from the dead. Or, as Paul writes in Romans 14:9, 'Christ died and returned to life so that he might be the Lord of both the dead and the living.'

What is implicit is now made explicit. For the hymn continues, *so that in everything he might have the supremacy* (v. 18c). Jesus rose as the firstborn from the dead in order that he – and he alone (the

231

Greek employs the personal pronoun and is emphatic at this point) – might be supreme. As in Romans 10:9 and Philippians 2:9–11, the resurrection forms the basis for the lordship of Jesus. Jesus is Lord by virtue of the fact that God raised him from the dead. It is important to note that the hymn allows for no exception to his rule. Literally, it asserts that Jesus rose from the dead 'in order that he might be first in all things'. The 'all things' refers to the whole creation – *all things . . . in heaven and on earth, visible and invisible, whether thrones or powers or rulers or authorities* (v. 16). Nothing is to be exempt from his rule. The hymn does not suggest that this is already a reality. Rather, the mood and tense of the Greek verb suggest that this is simply in the process of happening. The outcome, however, is not in doubt – Jesus is Lord!

This theme of resurrection power is taken up yet again in the sentence that follows. The superiority of Jesus in the new creation is founded upon the fact that *God was pleased to have all his fulness dwell in him* (v. 19). This is an extraordinarily difficult phrase to interpret. Indeed, the NIV, in its translation, has already opted for an interpretation. For the hymn itself simply speaks of *all the fulness* (*plērōma*), a term which may or may not be the subject of the verb. Some scholars believe that the hymn is borrowing a Stoic term, which referred in the first place to the universe rather than to God himself, and they therefore see Jesus as the second Adam in whom 'the whole universe was pleased to dwell'! The parallels for this use of the term, however, are all much later than the first century. The same is true for those who argue that here Paul is borrowing and reinterpreting a term used by the Colossian syncretists of his day: the parallels they draw all derive from second-century Gnosticism.

Traditionally this statement is interpreted as reinforcing the divinity of Christ. The NIV translation follows the traditional interpretation. A parallel is often drawn with Colossians 2:9, where Paul writes, 'For in Christ all the fulness of the Deity lives in bodily form.' The hymn itself, however, does not appear to be concerned to highlight the divinity of Jesus. Even the opening statement of the hymn, *He is the image of the invisible God*, is probably less concerned with who Jesus is than with what he does. For to be created in the image of God is to be created to rule over creation; as Genesis 1:26 makes clear, 'dominion' is a consequence – if not a constitutive part – of being in the image of God.

The key to the interpretation of this phrase is found in the fact that here in the hymn verse 19 depends on verse 18: *he is the beginning and the firstborn from among the dead . . . For God was pleased to have all his fulness dwell in him*. The fullness in question here is linked with the resurrection of Jesus. It would appear that the resurrection is the moment when the totality of the divine fullness finds its dwelling place in Jesus. If this is so, the hymn is concerned not so much with emphasizing the divinity of Jesus as with focusing on his lordship. The fullness in question is not the fullness of God's essence; it is the fullness of God's power. In raising his Son from the dead and exalting him to his right hand, God confers power upon his Son. The same idea, although not the same language, is found in Philippians 2:9–11, where the events of the resurrection and ascension are described as the moment when *God exalted him to the highest place*. As in Philippians 2, so in Colossians 1, the resurrection is the moment when Jesus is endowed with a new status, with new power. Perhaps a closer parallel to this line of the Colossian hymn is found in Colossians 2:9–10, where the statement that 'in Christ all the fulness of the Deity lives in bodily form' is followed by the assertion that 'Christ . . . is the Head over every power and authority'. The risen Jesus is Lord!

The consequences of the divine 'in-filling with power' are worked out in the closing lines of the hymn: 'and through him to reconcile to himself all things, whether things on earth or things in heaven, by making peace through his blood, shed on the cross' (1:20). The apparent universalism here has caused great difficulties. For at first sight verse 20 appears to envisage the salvation of all, humans and powers alike – for *all things* includes both *things on earth* and *things in heaven*. Indeed, it was on the basis of this text that the third-century theologian Origen talked of even the devil himself being saved. But such an interpretation runs counter to the teaching of the rest of the New Testament. In Colossians 2:15, for example, Paul talks of Christ triumphing over the powers rather than reconciling them.

The solution to the problem lies in an awareness of the verb used. For close examination of the text reveals that the hymn was talking not so much about 'reconciliation' as about 'restoration'. The Greek verb (*apokatallassō*) is significantly not the usual one Paul uses when he writes of reconciliation (*katallassō*). Rather, it has an additional prepositional prefix (*apo*) which is the Greek equivalent of the Latin *re-*, 'again'. This changes the meaning: the emphasis is on restoration, not reconciliation. The hymn is speaking about a return to cosmic harmony – about 'law and order' being re-established in the universe. The powers of evil are to be brought to heel. Rebellion in every shape and form is to be done away with. The GNB rightly translates, 'Through the Son, then, God decided to bring the whole universe back to himself.'

In this respect we may fittingly compare Acts 3:21, where the same prefix (*apo*) plays a similar role and where Peter refers to the re-establishing or restoration of all things (*apokatastaseōs pantōn*).

Likewise in Ephesians 1:10 a similar prefix (*ana*) bears a similar force: the creation again comes under the headship of Christ. This idea of restoration is also found in Romans 8:19–21, where Paul envisages the salvation of humankind within a cosmic context: 'The creation waits in eager expectation for the sons of God to be revealed' (v. 19). The Colossian hymn, far from standing at odds with the rest of the New Testament, is at one with it. The hymn looks forward to the restoration of the whole of creation, with Jesus as Lord. In the words of the Christ-hymn of Philippians 2, then every knee will bow and every tongue confess that Jesus Christ is Lord!

Throughout the second half of the hymn the emphasis is on Jesus as the risen Lord. However, the risen Lord is also the crucified Saviour. Cosmic harmony is in the process of being brought about as a result of Jesus *making peace through his blood shed on the cross* (v. 20b). The structure of the hymn may suggest that this line did not belong to the original hymn. Indeed, it may well be that Paul, who 'resolved to know nothing . . . except Jesus Christ and him crucified' (1 Cor. 2:2), himself inserted this reference to the cross, as a reminder that it was by means of Christ's death on the cross as well as by his resurrection that he set the process of universal restoration in motion.

Nevertheless, vital as the cross of Jesus is, in the Colossian hymn the resurrection is to the fore. Jesus is above all the risen Lord. Once again we see the importance of the resurrection in the thinking of the early church. The resurrection was not simply one of a number of tenets of the Christian faith – it was *the* faith. What is more, for the first Christians the resurrection had cosmic significance. As a result of the resurrection of Jesus the world was no longer the same. In the thinking of the Colossian hymn, for instance, the resurrection is portrayed not as affecting the individual destinies of believers, but rather as affecting the overall destiny of the world. The risen Jesus is Lord of all.

The implications of this thinking are revolutionary. If Jesus is Lord of all, no aspect of life today can be beyond his jurisdiction. If Jesus is Lord of all, as Christians we are called to be concerned not just with the affairs of the church, but with the affairs of the world: the struggle for human dignity and for justice, the issues of ecology and the use of resources – even the question of space colonization comes on to the Christian agenda!

4. Jesus, risen, ascended and glorified (1 Tim. 3:16b)

Our final example of the way in which the resurrection permeated the hymns and confessions of the early church is found in

1 Timothy 3:16. Here we have an early Christian credal hymn, sung or recited in worship, celebrating the 'mystery' (v. 16a) of the risen Lord Jesus. Its hymnic qualities may not be easily discernible in our English versions – but they are apparent in the original Greek form of the hymn, not least as a result of the deliberate assonance of the six third-person singular aorist passive verbs, each of which stands at the beginning of its respective line. Furthermore, with the exception of the third line, all the verbs are followed by the same preposition (*en*), and each line is rounded off by a noun in the dative case.

> He appeared in a body,
>> was vindicated by the Spirit,
> was seen by angels,
>> was preached among the nations,
> was believed on in the world,
>> was taken up in glory.

While questions of its structure are not easy to resolve, that the hymn is made up of six lines similar in construction is obvious. Less obvious, however, is how these six lines should be grouped. Many have tended to arrange the hymn into three antithetical couples, which combine in chiastic fashion – ABBAAB – in which A denotes an affirmation about an event in this world, and B an event in the transcendent world. On this arrangement, however, the last two lines can be taken together only with difficulty. It therefore seems better to divide the hymn into two verses of three lines each. The first and second lines, with their contrast between 'flesh' (NIV *body*) and *Spirit*, go well together, as also the fourth and fifth lines (*preached* and *believed*). The third and sixth lines are, we shall see, in many ways parallel, and may perhaps be viewed as forming a 'refrain', adding to each verse a final note of triumph.

Our prime concern, however, is not with structure, but with content. Within the space of these six short lines six important affirmations are made about Jesus. Not all of them relate to the risen Jesus but, as we shall see, most do.

a. Jesus is God's Son

He appeared in a body. Right at the beginning of this early Christian hymn we have a reminder that Jesus was no ordinary man. For whereas we humans came into being when our parents made love, Jesus was already in being long before he entered his mother's womb. Before time was, Jesus was. But, in the memorable words of

John in his Gospel, 'the Word became flesh' (John 1:14). Or, as the hymn puts it here, God came and 'was revealed in flesh'.

The reference is clearly to the incarnation. In the light of our interest in the resurrection, we note that some have seen in this phrase a reference to the Easter appearances of Jesus. Nowhere, however, is this Greek verb (*phaneroō*) or any of its cognates used of the post-resurrection appearances of Jesus; whereas the same verb is on several occasions applied to the incarnate Christ (see 2 Tim. 1:10; Heb. 9:26; 1 Pet. 1:20).

Why did God reveal himself in Jesus? Why did God come to us in human form? Here in 1 Timothy 3:16, nothing is said about the purpose of the coming of Jesus. In 2 Timothy 1:10, however, Paul speaks of 'the appearing of our Saviour, Christ Jesus, who has destroyed death and has brought life and immortality to light through the gospel'. This reminds us that the incarnation had the cross and, above all, the resurrection in view. Jesus came into this world to free us from the power of death, which holds us all in its icy grip. Left to our own devices, death would be the end of us. In the words of the French philosopher Blaise Pascal, 'The incarnation shows man the greatness of his misery by the greatness of the remedy which he required.' But Jesus was 'revealed in the flesh' – he *appeared in a body* – to save us from sin and death. Jesus, the Son of God, came to be our Saviour. All this is by implication summed up in the first line of the hymn.

b. Jesus rose from the dead

He *was vindicated by the Spirit*. As far as his contemporaries were concerned, Jesus was a failure. For he ended his life on a cross. The obvious conclusion to be drawn from this as far as any Jew was concerned was that the crucified was under the curse of God (see Deut. 21:23; Gal. 3:13). In his account of the crucifixion, Matthew tells us, 'Those who passed by hurled insults at him, shaking their heads and saying, ". . . Come down from the cross, if you are the Son of God!"' In similar vein the priests and scribes mocked Jesus, saying, 'He trusts in God. Let God rescue him now if he wants him, for he said, "I am the Son of God"' (Matt. 27:39–43). But God did not deliver him. Jesus did not come down from the cross. The logic of the situation therefore seemed to say that in no way was Jesus what he claimed to be. Jesus, if anything, was a charlatan.

But this is where the passers-by and the religious leaders were wrong. For God raised Jesus from the dead on the third day, and in raising him from the dead by the power of his Spirit God vindicated the claim of Jesus to be his Son. In the words of the GNB: 'He was shown to be right by the Spirit', who raised him from the dead (see Rom. 8:11). In the resurrection of Easter Day Jesus the crucified was proved to be God's 'Righteous One' (Acts 3:14; 7:52; see also 1 John 2:1, 29; 3:7).

This point was hammered home by Peter in his sermon on the day of Pentecost: 'This man . . . you, with the help of wicked men, put . . . to death by nailing him to the cross. But God raised him from the dead' (Acts 2:23–24). Good Friday was no horrible accident; it was in fact all part and parcel of the purposes of God. Jesus was no failure; rather, he achieved what he set out to do. But this became clear only in the light of Easter Day. The resurrection was the moment when God's initiative in the incarnation was seen to be vindicated.

c. Jesus is the risen, ascended Lord

He *was seen by angels*. When was Jesus seen by angels? Several suggestions have been made. Bearing in mind that the Greek word for 'angel' literally means 'messenger' (see Luke 7:24 and Jas. 2:25), one suggestion has been that here we have a reference to Christ's post-resurrection appearances to the apostles (i.e. 'the sent ones'). However, although the Greek verb (*ōpthē*) is found in such a setting (1 Cor. 15:5–8), the Greek noun (*angelos*) is nowhere in the New Testament used of the apostles. The natural meaning of 'angel' is far too common a meaning in the New Testament to be lightly set aside.

Another possibility is to take this line to refer not to one occasion in particular, but rather to the whole of Jesus' earthly life. For instance, angels greeted his birth (Luke 2:13), attended him in the wilderness at the time of his temptation (Matt. 4:11; Mark 1:13), strengthened him in the Garden of Gethsemane (Luke 22:43), and were present at the tomb on Easter Day (Matt. 28:2ff; Mark 16:5; Luke 24:4) and at the ascension (Acts 1:10). Once the second line is interpreted as speaking of the resurrection, however, this suggestion fails to compel, in so far as the chronology of the events is not respected – the incarnation comes before, and not after, the resurrection.

The most likely suggestion is that this is a reference to the ascension. In ascending to his Father, the risen Lord appeared in all his glory to the angelic powers. This suggestion is reinforced by the fact that the Greek verb (*ōpthē*) nearly always means the self-exhibition of the subject: Jesus was not primarily 'seen by angels'; rather, 'he appeared to angels'. Jesus is the one who took the initiative in appearing to the angels. A second-century parallel to this interpretation is in the *Ascension of Isaiah* (10:12ff.; 11:23ff.), where

Jesus is seen by the angels to be the Lord only on his ascension, when they worship him as the Lord of glory. In the New Testament we have a parallel in 1 Peter 3:19, where Jesus goes and preaches to 'the spirits in prison'. Modern New Testament scholarship has shown that this is not a preaching to the dead, but rather an announcement by the ascending Christ to the angelic spirits of his victory over them in the cross and resurrection.[3] This idea is not far removed from that in the Christ-hymn of Philippians 2:6–11, where we read that

> God exalted him to the highest place
>   and gave him the name that is above every name,
> that at the name of Jesus every knee should bow,
>   in heaven and on earth and under the earth,
> and every tongue confess that Jesus Christ is Lord.

d. Jesus is the Saviour of the world

He *was preached among the nations.* It is significant that the day the church was born was the day when the good news was preached to men and women from 'every nation under heaven' (Acts 2:5). In Luke's account of Pentecost we read that Peter preached to 'Parthians, Medes and Elamites; residents of Mesopotamia, Judea and Cappadocia, Pontus and Asia, Phrygia and Pamphylia, Egypt and the parts of Libya near Cyrene; visitors from Rome . . . Cretans and Arabs' (Acts 2:9–11). From the very beginning Jesus has been good news for all. It is said that in the wars of religion in France, the English soldiers used to shout, 'The Pope is French but Jesus Christ is English!' What nonsense! Jesus can never be the exclusive preserve of any one group, nation or race – he is the Saviour of the world.

It may be that the hymn specifically had Pentecost in mind, for Pentecost was the event that connected Christ's exaltation to God's right hand (i.e. above all angelic beings) with the inauguration of the apostolic preaching to 'the nations' (Acts 2:33–36). The Greek aorist past tense initially suggests a one-off event. But it is more likely that we have here a 'prophetic past'. Possibly the author of the hymn was so carried away with the success of the early Christian mission that he viewed it as already coming to a successful conclusion (see Rom. 15:19–23; Col. 1:23).

---

[3] This is supported by the fact that within the same context we find reference to such spirit powers (1 Pet. 3:22), while within the General Epistles as a whole, Jude 6 and in particular 2 Pet. 2:4 point in the same direction. Both elsewhere in the New Testament (see Luke 10:20; Heb. 1:14; Rev. 1:4; 3:1) and in Jewish apocalyptic literature (see especially *1 Enoch* 10:15; 13:6; 15:4, 6, 7, 8, 9, 11, 12; 16:1; 19:1), 'spirits' (*pneumata*) is used of angelic beings, both good and evil.

e. Jesus is the Saviour of those who believe

He *was believed on in the world*. Not only has the gospel been preached; it has also met with acceptance. Again the Greek aorist past tense is used. In all probability this is another 'prophetic past'. The hymn again anticipates the successful outcome of gospel preaching. It celebrates the transformation of a small Jewish sect into a worldwide movement. In many ways that vision has already been realized. Numerically Christianity is well ahead of all world religions. On one reckoning one out of every four human beings is at least a nominal Christian. Some years ago it was estimated that every day there is a net increase of over 64,000 Christians. Jesus has indeed been 'believed on in the world'.

This celebration of the worldwide dimension of Christian believing does not need to be equated with universalism. The NIV is right to translate the Greek preposition employed here (*en*) in a local rather than an instrumental sense: that is, he has been believed on 'in' (or 'among') the world, as distinct from having been believed on 'by' the world. Sadly, the world as a whole does not believe – nor is it likely to believe. In this respect some words of Paul in 1 Timothy 4:10 are relevant: 'We have put our hope in the living God, who is the Saviour of all men, and especially of those who believe.' Faith is the catalyst that turns the potential into actual. Salvation becomes a reality where men and women put their trust in Jesus as the Saviour of the world. Such faith, however, cannot be commanded or enforced. The glory and the tragedy of humankind is that we are free to believe – or not to believe.

f. Jesus shares in the Father's glory

He *was taken up in glory*. The hymn ends by celebrating again the ascension of Christ (see Acts 1:11). The sixth line of the hymn thus corresponds to the third line. Indeed, I have suggested that these two lines might form a 'refrain' to the hymn.

Some people have thought this affirmation of Christ's ascension to be out of chronological order – for clearly the preaching and the believing took place after Jesus was taken up in glory. The emphasis here, however, is not so much on the ascension as a past event as on the truth that even now Jesus shares in his Father's glory. In this sense there is in this final line a sense of progression over against the third line. The risen and ascended Christ has not only appeared to angels, but has also been received up *in glory*. The Greek preposition (*en*) does not denote movement (by contrast with Luke 24:26 where another preposition, *eis*, is used of Jesus' entering his glory). True, the phrase *in glory* could be construed adverbially: Jesus was taken up 'with glory'. It may, however, refer to the glory in which Jesus shares even now. God's throne is the throne of his glory (see Jer. 14:21; 17:12). Certainly this interpretation would cause the hymn to end on a magnificent note. The risen Lord now sits at God's right hand, and enjoys a state of splendour beyond all imagining.

Yet again the risen Lord is to the forefront of an early Christian hymn. While not every line of the hymn in 1 Timothy 3:16 celebrates the resurrection of Jesus, the resurrection surely forms the foundation of the hymn. The implications of the resurrection are not fully worked out in this particular composition. Nevertheless no-one can doubt its centrality to Christian believing.

In all four of the pre-Pauline hymns and creeds we have examined, the resurrection of Jesus from the dead and his subsequent exaltation to the right hand of God form the basis for Jesus's lordship over the world. Thus in Romans 10:9 the primal confession 'Jesus is Lord' is paralleled by the belief that 'God raised him from the dead'. This confession and belief are inseparable parts of one whole, like two sides of the one coin. In the Christ-hymn of Philippians 2 the exaltation of Jesus marks his appointment to a higher position than he had before. Because Jesus refused to snatch at equality with God, but was obedient to the uttermost, God raised him to the heights and gave him the new name of 'Lord'. The name refers not only to a new dignity, but to a new office: Jesus is here given the 'divine' function of rulership over the cosmos. The resurrection marks the beginning of his kingdom. In the hymn to the cosmic Christ in Colossians 1:15–20 there is a similar theme. As the 'beginning' Jesus initiates the new creation of which he is Lord (1.18). He is 'the firstborn from among the dead' (1:18) and so Lord by virtue of his resurrection from the dead. Furthermore, the indwelling of the fullness (1:19) of divine power appears to be linked with the resurrection. The second half of the hymn celebrates Jesus as the risen Lord. Finally, in 1 Timothy 3:16 the exaltation of the risen Jesus is the moment of divine vindication, when the incarnate Christ is seen to have come from God. For the evil angels at least, this moment of truth comes when the ascending Christ appears to them in his risen glory: their doom is sealed. In so far as the exaltation/ascension of Jesus is central to the credal hymn (it is mentioned in lines 2, 3 and 6), it is probable that the successful completion of the mission of the church is the expression of the lordship of the exalted Lord.

From all these examples we see that the resurrection is celebrated as the foundation of the lordship of Jesus. In the words of the German scholar Ernst Käsemann: 'The content of the Resurrection is primarily not anthropological at all, but Christological. It is the work of the Second Adam and therefore its meaning is not immediately and primarily our reanimation, but the lordship of Christ. "Christ must reign": that is the nerve centre of the design and the firm ground that gives us confidence concerning our own destiny.'[4]

The centrality of the resurrection to early Christian worship poses a challenge to the way in which we worship. To what degree is the resurrection central to our worship? Are Easter hymns to be sung only on Easter Day? And even if they are not, to what extent do we in fact sing Easter hymns at other times of the year? If the early Christian hymns are anything to go by, then we should be singing Easter hymns every week of the year!

The centrality of the resurrection does not, of course, rule out the centrality of the cross. Although it is true to say that in these pre-Pauline hymns and creeds it is the resurrection that is emphasized, in their present form at least, there are a number of references to Jesus' death.[5] In Philippians 2:8 Jesus is described as 'obedient to death', and in Colossians 1:20 the hymn speaks of Jesus 'making peace through his blood, shed on the cross'. Although the cross receives no direct mention in 1 Timothy 3:16, the reference in the second line to vindication certainly alludes to it. It is good to remind ourselves that the Jesus who sits at God's right hand and shares in his Father's glory is also the crucified Jesus. Because he bears on his hands and in his side the scars of his suffering, he is more than able to intercede for us.

---

[4]E. Käsemann, *New Testament Questions for Today* (ET SCM, 1969), p. 133.

[5] For other probable pre-Pauline confessions or creeds where the death of Christ is central, see, e.g., Rom. 3:24–25 and 1 Cor. 15:3–5.

8. The witness of theologians to the resurrection

The witness of theologians to the resurrection of Jesus has been extraordinarily mixed. In the second half or so of the past century many theologians displayed an amazing degree of scepticism toward the New Testament documents in general, and toward the accounts of the resurrection in particular. Conversely, there have always been those prepared to defend the reliability of the New Testament witness to the resurrection of Jesus.

While recognizing that it will inevitably be limited, in this chapter we shall engage in a brief overview. In the words of the Preacher of old, 'Of making many books there is no end' (Eccles. 12:12), not least of books on the resurrection!

1. Doubts raised

We begin with Rudolf Bultmann, the German New Testament scholar, who, in seeking to 'demythologize' the gospel with a view to making it 'believable', wrote in 1941 of 'the incredibility of a mythical event like the resuscitation of a corpse – for that is what the resurrection means'. He went on: 'If the event of Easter Day is in any sense an historical event additional to the event of the cross, it is nothing else than the rise of faith in the risen Lord ... All that historical criticism can establish is the fact that the first disciples came to believe in the resurrection.'[1]

In the 1960s there was a flurry of books and articles on the resurrection of Jesus. In 1964, for instance, Willi Marxsen caused a stir in the German Lutheran church with a paper on 'The Resurrection of Jesus as a Historical and Theological Problem',[2]

---

[1] R. Bultmann, *Kerygma and Myth* (ET SPCK, 1953), pp. 38–42.
[2] Published in English in C. F. D. Moule (ed.), *The Significance of the Message of the Resurrection for Faith in Jesus Christ* (SCM, 1968), pp. 15–50.

subsequently followed up with a more popular presentation in *The Resurrection of Jesus of Nazareth*.[3] Marxsen maintained that we cannot answer the question of historicity simply by appealing to the texts, any more than we can answer the question about how the world came into being by appealing to the book of Genesis without taking into consideration the conclusions of natural science.[4] Somewhat surprisingly, Marxsen argued that, for Paul, belief in the resurrection of Jesus was a deduction as contrasted with 'something which he considers to have taken place'.[5] As for the appearances of the risen Jesus to his disciples, Marxsen believed them to be subjective visions, derived from the faith of the disciples, rather than objective in nature.[6]

In 1968 Geoffrey Lampe, the Regius Professor of Divinity at the University of Cambridge, maintained that 'although Jesus was actually raised from the dead', this did not necessitate an empty tomb. Indeed, he went on to argue that 'the fact that Christ's Resurrection is the assurance that we too shall rise from the dead' implies 'that his Resurrection was not different in kind from what we may hope for through him'. If, however, his body 'was raised physically from the grave and did not see corruption, or if his body was transformed after death into something different, in such a way that in itself it was annihilated, then he did not experience the whole of our human destiny'.[7] But as Donald MacKinnon, Lampe's Cambridge colleague, rightly pointed out, 'the apparent inability of the opponents of the early Christian preaching to silence the message of the Resurrection once and for all by producing its remains' is in itself an argument for the empty tomb.[8]

In 1970 a detailed study of *The Resurrection and the New Testament* was produced by Christopher Evans, Professor of New Testament at the University of London.[9] Evans believed not only that it was impossible to harmonize the various accounts of the resurrection of Jesus, but also that there was no way in which we could know what had actually happened that first Easter Day: 'The events themselves . . . both the resurrection appearances and the empty tomb, lie so deeply concealed within the traditions that they can be glimpsed only very indirectly, so that the principal difficulty

---

[3] W. Marxsen, *The Resurrection of Jesus of Nazareth* (SCM, 1970).

[4] Marxsen, 'The Resurrection of Jesus' as a Historical and Theological Problem, p. 16.

[5] Ibid., pp. 23–24.

[6] Ibid., p. 30.

[7] G. W. H. Lampe and D. MacKinnon, *The Resurrection: A Dialogue* (Mowbray, 1966), 58–59.

[8] Ibid., p. 84.

[9] C. F. Evans, *Resurrection and the New Testament* (SCM, 1970).

here is not to believe, but to know what it is which offers itself for belief.'[10]

In the 1980s David Jenkins, who prior to his appointment as Bishop of Durham had been theological professor at the University of Leeds, startled the British public by making a number of controversial statements appearing to deny the resurrection of Jesus. According to Jenkins, Jesus rose, not bodily from the grave, but spiritually (although none the less really) in the minds of the disciples.[11] In April 1984, just prior to his enthronement as Bishop of Durham, he said in a television interview: 'It doesn't seem to me, reading the records as they remain both in the Gospels and what Paul says in 1 Corinthians, that there was any one event which you could identify with the resurrection.'[12] More starkly, in July 1986, at the York meeting of the General Synod of the Church of England, he gave an impassioned defence of his views of the resurrection, in which he accused those who believed in the empty tomb of worshipping 'a cultic idol' or 'the very devil'. His central argument was that people should not believe in a God who worked miracles on some occasions, yet stood by and did nothing miraculous to prevent horrors like Auschwitz and Hiroshima:

> We are faced with the claim that God is prepared to work knock-down physical miracles in order to let a select number of people into the secret of his Incarnation, Resurrection and salvation, but is not prepared to use such methods in order to deliver from Auschwitz, prevent Hiroshima; overcome famine, or bring about a bloodless transformation of apartheid. Such a God is surely a cultic idol. That is to say he is a false and misdeveloped picture of the true and gracious God, drawn up by would-be worshippers, who have gone dangerously astray.[13]

To put it mildly, this statement was misleading. The purpose of the incarnation and resurrection, for instance, was that salvation might come to all, and not to the few![14]

In 1988 David Jenkins again scandalized many by describing the doctrine of the bodily resurrection of Jesus as 'a conjuring trick with bones', clearly indicating that he did not believe that the resurrection involved the transformation of the body of Jesus.

---

[10] Ibid., p. 130.

[11] M. J. Harris, *Easter in Durham* (Paternoster, 1985); also *From Grave to Glory: Resurrection in the New Testament* (Zondervan, 1990), pp. 337–353.

[12] *Credo*, London Weekend Television, 29 April 1984.

[13] Cited by R. Harries, *Christ is Risen* (Mowbray, 1987), p. 76.

[14] For a critique see Harries, *Christ is Risen*, pp. 76–80.

Equally controversial views were put forward in 1987 by Peter Carnley, Anglican Archbishop of Perth, Western Australia.[15] For him the central claim of 1 Corinthians 15 and the Gospel narratives is that 'seeing' is the basis of the affirmation of resurrection belief. It was this experience that 'provided the experiential ground for the inference that Jesus had been raised in the tomb and also for theological speculation concerning the heavenly place where Jesus had gone'.[16] This 'seeing' however was not a literal 'seeing' in terms of 'seeing a material object through the natural mechanism of the eye',[17] but rather something more akin to – but not identical with – intellectual apprehension. Carnley is not interested in the resurrection as a past event – indeed, he is quite sceptical about the possibility of piecing together the various accounts.[18] Like David Jenkins, he lays emphasis on present experience. Therefore for him the 'Easter stories . . . are not proofs, but pointers . . . to a possibility of present experience.'[19] Easter faith, he says 'involves a post-mortem experience of encounter with the raised Christ', who is known as the Spirit.[20] 'Faith is . . . the apprehension and identification of the presence of the Spirit in the Christian fellowship as the presence of Christ.'[21] Carnley's reconstruction of Easter faith is quite ingenious; however, it involves a substantial divergence from the witness of the New Testament.

More recently, Gerd Ludemann, Professor of New Testament and Director of the Institute of Early Christian Studies at the University of Göttingen, has created a furore in his native Germany with an erudite study on the resurrection of Jesus, in which he has sought to demolish totally the historicity of the resurrection.[22] He concludes: 'We can no longer understand the resurrection of Jesus in a literal sense . . . for historically speaking we do not know the slightest thing about the tomb (was it empty? was it an individual tomb at all?) and about the fate of Jesus' corpse: did it decay?'[23] Somewhat improbably, Ludemann suggests that belief in the resurrection of Jesus came about as a result of Peter's seeing Jesus in a 'vision', which thereupon proved 'infectious' and was followed by others![24]

---

[15] P. Carnley, *The Structure of Resurrection Belief* (Clarendon, 1987).
[16] Ibid., p. 225.
[17] Ibid., p. 227.
[18] Ibid., p. 18.
[19] Ibid., p. 367.
[20] Ibid., pp. 200, 266.
[21] Ibid., p. 326.
[22] G. Ludemann, *The Resurrection of Jesus: History, Experience, Theology* (ET SCM, 1994).
[23] Ibid., p. 180.
[24] Ibid., p. 174.

Less negative in tone, but ultimately no less negative in conclusion, is the investigation of A. J. M. Wedderburn, Professor of New Testament in the Protestant Faculty of the University of Munich. After an in-depth survey of the resurrection narratives, he writes: 'As far the resurrection of Jesus itself is concerned, a decisive historical judgment is to my mind epistemologically improper and impossible.' Instead, he argues for a 'reverent agnosticism' as being 'the surest and the most soberly scientific and scholarly policy'.[25] Wedderburn's version of the Christian faith centres not on the resurrection of Jesus, but rather on 'the life Jesus lived and the message that he delivered'.[26] Wedderburn admits that such a version of the faith can create pastoral difficulties, for to those who are suffering or who are experiencing bereavement it offers no comfort of another life.[27] All we can do in the dark moments of life is to throw ourselves 'upon the love and mercy of God who, if we can learn anything about the divine nature from the fate of Jesus, above all suffers with us'.[28] What a travesty of the good news!

2. Faith affirmed

Fortunately, not all theologians are sceptical of the resurrection of Jesus. Over the years many have examined the evidence, and found it not to be wanting. For example, in 1947 George Beasley-Murray, then a young New Testament scholar, wrote an apology for the resurrection, in which – among other things – he examined six facts pointing to the resurrection of Jesus, namely the empty tomb, the appearances of Jesus after his death, the existence of the church and the worship of Jesus, the testimony of Christian experience, the predictions of Jesus, and the congruity of the resurrection with the biblical revelation. He wrote:

> The first converts to Christianity were convicted by the assertion that the Messiah they had rejected had been raised from the dead by God, and they repented of their wickedness and exulted in their new life. There is no reason why the joyous certainty of that primitive Church should not be shared by the modern Church. For clearly, if Christ is alive the world is mistaken. Spinoza, the famous philosopher, said that he would renounce his system if he could be made sure that Lazarus had risen. Owing to the nature of the circumstances it cannot be proved that Lazarus was revived;

[25] A. J. M. Wedderburn, *Beyond Resurrection* (ET SCM, 1999), p. 98.
[26] Ibid., p. 221.
[27] Ibid., pp. 221–222.
[28] Ibid., p. 225.

Spinoza accordingly stuck to his system and remained a Jew. What a tragedy it was that no one asked him to reconsider the evidence for the belief that Christ had risen from the dead and is alive for evermore! I believe that the evidence for the truth of the resurrection of Christ is overwhelming to any unprejudiced observer; so do most scholars who have examined the problem, but the Church is not sure and the world is wholly ignorant of our reasons. It is our duty to know why we believe this, the central tenet of our Faith, and to be able to pass on our convictions to our fellows.[29]

In 1961 the revised edition of Michael Ramsey's book *The Resurrection of Christ* appeared and received a good deal of publicity, for by then its author, formerly a professor of divinity at Durham and later at Cambridge, was Archbishop of York, soon to become Archbishop of Canterbury.[30] In the chapter dealing with 'History and Criticism', Ramsey made the important point that no-one can approach the study of the New Testament without presuppositions. 'A historian must needs bring to his task a certain view of the world and a certain mental furniture of his own.'[31] For some, for instance, the underlying presupposition might be that history can be understood only within the terms of this world, a world in which miracles are not deemed to happen; whereas for others the underlying presupposition might be the uniqueness of Jesus.

Ramsey acknowledged that he was working with two presuppositions: the first was the 'Biblical belief in the living God', and the other that 'the events must be such as account for the Gospel which the Apostles preached and by which the first Christians lived'. He went on:

If the evidence is pointing us towards a Resurrection of an utterly unique sort, we will not be incredulous, for the Christ is Himself a unique and transcendent fact in history. If the evidence is pointing us towards a miracle we will not be troubled, for the miracle will mean not only a breach of the laws that have been perceived in this world but a manifestation of the purpose of the creator of a new world and the redeemer of our own. And if the evidence is pointing us towards an act wherein spirit and body are

---

[29] G. R. Beasley-Murray, *Christ is Alive* (Lutterworth, 1947), pp. 14–15. See also his *The Resurrection of Jesus Christ* (Oliphants, 1964).

[30] A. M. Ramsey, *The Resurrection of Christ: A Study of the Event and its Meaning for the Christian Faith* (reissued Fontana, 1961).

[31] Ibid., p. 54.

strangely blended and exalted, our minds will have no terrors: for the message of the New Testament is pervaded through and through by the belief that the spiritual and material are interwoven in the person of the Word-made-flesh. Why is it judged incredible with you, if God should raise the dead?[32]

In 1965 Daniel Fuller, a member of the dynasty that founded Fuller Theological Seminary in Pasadena, California, published his Basle PhD thesis. This involved a detailed survey of the various philosophical and critical approaches to the resurrection over the previous 250 years, which he then went on to link with Luke's depiction of the resurrection of Jesus.[33] Fuller argued that 'Man's ability to believe, due to sin and Satan, is not owing to the fact that he lacks the evidences necessary to believe the resurrection until he is illumined by the Holy Spirit, but to the fact that he does not want to own up to the inescapable evidences when confronted with them.'[34] Such evidences include the historical origins of the Christian faith, but also include the reality of changed lives, which in turn can be explained only by reference to the risen Christ.[35]

In 1967 S. H. Hooke, Professor of New Testament at London University, published a major work on the resurrection of Jesus, in which he reviewed at length the New Testament material.[36] Although he viewed the resurrection as ultimately incapable of historical verification, in so far as it was 'a transaction which took place between the Father and the Son, unlimited by time, incapable of being witnessed by any human witness',[37] he unreservedly accepted the reality of the resurrection of Jesus and for the most part accepted the reliability of the witness of the Gospels. Indeed, in his final chapter, entitled 'An Anchor of the Soul', he wrote: 'It is because Christ, having met and overcome death, has entered upon a new kind of life, the life of new creation, that hope has become possible for those to whom death was the blank end of everything.'[38]

In 1973 Norman Anderson, a distinguished lawyer and able lay theologian, reviewed some of the then current theological debates, and in particular devoted two chapters to the resurrection of Jesus.[39]

---

[32] Ibid., p. 56.
[33] D. Fuller, *Easter Faith and History* (Tyndale Press, 1968).
[34] Ibid., p. 233.
[35] Ibid., p. 260.
[36] S. H. Hooke, *The Resurrection of Christ as History and Experience* (Darton, Longman & Todd, 1967).
[37] Ibid., p. 130.
[38] Ibid., p. 190.
[39] N. Anderson, *A Lawyer Among the Theologians* (Hodder & Stoughton, 1973), pp. 66–149.

In his introduction he expressed his astonishment at the way in which theologians 'handle their evidence, at the pre-suppositions and *a priori* convictions with which some of them clearly (and even on occasion, on their own admission) approach the documents concerned, and by the positively staggering assurance with which they make categorical pronouncements on points which are, on any showing, open to question and on which equally competent colleagues take a diametrically opposite view'. He contrasted the cavalier way in which some theologians did their work with that of lawyers, who 'are predisposed by their training to accept the propositions that documentary evidence should, as far as possible, be allowed to speak for itself; that an honest attempt should be made to sift and assess oral testimony and not to jump to any premature conclusions that are mutually contradictory; and that circumstantial evidence may, on occasion, be exceedingly persuasive'.[40] After examining the basic historicity of the resurrection and the biblical evidence for it, he ended with a quotation from another lay theologian, Dorothy L. Sayers, concerning the apparent divergences of the accounts of the resurrection:

> The divergences appear very great on first sight; and much ink and acrimony have been expended on proving that certain of the stories are not 'original' or 'authentic', but are accretions grafted upon the first-hand reports by the pious imagination of Christians. Well, it may be so. But the fact remains that all of them, without exception, can be made to fall into place in a single orderly and coherent narrative without the smallest contradiction or difficulty, and without any suppression, invention or manipulation, beyond a trifling effort to imagine the natural behaviour of a bunch of startled people running about in the dawnlight between Jerusalem and the Garden.[41]

In 1975 the contribution of George Eldon Ladd, then Professor of New Testament at Fuller Theological Seminary, to the 'I Believe' series appeared: *I Believe in the Resurrection*.[42] After a careful analysis of the witness of the New Testament to define as clearly as possible the nature of the resurrection, he went on to survey

---

[40] Ibid., p. 15.
[41] D. L. Sayers, *The Man Born to Be King* (Hodder & Stoughton, 1943), p. 35. A sustained attempt at harmonization is provided in particular by J. Wenham in his book *Easter Enigma* (Paternoster, 2nd edn 1992); and also more recently and somewhat popularly by P. Walker, *The Weekend that Changed the World: The Mystery of Jerusalem's Empty Tomb* (Marshall Pickering, 1999), pp. 42–55.
[42] G. E. Ladd, *I Believe in the Resurrection* (Hodder & Stoughton, 1975).

modern so-called historical explanations for the resurrection, all of which he found lacking in credibility. He concluded that section with a personal statement:

> In the end, I accept the biblical witness to the resurrection not because of logical proof or historical reasoning, but because of an inner quality of the gospel, namely its truthfulness. It so overpowers me that I am rendered willing to stake the rest of my life on that message and live in accordance with it. My faith is not faith in history, but faith in the God who acts in history . . .
>
> Does such faith mean a 'leap in the dark'? Does historical reasoning have no place in my experience? By no means. For in fact, only the 'hypothesis' of actual bodily resurrection adequately explains the known facts.[43]

In 1983 Murray J. Harris, a New Testament scholar from New Zealand, reviewed the evidence yet again.[44] In so doing he made the interesting point that 'The New Testament writers do not set out to give historical proof of the empty tomb, but to testify to its theological significance. That is, the question "To what does the empty tomb point?" is more their concern than the question "Was the tomb empty?"'[45] After a rigorous investigation he concluded his review: 'While the exaltation of Jesus to God's right hand (one aspect of the Resurrection in its wider sense) is an item of faith whose factual reality cannot be investigated, there are compelling historical evidences that encourage and validate the belief that, at the latest, some 36 hours after his death and burial, Jesus rose from the dead in a transformed bodily state.'[46]

At around the same time a most astonishing book exploded on the scene, in which Pinchas Lapide, a leading orthodox German Jew, announced his acceptance of the resurrection of Jesus not as an invention of the early church but as a historical event.[47] The book makes for fascinating reading, and all the more so in so far as Lapide refused to accept the messiahship of Jesus.[48]

As a Jewish New Testament scholar Lapide listed what he called 'traces of authentic Jewish experience' to be found in the Gospel accounts of the resurrection. For example, he writes: 'In a purely

[43] Ibid., p. 140.
[44] M. J. Harris, *Raised Immortal: Resurrection and Immortality in the New Testament* (Marshall, Morgan & Scott, 1983).
[45] Ibid., p. 37.
[46] Ibid., p. 71.
[47] P. Lapide, *The Resurrection of Jesus: A Jewish Perspective* (ET SPCK, 1984).
[48] Ibid., pp. 152–154.

fictional narrative one would have avoided making women the crown witnesses of the resurrection since they were considered in rabbinic Judaism as incapable of giving valid testimony.'[49] Furthermore, 'The circumstance that the same women wanted to anoint the dead Jesus right after his burial, as Jewish custom demanded, proves that basically none of the disciples nor the women themselves . . . expected his resurrection.'[50] 'Even more eloquent is the silence of the evangelists concerning the resuscitation of the dead Nazarene . . . How easy it would have been for them or their immediate successors to supplement this scandalous hole in the concatenation of events by fanciful embellishments.'[51]

Later Lapide goes on:

> In regard to the future resurrection of the dead, I am and remain a Pharisee. Concerning the resurrection of Jesus on Easter Sunday, I was for decades a Sadducee. I am no longer a Sadducee since the following deliberation has caused me to think this through anew. In not one of the cases where rabbinic literature speaks of such visions did it result in an essential change in the life of the resuscitated or of those who had experienced the visions.[52]

Lapide confesses himself mystified by 'the strange paraphrases' used by theologians for the resurrection, which are 'too abstract and scholarly to explain the fact that the solid hillbillies from Galilee who, for the very real reason of the crucifixion of their master, were saddened to death, were changed within a short period of time into a jubilant community of believers'. Clearly, something 'concrete' had happened.[53] This refusal of certain Christian theologians to believe in the resurrection of Jesus caused Lapide to lambast what he perceived as unwarranted scepticism:

> Neither the Twelve nor the early church believed in the ingenious wisdom of theologians. Indeed, they would hardly have understood what the gentlemen of scholarship went on to say in such a roundabout manner . . . For all these Christians who believe in the incarnation (something which I am unable to do) but have difficulty with the historically understood resurrection,

---

[49] Ibid., p. 95.
[50] Ibid., p. 96.
[51] Ibid., p. 97.
[52] Ibid., p. 125.
[53] Ibid., pp. 128–129.

the word of Jesus of the 'blind guides straining out a gnat and swallowing up a camel' (Matt. 23:34) probably applies.[54]

Faith in the 'personal and bodily' resurrection of Jesus from the dead has also been clearly articulated by the Jesuit priest Gerald O'Collins, not least in his book *Jesus Risen*, published in 1987.[55] There, after a lively review of the way in which scholars have sought to deal with the New Testament evidence for the resurrection, he puts forward five tests by which we can validate the confession of Easter faith:[56] (1) *Partial continuity* – did the new truth ('Jesus has been raised from the dead') stand in some continuity with what Jewish people already knew of God? (2) *Coherence* – can the various levels and patterns of meaning in the event of Christ's resurrection be systematically related in ways that are mutually consistent? (3) *Reliable historical witness* – can the various accounts of the resurrection hold water? (4) *Vindication in public practice* – are there signs of the risen Christ's activity in the contemporary life of the Christian community and the wider world? (5) *Personal experience* – does this belief illuminate my present reality, human concerns and future hopes?

O'Collins leaves his readers in no doubt that to each a ringing affirmative can be made. For him, 'faith in the risen Jesus is an intellectually valid choice'.[57] Furthermore, in the words of his most recent contribution to the resurrection debate, 'Belief in the resurrection of Jesus has carried the church for nearly twenty centuries. If Christians as a whole ever stop believing in, and living from, his resurrection, that will be when the Church stops being the Church of Jesus Christ.'[58]

In 1993 Stephen T. Davis, who is a philosopher rather than a New Testament scholar, produced a highly readable book in which he examined the two central Christian resurrection claims – namely that Jesus was bodily raised from the dead and that we shall be raised from the dead – and found them to be defensible.[59] Over against those theologians who believe that the question of the historicity of Jesus' resurrection is secondary to its meaning – and indeed is of

---

[54] Ibid., p. 30. For a similar critique, see also M. Green, *The Empty Cross of Jesus* (Hodder & Stoughton, 1984), pp. 155–158.

[55] *Jesus Risen* (Darton, Longman & Todd, 1987).

[56] Ibid., pp. 137–146.

[57] Ibid., p. 146.

[58] G. O'Collins, 'The Resurrection: The State of the Questions', in S. T. Davis, D. Kendall and G. O'Collins (eds.), *The Resurrection: An Interdisciplinary Symposium on the Resurrection of Jesus* (Oxford University Press, 1997), p. 28.

[59] S. T. Davis, *Risen Indeed: Making Sense of the Resurrection* (SPCK, 1993).

little interest – Davis argues that the latter is clearly dependent upon the former:

> I am convinced that the resurrection means little unless it really happened. If the resurrection of Jesus turns out to have been a fraud or a pious myth or even somehow an honest mistake, then there is little reason to think about it or see meaning in it. Perhaps it would provide some lessons about courageously facing death, but that would be about all.[60]

In his final chapter, 'Resurrection and Meaning', Davis develops the difference that the resurrection makes to the death each of us must face, and in so doing provides rich pastoral resources. He shows that while we may fear death (it is inevitable and mysterious; we have to face it alone; in death we shall be separated from our loved ones; in death our personal hopes and aims will not be realized; death raises the real and frightening possibility that we shall be totally annihilated), Jesus' resurrection from the dead is a promise or guarantee of our resurrection from the dead:

> So there is only one bit of evidence for life after death that is convincing to Christians. It is not philosophical arguments for the immortality of the soul. It is not supposed spiritualist conversations at seances with loved ones who are (as they say) 'on the other side'. It is not medical testimony about out-of-body experiences or the interesting stories told by people who were near death and then resuscitated. It is that Jesus was dead for three days and lived again.[61]

Most recently Tom Wright, Canon-Theologian at Westminister Abbey and a leading New Testament scholar, in a debate with Marcus Borg, a liberal American scholar, makes a very reasoned defence of the empty tomb and of the bodily resurrection of Jesus.[62] He points out that 'for Paul, the Pharisee, saying that "he was raised, leaving an empty tomb", would have been tautologous'.[63] Furthermore, as Paul develops his argument in 1 Corinthians 15, he 'is not asking whether the resurrection state is physical or non-physical; that is our late-modern question. His question is, rather, Granted that the resurrection body is of course physical, what sort

---

[60] Ibid., p. ix.
[61] Ibid., p. 207.
[62] N. T. Wright and M. Borg, *The Meaning of Jesus: Two Visions* (SPCK, 1999).
[63] Ibid., p. 119.

of physicality is it? It is, he says, a transformed physicality'.[64] As for the different Gospel resurrection narratives, 'the surface discrepancies do not mean that nothing happened; rather, they mean that the witnesses have not been in collusion'.[65]

3. Responding to the inconceivable

To believe in the resurrection of Jesus from the dead is to accept that God has gone beyond the bounds of rationality. Dead men do not rise from the dead. The claim that God raised Jesus from the dead strains credulity to the limit. For this reason it is perhaps not surprising that the witness of theologians to the resurrection of Jesus has not always been united. Many of the apparently 'doubting' theologians are happy to repeat the words of the creed and affirm that 'on the third day he rose again from the dead', but on closer inspection, the plain meaning of that affirmation has not been accepted by all.

Where lies the problem? Is it to be found within the New Testament documents themselves? Is their witness ambiguous? I believe not. The fact is that time and again the diversity of theological interpretation is due to the varying presuppositions with which theologians approach the resurrection texts. Stephen Davis is indeed right when he notes: 'The odd thing is that most people adopt their belief in the resurrection on the basis of something other than the relevant historical evidence, pro or con.'[66] Davis has in mind those who approach the New Testament with a 'naturalist' or 'supernaturalist' frame of mind. This is not, however, the only difference in presupposition. For instance, those who have little respect for the integrity of the New Testament documents will inevitably tend to be more cavalier in their approach to the resurrection narratives.

A similar point is made somewhat scathingly by Tom Wright:

If Christianity is only going to be allowed to rent an apartment in the Enlightenment's housing scheme, and on its terms, we are, to borrow Paul's phrase, of all people the most to be pitied – especially as the Enlightenment itself is rumoured to be bankrupt and to be facing serious charges of fraud . . . Once you allow that something remarkable happened to the body that morning, all the other data fall into place with ease. Once you insist that nothing

[64] Ibid., p. 120.
[65] Ibid., p. 122.
[66] Davis, *Risen Indeed*, p. 19.

so outlandish happened, you are driven to ever more complex and fantastic hypotheses.[67]

For those who come with truly open minds, the evidence is there. There is no other conclusion than that God raised Jesus from the dead. The empty tomb is a sign for all to see that God has been at work, and it is awe-inspiring. God has done the unthinkable; he has done immeasurably more than we could ever have imagined. No wonder Thomas cried out, 'My Lord and my God!' The only response we can make is one of worship and adoration. Gerald O'Collins is right: 'Christ's resurrection remains far more than the sum of any or all descriptions. At some point we will find no words to say. Then we can do no more than pay silent homage to the awesome nature of this resurrection from the dead, the beginning of God's new creation.'[68] The only proper theological response to the resurrection of Jesus from the dead is doxology – to God be the glory!

[67] Wright and Borg, p. 124.
[68] G. O'Collins, *The Easter Jesus* (Darton, Longman & Todd, 1973), p. 138.

Endword

'Paint Christ not dead but risen!' cried Tomaso Campanella to the Italian painters of his day. 'Paint Christ, with his foot set in scorn on the split rock with which they sought to hold him down! Paint him the conqueror of death! Paint him the Lord of life! Paint him as what he is, the irresistible Victor who, tested to the uttermost, has proved himself in very deed mighty to save.'

Christ is risen! He is risen not just in the hearts of men and women, but risen from the dead. As we have seen, the evidence for the resurrection of Jesus is not only strong, it is also overwhelmingly compelling. Jesus, wrote Luke, 'gave many convincing proofs that he was alive' (Acts 1:3), and in so doing used *tekmērion*, the strongest term possible to convey the sense of 'proof beyond doubt'.

From first to last the New Testament witnesses to the resurrection of Jesus. The resurrection is not part of the Christian faith; it is the very heart of the Christian faith. For this reason we cannot restrict the resurrection of Jesus to Easter Sunday. Rightly understood, every Sunday Christians come together to celebrate the resurrection of Jesus from the dead. Whereas the Jews met for worship on the seventh day of the week to commemorate the day when God rested from his work in creation, we Christians meet together on the first day of the week to commemorate God's work of new creation. Jesus lives and, because he lives, we too may live (John 14:19).

The resurrection is good news. To a dying world we can proclaim the good news of life in Christ. Death no longer need have the last word, for Jesus is risen from the dead, and in rising has brought life and immortality to light. The atheist Bertrand Russell, who sought to give a philosophical undergirding to the permissive society of the 1960s, wrote in his autobiography as he came to the end of his life: 'No dungeon was ever constructed so dark and narrow as that in which the shadow physics of our time imprisons us; for every prisoner has believed that outside his walls a free world existed; but now the prison has become the whole universe. There is darkness without and when I die there will be darkness within. There is no splendour, no vastness, anywhere; only triviality for a moment, and then nothing.'[1] But Russell was wrong. There is purpose, there is hope, there is life for men and women of faith.

I find it significant that while many people no longer mark the birth of a child with any religious ceremony, or indeed bother to go to a church to be married, few people do without a minister or priest at the point of death. Although it is possible to hold a secular or humanist ceremony, few do so. Why? Because at heart most people want to believe in life after death. Even in this secular age it seems as if there is an innate conviction that death is not the end. Indeed, in a survey conducted in a Gallup poll in 1990, 64% of the British population believed in a soul, 53% in heaven, 44% in life after death, and 32% in the resurrection of the dead.[2] 'From the incompleteness of human life (and especially all young lives tragically cut short), from the crying injustices of this world (and especially the sufferings of the innocent), from the greatness as well as the misery of man, all have concluded, "There must be another world in which all lives will come to fruition, all wrongs will be redressed, all mysteries will be made plain."'[3] Indeed, even H. G. Wells, who in other contexts evinced no religious belief whatsoever, once said, 'If there is no larger life after death, then this life is a huge ugly joke. Man is like an ass braying across the scenes of history.'

The good news, of course, is that Jesus has broken through death's defences. Jesus, in rising from the dead, has carved a trail through the valley of the shadow of death, and through faith we may follow him. Or, in the words of C. S. Lewis, 'He is the "first fruits", the "pioneer of life". He has forced open a door that has been locked since the death of the first man. He has met, fought and beaten the King of Death. Everything is different because He has done so. This is the beginning of the New Creation: a new chapter in cosmic history has begun.'[4] Unfortunately, although a 1997 survey of 1,500 people in Britain found 50% who answered Yes to the question 'Do you believe that Jesus actually rose from the dead?',[5] many fail to see the relevance for themselves. What was true of E. M. Forster's famous summing up of his book *Howard's End*, 'Only connect,'[6] is

---

[1] *The Autobiography of Bertrand Russell* (Unwin, 1978), p. 393.

[2] *European Values Study* (Gallup, 1990), cited in the *UK Christian Handbook 1998/1999*, Vol. 1: *Religious Trends* (Paternoster, 1997), 2.5.

[3] A. M. Hunter, *Taking the Christian View* (St Andrew Press, 1974), p. 51.

[4] C. S. Lewis, *Miracles*, in *Selected Works of C. S. Lewis* (HarperCollins, 1999), p. 1210.

[5] *Sunday Times*, March 1996, cited in the *UK Christian Handbook 1998/1999*, Vol. 1: *Religious Trends* (Paternoster, 1997), 2.5.

[6] E. M. Forster, *Howard's End* (Penguin, 1992).

also true of the life, death and resurrection of Jesus: many people have yet to 'connect'.

As it is, for many people much confusion surrounds the afterlife. This confusion is well illustrated by the story of a family who wished the ashes of their father to be scattered on the local football pitch, so that he could continually catch the atmosphere of each Sunday's match![7] Add to this the growing belief in reincarnation, as well as a wide spectrum of belief in the immortality of the soul, and the task of preaching the message of the resurrection today becomes all the more urgent. In a dying world there is a desperate need for the good news of Jesus.

But, as we have seen, the resurrection of Jesus is not just good news for the future; it is also good news for the present. The risen Saviour offers not just hope for the world to come, but also the resources of his power and grace in the here and now. 'I want to know Christ and the power of his resurrection,' wrote Paul (Phil. 3:10). The power Paul had in mind was power for living, power for overcoming even the most difficult of obstacles. Hence he could write a little later that in all the ups and downs of life 'I can do everything through him who gives me strength' (Phil. 4:13). By contrast with some modern theologians, for Paul the gospel of Easter did not create a problem – rather it meant the dispelling of problems.

The risen Lord Jesus has promised to be with his people not just 'at the end', but also 'to the very end' (Matt. 28:20). Life does not have to be lived in our strength, therefore, but in his strength. His invitation of old applies to the here and now: 'Come to me, all you who are weary and burdened, and I will give you rest. Take my yoke upon you . . . and you will find rest for your souls' (Matt. 11:28–29). Here is good news indeed for a world marked by loneliness, stress and pressure of every kind.

The story is told of how the first native Indian bishop of the Church of South India, Bishop Azariah, was once asked: 'If you were in a village where they had never heard of Christ, what would you preach upon?' Without hesitation the bishop replied: 'The resurrection.' In the global village that is our world today, we too need to preach the message of the resurrection.

---

[7] Cited by I. Bunting, *Preaching at Funerals*, (Grove, 1978).

Study guide

The aim of this study guide is to help you get to the heart of what the author has written and to challenge you to apply what you learn to your own life. The questions have been designed for use by individuals or by small groups of Christians meeting, perhaps for an hour or two each week, to study, discuss and pray together.

The guide provides material for each of the sections of the book. When used by a group with limited time, the leader should decide beforehand which questions are most appropriate for the group to discuss during the meeting, and which should perhaps be left for group members to work through by themselves or in smaller groups during the week.

In order to be able to contribute fully and learn from the group meetings, each member of the group needs to read through the section or sections under discussion, together with the Bible passages to which they refer.

It's important not to let these studies become merely academic exercises. Guard against this by making time to think through and discuss how what you discover *works out in practice* for you. Make sure you begin and end each study by focusing on God in praise and prayer. Ask the Holy Spirit to speak to you through your discussion together.

1. The witness of Mark to the resurrection (pp. 21–42)

1. The empty tomb (16:1–8)

1 What do you make of this Gospel's abrupt ending? If Mark intended to finish at verse 8, what might he have been trying to communicate?

2 How do the actions of the women challenge your own level of devotion to Christ? Can you think of times when you have been brought up short by the faith of 'insignificant' Christians?

> *'The powers of evil did their worst, but they did not*
> *– and never will – have the last word'* *(p. 29).*

3 Why is the resurrection's 'note of vindication' (p. 29) important in our everyday lives?

4 What is significant in the fact that Jesus rose *on the first day of the week* (v. 2)? How do you think we should carry this significance over into our own weekly routine?

5 What lessons can be drawn from the angel's message to the disciples – and Peter?

2. *Jesus appears to his disciples (16:9–20)*

6 Paul Beasley-Murray highlights two of Mark's favourite terms: *good news* and *preach*. What do you think it means to 'preach the gospel'?

> *'Jesus is more than a personal saviour – he is Lord of*
> *the world. Jesus, through his death and resurrection,*
> *has begun to take up his reign. Here is good news!'*
> *(p. 38).*

7 Verse 16 speaks of two possible responses to the gospel, and their consequences. What factors in the relativistic culture around us might make us uncomfortable with these uncompromising words? How can we inject a note of urgency into our sharing of the gospel while remaining sensitive to those to whom we speak?

8 Paul Beasley-Murray regards verses 17–18 as descriptive, not prescriptive. Do you agree? Why or why not? If they are descriptive, how can they be seen as relevant to us today?

2. The witness of Matthew to the resurrection (pp. 43–59)

1. *The empty tomb (28:1–10)*

1 What information about the resurrection does Matthew add to Mark's account? How are we to understand the earthquake?

2 How can we help people in our church or Christian group to get beyond the 'just looking' stage which Paul Beasley-Murray describes?

'. . . *Christ's resurrection power is not buried in some time capsule, but rather is available to us today*' (p. 48).

2. *The report of the guard (28:11–15)*

3 '*His disciples came . . . and stole him away*' (v. 13). Here is one explanation for the empty tomb. What flaws are there in this theory?

4 What other explanations have been put forward? How might they be refuted?

3. *Jesus appears to his disciples (28:16–20)*

5 What does this passage teach us about (a) the Lord who issues the Great Commission, and (b) the nature of the Commission itself? What gives us 'confidence' (p. 58) as we carry it out?

3. The witness of Luke to the resurrection (pp. 60–82)

1. *The empty tomb (24:1–12)*

1 What does Luke add to Mark's account? What are we to make of the divergences? How does Luke's account add to the evidence for the historicity of the resurrection?

'*The minds and hearts of the disciples were changed because they discovered that the body of Jesus had been transformed through resurrection*' (pp. 64–65).

2 What does Easter say to us about (a) death, (b) the identity of Jesus, and (c) the future? How does this compare with generally accepted views in our culture?

3 How does Luke's resurrection narrative fulfil his intention in writing, as set out in his prologue (1:1–4)?

2. *Jesus appears on the road to Emmaus (24:13–35)*

4 What might Luke intend us to understand by the two disciples' inability to recognize Jesus?

5 Paul Beasley-Murray suggests three ways in which the risen Christ meets us today (p. 74). What are they? Recall times when they have proved true in your own experience.

6 How can we open ourselves to encounter the risen Lord? What practical measures can we take in order to do so?

3. Jesus appears to his disciples (24:36–43)

7 Trace the disciples' reactions from fear and disbelief to understanding that Jesus was really in their midst. How would you try to convince a sceptic that such appearances were not just hallucinations?

4. Jesus instructs his disciples (24:44–49)

'. . . the Christian gospel was no innovation, but rather the fulfilment of the Scriptures' (p. 81).

---

8 What does this passage teach us about our role as 'witnesses'? Think about your family, friends, neighbours and colleagues. How far have you fulfilled this role among them? How might you go further?

4. The witness of John to the resurrection (pp. 83–119)

1. The empty tomb (20:1–10)

1 What evidence for the physical reality of Jesus' resurrection does this passage give us?

2 Think of people you know who, like the three mentioned here, are at different points in the process of coming to faith. How might you help each one to 'see and believe'?

2. Jesus appears to Mary Magdalene (20:11–18)

3 Why was Mary so grief-stricken outside the empty tomb? How do her responses challenge us?

'Where there is no belief in the risen Christ, there is no joy. Nor is there any hope' (p. 91).

---

4 '*Do not hold on to me . . . Go instead . . .*' (v. 17). What can we learn from those words of Jesus to Mary?

3. *Jesus appears to his disciples (20:19–23)*

5 What do Jesus' words tell us about the nature of our mission as his disciples?
6 *He breathed on them* (v. 22). What did Jesus' action mean? How might John's account of the bestowal of the Holy Spirit relate to the Pentecost account in Acts 2?

4. *Jesus appears to Thomas (20:24–29)*

7 Trace Thomas's journey to belief. How does it compare with yours?
8 Think about any doubts you may be experiencing now or which a friend may have expressed to you. According to Paul Beasley-Murray, how can they be turned to faith?

'For many, doubt is the pathway to belief. Indeed, faith is often the stronger because of the doubt' (p. 103).

5. *Jesus appears to seven of his disciples (21:1–14)*

9 What do you think this story tells us about the character of Peter? Can you identify with his responses? How?
10 Why does Paul Beasley-Murray suggest that this 'may very well have been a story about winning the world for Jesus' (p. 110)? How can it be applied to our evangelistic efforts?

6. *Jesus and Peter (21:15–25)*

11 How does Jesus both force Peter to confront his earlier denials and restore him to leadership? What does this tell us about the nature of forgiveness?
12 What can we learn about Christian leadership in this passage?

5. The witness of Paul to the resurrection (pp. 120–170)

1. *The resurrection of Jesus (1 Cor. 15:1–11)*

1 Paul *passed on* to the Corinthians what he himself had *received* (v. 3). What evidence is there in the 'creed' of verses 3–5 that these traditions about Jesus' death and resurrection are very early?

2 What are the two main propositions of Paul's gospel? Why does he add the phrase *according to the Scriptures* to each?

3 Paul says that Christ died *for our sins* (v. 3). How would you explain this to a non-Christian friend?

4 How does Jesus' resurrection differ from a resuscitation?

2. The resurrection of the dead (1 Cor. 15:12–34)

5 According to verses 12–19, what implications follow if *there is no resurrection of the dead*? In the light of Paul's words, what do you make of preaching that denies Christ's bodily resurrection and interprets the event in purely 'spiritual' terms?

6 Verses 20–28 give rise to several debatable points of interpretation, but the focus is on Jesus' kingship, especially over death. How do these truths encourage you in your own situation and as you look at the world around?

7 In verses 29–34 Paul returns to the folly of certain practices if there is no resurrection. Can you state his threefold argument in your own words? How does the prospect of resurrection provide a basis for morality?

3. The resurrection of the body (1 Cor. 15:35–58)

8 What do Paul's analogies of 'seeds' and 'bodies' tell us about the resurrection of the body? How does this doctrine differ from belief in the immortality of the soul?

9 On the basis of Genesis 2:7, Paul develops his analogy of Christ and Adam (begun in vv. 21–22). What points is he making?

10 In what ways is death conquered, according to verses 50–57? How does this victory relate to our service for the Lord (v. 58)?

'Already the sting of death has been removed . . . Christ has drawn out the poison, however, by drawing it, as it were, into himself' (p. 142).

---

4. Resurrection – present and future (2 Cor. 4:7 – 5:10)

11 Paul speaks of *this all-surpassing power* (4:7). What power? To do what? (Look back at 4:1–6 as well as at 4:7–19.) Spend some time reflecting on the fact that this power is in you, a 'common clay pot'. How does this truth encourage you in your particular situation?

12 How was this power demonstrated in Paul's ministry? Can you identify with his experience? In what ways?

13 How does Paul's testimony in this passage speak to the triumphalist tendency that crops up from time to time among Christians? How do his words help us to recognize ministry that is truly empowered by God?

14 Paul uses two metaphors in 5:1–5: *tent/building* and *naked/clothed*. What is he saying here about our future hope as Christians? What is he *confident* about (5:6, 8), and why?

15 Can you honestly say with Paul that you long for heaven (5:2), and that the prospect of appearing before *the judgment seat of Christ* (5:10) motivates your behaviour in this present life? Why do you think today's Christians, at least in the West, tend to give so little thought to judgment and heaven?

'We don't have to be special people to experience God's power. God specializes in working in the lives of weak and ordinary people, who feel that not only do they have feet of clay, but clay characterizes all they do and are' (p. 155).

---

5. The resurrection life (Col. 3:1–4)

16 'The use of tenses in this passage is highly significant.' What do they teach us about 'the theological implications of baptism' (p. 157)?

17 What rationale does Paul give for his exhortation to *set your hearts* and *minds on things above*, and what does this mean?

6. The resurrection hope (1 Thess. 4:13–18)

18 What questions had been bothering the Thessalonians? In his response, what does Paul teach here about the Lord's return? Note the events in order, with their significance.

19 Explore the differences between 'grieving with hope' and 'grieving with no hope' in the face of death. What is the content of the 'hope', and how can we be sure of it? How can we *encourage* a bereaved Christian *with these words* (v. 18), without appearing to trivialize or rebuke his or her grief?

6. The witness of Peter and his friends to the resurrection (pp. 171–216)

1. Preaching the resurrection in Jerusalem (Acts 2:22–32)

1   In what terms does Peter describe Christ's resurrection in verse 24, and what do these statements mean? How does he use the quotation from Psalm 16 to support his assertions?

2   Two thousand years after the event, in what sense are Christians today witnesses to Christ's resurrection? What do you think should characterize such witnesses? Does this train of thought lead you to any aspect of your life (or of your church's life) where the evidence might be less than credible? How can you work on this?

'If our lives are full of the fragrance of the risen Lord Jesus, then people will be drawn to the message we preach' (p. 177).

---

2. Preaching the resurrection in Athens (Acts 17:16–21, 30–32)

3   What similarities do you detect between the Athenian society that Paul encountered and our own?

4   How can Paul's example here help us as we share the gospel with those around us? Think of (a) the opportunities he sought; (b) the way he approached his hearers and explained the message to them; and (c) the points he emphasized.

3. A resurrection benediction (Heb. 13:20–21)

5   How does this benediction link God's work in us with his 'bringing back from the dead' our Lord Jesus? What points is the writer making?

4. Resurrection joy (1 Pet. 1:3–9)

6   How was it possible for Peter's readers to experience *grief* and *trials* (v. 6) at one and the same time as *hope* (v. 3) and *an inexpressible and glorious joy* (v. 8)? How could Peter see grounds to *praise* God in their situation (v. 3)?

7   What attitudes to death have you encountered among non-Christians around you and in the media? How do they contrast with the *living hope* which Christians have through the resurrection of Jesus Christ (v. 3)?

5. A vision of the risen Lord (Rev. 1:9–18)

8 Read John's description in verses 13–16 and Christ's words in verses 17–18. What does the terminology tell us about the risen Lord?

9 How does this vision of the Lord strengthen and encourage us in the *suffering and kingdom and patient endurance that are ours* as Christians (v. 9)?

'... the implication of the fact that the Lord is the First and the Last, the Alpha and the Omega, is that ... he is Lord of history and sovereign of all' (p. 198).

---

6. Life before the throne (Rev. 7:9–17)

10 What does John's symbolic description tell us about the past, the present and the future of those who constitute the *great multitude* (v. 9)?

11 How can we be sure that our hope of heaven is not just pie in the sky when we die?

7. Life in the new city (Rev. 21:1–5)

12 List (a) what *won't* be in the new Jerusalem, according to this passage, and (b) what *will* be there. What do the various elements mean, both in John's imagery, and to you in your own situation?

13 What does John's depiction of heaven as a city – Jerusalem – tell us about it?

7. The witness of other voices to the resurrection (pp. 217–241)

1. Jesus is Lord (Rom. 10:9)

1 What did this confession mean to the first Christians? How does Jesus' lordship relate to his resurrection?

2 What does this confession say to us twenty centuries later?

2. Jesus is Lord of all (Phil. 2:9–11)

3 How does this hymn depict the position of the risen Jesus? What do the phrases *God exalted him, highest place* and *name that is above every name* mean?

4 Reflect on the cosmic implications of Jesus' lordship and the universal homage that will be offered to him. Why do you think we, as individuals and as local churches, often lack the confidence that these truths ought to give us in our mission in the world? How can we get a bigger vision of Jesus' lordship?

'We need to recover the faith of the early church and see what difference the risen Jesus has made to the world – and then go out and claim the world for him!' (p. 228).

---

3. Jesus is Lord of the world (Col. 1:15–20)

5 How are we to understand the assertions about Jesus in verses 17–18?

6 How does Paul Beasley-Murray suggest we should understand the difficult verse 19?

7 What are the consequences of Jesus' supremacy? How would you respond to someone who cited verse 20 in support of the belief that God will save everyone in the end?

4. The risen, ascended and glorified Lord (1 Tim. 3:16b)

8 Trace the 'story' of Jesus' glorification in the six assertions of this hymn. To what events do they refer?

8. The witness of theologians to the resurrection (pp. 242–255)

1. Doubts raised

1. The theologians whose views are summarized here point to a number of problems which they perceive to attach to the historicity of Christ's bodily resurrection. What are they?

2. In what ways do they reinterpret the resurrection? What motives for such reinterpretations can you pick out of these summaries?

2. Faith affirmed

3. Page 247 refers to an 'important point' made by Michael Ramsey. What was it? What presuppositions do you think underlie the sceptical views just surveyed?

4. What insights do the quotations from Norman Anderson (p. 249) contribute on this point about presupposition?

5. What was 'most astonishing' (p.250) about the book by Pinchas Lapide? What did he make of the scepticism of certain theologians?
6. How do Stephen Davis and Tom Wright (pp. 252–254) respond to the idea of a meaningful, but non-bodily, resurrection of Christ?

3. Responding to the inconceivable

7. Think about the quotation from Stephen Davis on p.253. Before working through this book, on what did you base your belief in the resurrection? Would you say that your belief is now more soundly based? In what respects, in particular?
8. Slowly reread the closing paragraph of this chapter. Allow it to lead you into a time of adoration of 'your risen Lord and your God'.

'To a dying world we can proclaim the good news of life in Christ. Death no longer need have the last word, for Jesus is risen from the dead ... There is purpose, there is hope, there is life for men and women of faith' (pp. 256–257).
